Anglo-Spanish Rivalry
in North America

Anglo-Spanish Rivalry in North America

J. Leitch Wright, Jr.

University of Georgia Press, Athens

Library of Congress Catalog Card Number: 72–156039
Standard Book Number: 8203–0305–4

The University of Georgia Press, Athens 30601

Printed in the United States of America
by The TJM Corporation
Baton Rouge, Louisiana 70821

To Beth

Contents

Maps (following page 18)

Acknowledgments

The author is indebted to many people who assisted in the research and writing of this work—the staffs of the Public Record Office and British Museum in London; the Archivo General de Indias and the Archivo de Simancas in Spain; the Archivo General de la Nación and the Biblioteca Nacional in Mexico; the Public Archives of Canada; the Library of Congress; the William L. Clements Library; the libraries of Florida State University, the University of Florida, the University of Virginia and Randolph-Macon College. Members of the staff of the Manuscript Division of the Library of Congress and the entire staff of the Archivo General de Indias have been of particular assistance. Support from the Penrose Fund of the American Philosophical Society, the State of Virginia Society of the Cincinnati Historical Fund, the University Center in Virginia, the Shell Foundation, Randolph-Macon College and Florida State University helped make possible the research in various archives and libraries and the typing of the manuscript. Dr. Thomas P. Abernethy made valuable suggestions, and the typing was carefully done by Mrs. Sarah Wright who made few errors and corrected many. The author also recognizes that without the untiring efforts and criticism of his wife this book would not now be ready for publication and that by claiming sole credit for this work he is being less than honest.

Introduction

A Spanish ship, sails billowing, the banner of Castile at the masthead, and its captain scanning the horizon for signs of a new English settlement, sailed into Chesapeake Bay in 1611. As a student of colonial American history, immersed in the early hardships at Jamestown, the development of representative government, and the economic and political trials of the new colony, I found myself caught up in the distracting questions raised by the appearance of this Spanish ship. In my search for answers Jamestown became almost lost from view, and years of study and miles of travel intervened before this work assumed its present form.

Essentially it is a study of Spain's response to English intrusions into North America—that expanse north of the Rio Grande which I, if not geographers, define (for this book) as North America. It was an unequal contest and Spain steadily lost ground, but this is not surprising. The heart of English mainland America was on the North Atlantic coast; the important part of Spanish America was south of the Rio Grande. Spanish provinces above that river—Florida, Louisiana, Texas, California—usually were unprofitable and were occupied primarily to keep them out of foreign hands. They were frontier buffer colonies designed to protect Mexico and to safeguard strategic sailing routes. Though they served their purpose reasonably well over the centuries, it is not astonishing, since they were a financial drain, that Spain did not expend more of her resources to defend them.

This study divides itself into two distinct periods—1492–1763 and 1783–1821—with a confusing twenty-year interval between 1763 and 1783. Prior to 1763 one could assume that British "manifest destiny," sustained by a robust national economy and an expanding population, and legally buttressed by the doctrine of effective occupation, would thrust British colonists from the Chesapeake Bay down to the Florida peninsula. In the unsettled 1763–1783 period British "manifest destiny" focused west of the Mississippi River on Spanish Louisiana, while at the same time a reinvigorated Spanish monarchy determined to repel British advances and regain lost ground. Spain was successful during the wars of the American Revolution, and by 1783, through conquest and diplomacy, she had re-acquired the Floridas.

In the post–1783 period Britain assumed France's previous role in North America: she controlled the St. Lawrence-Great Lakes-Hudson Bay river systems and was attempting to keep the Americans from expanding west of the mountains. Assorted British subjects, like Frenchmen at an earlier date, argued that the regime in Quebec should also command New Orleans and the entire Mississippi Valley. Since Spain occupied both Louisiana on the Mississippi's west bank and New Orleans and the Floridas to the east, it was only natural that Anglo-Spanish rivalry continued after 1783, but with new dimensions. The dynamics of the American and French revolutions further complicated matters, and England and Spain alternated between vying for control of the interior of North America and cooperating to stamp out the spread of Jacobinism in the heart of America. Indeed, in the final episode of this rivalry around 1820 Spain vainly pleaded with Britain to renew their alliance of the Napoleonic period and help Spain keep the Americans, whose principles were like Napoleon's, out of Florida.

Fortunately many documents have been preserved relating to the British and Spanish colonial empires. The Archivo de Indias, the Archivo de Simancas, and the Archivo Histórico National in Spain; the Public Record Office and British Museum in London; the Library of Congress in Washington; the Archivo General de la Nación in Mexico City; and the Public Archives of Canada; along with numerous other depositories on both sides of the Atlantic contain millions of manuscripts pertaining to the colonial period. I do not pretend to have exhausted these sources. My objective throughout has been to examine the most significant categories of documents, and throughout I have attempted to utilize those sources that illustrate both the English and Spanish points of view. The reproductions and transcripts of Spanish manuscripts in libraries in the United States, usually well catalogued, were invaluable, though in most instances the originals in Mexican and Spanish archives were consulted and cited in the notes. Since reproductions in the United States of manuscripts from the Archivo de Indias are frequently still classified according to the old system in use until 1929, for simplicity I have retained the old system in certain cases in referring to both reproductions in the United States and to the originals in Seville. The bibliography is not comprehensive and includes only those works cited in the footnotes with a few important additions.

Spain Comes
to the New World

Chapter 1

The nations of western Europe were stirring and restless at the end of the fifteenth century. They were making rapid strides toward consolidating power in a centralized monarchy, achieving well-defined geographical boundaries, and developing a national consciousness. At the same time that the heady ideas of the Renaissance were disseminated, nautical and cartographical improvements led to the physical spread of European culture. The rising nation states commissioned bold mariners to venture into the uncharted ocean to discover and claim new lands or to seek a water route to Cipango and Cathay. These voyages added to the store of human knowledge, and, more to the point, enriched both public and private coffers.

Nowhere were these forces more in evidence than on the Iberian peninsula. Prince Henry of Portugal, from his court at Sagres on the peninsula's southwestern tip, had urged hesitant mariners to probe further and further along the African coast. Though at first Portugal was the leader in charting new lands and in fathoming the ocean's mysteries, soon she was at least equaled by neighboring Spain, who was now successfully expelling the Moors after seven centuries of struggle. Granada, the last Moorish outpost, capitulated in 1492 to Ferdinand and Isabella—and this was only the beginning. The militant Spanish crusading spirit and the insatiable desire of the nobles for new lands no longer could be restricted to the peninsula, and it spread to North Africa, to other parts of Europe, and above all to America. Spain, exhilarated, confident, and optimistic after over-throwing the Moorish infidels, proceeded to gain an empire in the Old World and in the New.

In the same year as the fall of Granada the Catholic sovereigns commissioned a rash Italian mariner—a mariner heretofore unsuc-cessful in peddling to Portugal, England, or France his impractical scheme of sailing westward to the Indies—to take three ships and seek the Grand Khan of Cathay. Christopher Columbus, Admiral of the Ocean Sea, was to govern in behalf of the Catholic sovereigns in all islands or lands to be discovered, providing they were outside the Portuguese sphere.[1]

Weighing anchor in the tiny harbor of Palos in August, 1492, he took the well-known route to the Canaries, recently conquered by the Spaniards. From here he followed the setting sun, beset more by his mutinous crew than by the placid ocean, until finally he reached San Salvador in the Bahamas which was mistaken as an outlying island of the Indian mainland. Columbus established a colony on the island of Hispaniola and then returned to Spain where all the country, ex-cept for a few pessimists who believed he had not sailed far enough westward, extolled the discoveries of the valiant admiral. His re-maining three voyages, however, were anticlimactic: no appreciable amounts of gold, silver, silks, or spices were returned to the mother country; the Grand Khan was nowhere to be found; many colonists became dissatisfied with Columbus's administration; and privileges granted in the original commission were largely revoked by the Crown which desired not only the title but also the direct administration of the Indies in its hands. In 1506 Columbus, whose fame had waned, died neglected at Valladolid.[2]

In 1493, however, his dramatic return from the first voyage and glowing reports of his discoveries created a squabble on the Iberian peninsula. Portugal, which in 1488 had found a route to India via the Cape of Good Hope and which injudiciously had dismissed Colum-bus's scheme, now was alarmed and jealous that her monopoly of an all-water route to India had apparently been broken. As with prior similar disputes, the Pope stepped in to mediate. But the series of partisan bulls issued by the worldly Alexander VI in 1493 did little to settle the issue; in fact, they had the opposite effect. A native of Valencia and indebted to Spain, Alexander VI courted Spain's favor, and his bulls of demarcation were biased heavily in her favor.[3] It was not papal intercession but secular negotiation between the two crowns that pacified Portugal. The Treaty of Tordesillas in 1494 which moved the line of demarcation westward provided for a division of the world between the two nations: Portugal would have all lands lying east of a north-south line three hundred and seventy leagues west of the Cape Verde Islands; Spain would have all lands to the west. Their request that the Pope confirm these terms by still another bull was complied with after twelve years.[4] This papal donation and the right of first discovery became the cornerstones of Spain's claim to the New World. At times she put forth additional arguments to buttress these claims. And at times Spanish scholars and theologians denied the validity of these traditional claims to the New World. Nevertheless the papal donation, with its various interpretations, and the right of discovery, with considerable difference of opinion as to what had been discovered, remained the chief official Spanish title to the New World for over three centuries.

Columbus's successors, if not his contemporaries, soon discerned that the Admiral had greatly underestimated the globe's circumference and had reached not the Indies but some new and unsuspected land of enigmatical dimensions, yielding unknown treasure and blocking the path to Cathay. Soon a swarm of eager Castilians flocked to the New World seeking fame, excitement, and fortune; and there were zealous friars hopeful of a rich harvest of pagan souls. Spain at first concentrated her efforts in the Caribbean and its adjacent littoral. Then Spanish vessels began to skirt the uncharted coastline far to the north and south. The first area of settlement on the mainland was in northern South America and in the Isthmus of Panama. It was here that the headstrong Vasco Núñez de Balboa slashed his way across the almost impenetrable isthmus in 1513 and became the first white man to behold the "South Sea," claiming it for his sovereign. Far to the south, Ferdinand Magellan six years later threaded his way through the straits now bearing his name and reached the Orient.

While Magellan was attempting to circumnavigate the globe, Hernando Cortés, with an incredibly small band of soldiers, doggedly fought his way inland from Veracruz, capturing Montezuma in Mexico City and winning an empire. Now for the first time large amounts of gold and silver flowed eastward to Old Spain and immediately Cortés became famous. From the fertile Valley of Mexico he and his contemporaries extended Spanish dominion west to the Pacific, north to Sinaloa, and south to Honduras. From Panama ruthless Governor Pedrarias and others eagerly pushed northward through Central America, subduing the Indians and founding towns. Though all this area was not under absolute Spanish dominion, by 1550 Spain had explored, conquered, and organized into political units much of Mexico and Central America.

Whereas Cortés was the dominant figure in overthrowing the Aztec empire in Mexico, his counterpart to the south was Francisco Pizarro who with an even smaller band of soldiers captured an even wealthier empire—that of the Incas in Peru. It was here in South America and Mexico that the most significant Spanish exploits occurred, and it was here that the main stream of Spanish exploration, conquest, and colonization flowed. But in the early sixteenth century much of the New World was unknown; both North and South seductively awaited some conquistador to uncover their secrets and to win their treasures.

It was the lure of the unknown and a quest for riches—be they gold, pearls, or Indian slaves—that inspired Juan Ponce de León to seek the Island of Bimini and its fabled fountain of youth. Having secured a royal patent in 1512 authorizing him to discover, populate, and govern Bimini or adjacent islands not within the Portuguese sphere, Ponce de León set sail from Puerto Rico.[5] In April 1513 a low silhouette arose on the horizon, revealing upon closer scrutiny the "fair and pleasant . . . forests" of a land now christened "isla Florida." [6] The Spaniards made their first landing north of the future location of St. Augustine and then skirted the tip of Florida and sailed up its west coast. Because the Indians here were hostile, the expedition soon headed home, unsuccessfully searching along the way for the "fuente de Bimini" in the Bahamas.

Temporarily occupied with fighting Caribs in the West Indies, Ponce de León waited eight years to return to Florida. By then news of Cortés's dazzling achievements was spreading rapidly throughout the New World. Impatient to return and armed with a new patent authorizing him to settle "isla Florida" and to discover what lay beyond, Ponce de León set sail once more. His first expedition achieved only limited success; his second, none. Landing once more on Florida's west coast, his men were again attacked by Indians. Many Spaniards were killed, and Ponce de León himself limped back to Puerto Rico, crestfallen, wounded, and soon to die. This first Spanish attempt to settle the northern Gulf Coast had ended ignominiously and proved to be a harbinger of succeeding endeavors.[7]

In the ensuing years Spaniards outfitted many expeditions to explore, conquer, and Christianize *la Florida*, a "lande . . . like unto Peru," [8] which included not only the Florida peninsula but also the Gulf and Atlantic coasts, and extended inland an infinite way. In 1526 Lucas Vásquez Ayllón led six hundred men to the strange land called Chicora (the Carolinas), but fortune was unkind. The pilot went insane, the ships ran aground, the provisions were exhausted and the survivors considered themselves forunate when they were able to retire to Hispaniola.[9] At the same time Pánfilo de Narváez, who had been defeated when he attempted to supplant Cortés in Mexico, tried to settle on the Gulf Coast, but his fate here was even worse than that meted out by Cortés. In the 1540s Hernando de Soto and in the 1550s Tristán de Luna y Arrellano led even larger expeditions to Florida, and both failed.[10] In contrast to Mexico and Peru, Florida proved utterly uninviting. Her apparently barren interior yielded no quick riches, her Indians were hostile and ever ready to fight, and her shores were strewn with the wrecks of Spanish galleons. In March 1562, Philip II declared that no further attempts should be made to colonize Florida; it was valueless to Spain and no other European power had designs on it.[11]

By the end of the year it was obvious that he had erred. The attraction that had drawn Spaniards to Florida was the same that had drawn Cortés to Mexico and Pizarro to Peru. But to other European nations, particularly England and France, Florida offered another enticement—her strategic location. The return route of the Spanish fleets, transporting the treasures of New Spain and Peru, was from Havana, through the Bahama Channel via the swift Gulf Stream, and then eastward from the Florida coast to Spain.

Jean Ribault, a French Huguenot, constructed Charlesfort at Port Royal Sound in 1562 as a haven for persecuted Huguenots and as a future base to prey on Spanish possessions. This first French colony failed. René de Laudonnière, however, founded a second in 1564 in a new location and built Fort Caroline to the south on the St. Johns River. Against the orders of Laudonnière, who did not want to antagonize the Spaniards while his colony was in its infancy, part of his force made a swift raid into the Caribbean, capturing Spanish ships, and even holding the Governor of Jamaica for ransom.[12] Alarmed Spanish officials in both the Indies and Madrid agreed that these impetuous Frenchmen must be ejected. Thus it was not El Dorado, but foreign intrusion—England too had been closely associated with Ribault—which inspired the first permanent Spanish settlement in *la Florida.*

Philip II chose one of his finest seamen and ablest organizers, Menéndez de Avilés, for the job. Born in Asturias, he had spent his life fighting Spanish battles at sea and at this time was an outstanding example in the tradition of El Cid *Campeador* of a Castilian's battling for crown and church. His large armada left Spain in 1565, instructed first to expel the foreigners, then to colonize Florida. Surprise and timely aid from the elements allowed Menéndez to crush the Frenchmen. They surrendered unconditionally, and all but a few of the "Lutheran heretics," their hands bound behind them, "were put to the knife." [13]

Successfully completing the first part of his mission, Menéndez, who was governor, captain-general, and adelantado (royal deputy in an exposed frontier province), set about the second part—colonization. Aided by his "marriage" to a cacique's sister, he first established semi-friendly relations with the Indians, then he explored much of the Florida peninsula, and finally he established scattered missions and blockhouses. The principal area of settlement was on the east coast in the region of recent French activity. Here Menéndez founded St. Augustine in 1565 as a base to attack Fort Caroline. Nearby were two triangular wooden forts—one at San Mateo on the St. Johns River, the other farther north at Santa Elena on Port Royal Sound—which were manned by seven hundred and fifty men.[14]

His original commission had ordered him to explore as far north as Newfoundland,[15] and the adelantado envisioned occupying strategic points along the coast. Not only would there be a fort at Santa Elena but also another as far north as the Bahía de Santa María or Chesapeake Bay. Further scrutiny and occupation of the Atlantic Coast would have to disclose a route to the South Sea and the Orient —a route which hopefully would be safer and more serviceable than the Straits of Magellan.[16] Lingering in the background, of course, was the tantalizing dream that possibly de Soto and the others were wrong: perhaps there were treasures in the interior of *la Florida.*

Menéndez returned to Spain in 1574. As time passed the Spaniards discovered neither a Northwest Passage nor an El Dorado in Florida, they failed to erect the outposts envisioned by the adelantado, and they even abandoned some already established. The northernmost outpost on the Atlantic seaboard, a Jesuit mission rather than a blockhouse, was in the province of Jacán on the Chesapeake Bay, perhaps not too distant from the future Jamestown. The Indians quickly massacred these missionaires, however.[17] By the end of the century there was only one major settlement, at St. Augustine, and for a while Spain even considered abandoning it. From here missions and outposts extended southward throughout the peninsula and northward into Guale and Santa Elena. The Franciscans succeeded the Jesuits in Florida and their industry in converting the Indians, founding missions, and influencing the actions of thousands of Indian converts was an important factor in strengthening Spain's tenuous hold on Florida. The boundaries of *la Florida* always had been vague and disputed. At the end of the sixteenth century, they extended to Newfoundland in the north, to present-day Mexico in the southwest, and mystically merged into terra incognita in the northwest.[18] That Spain occupied only a fraction of this immense province—the Florida peninsula and the Atlantic Coast up to the future South Carolina—soon became painfully apparent.

During this century Spain wasted much blood and treasure in Florida, but not all of her ventures along the Atlantic Coast were fruitless. It was not gold from *la Florida,* but *bacalaos* or codfish from Newfoundland, "Tierra de los Bacalaos," that enriched Vizcayans and Guipúzcoans in Old Spain. The first Spanish vessel at Bacalaos probably arrived shortly before Ponce de León discovered Florida,[19] though Spain was the last West European power seriously to engage in this fishery. It was not until around 1540 that she took an active interest, and each year afterwards more and more Spanish ships appeared, manned by seagoing Basques, reaching a peak in the 1570s and 1580s.[20] In the year 1578 a hundred Spanish vessels were taking cod in Newfoundland, while nearby twenty to thirty others were whaling.[21] During this period mariners from San Sebastián and neighboring Basque ports had a large and highly-valued share of the fishery, which was an important reason why Menéndez and also England were so anxious to fortify Newfoundland. There was more incentive for England to make a settlement, because English fishermen customarily cured their fish ashore, while the Spaniards used a wet cure which required more salt but did not necessitate going ashore.

Spain had a number of thriving towns on or near the Pacific Coast in Central America; Guadalajara and Acapulco, port of the

Manila galleon, in Mexico; but there were only a few scattered settlements to the north. Spanish vessels had sailed up the coast to Oregon, however, while Francisco Vásquez de Coronado and Juan de Oñate had explored part of the interior to the south.

By 1600 the major characteristics of Spanish dominion in the New World had evolved. Spain had conquered the most advanced and most populous Indian civilizations and had substituted Spanish for native rule. She made an earnest attempt to Christianize the Indians and an even more earnest effort to see that American treasure safely reached Seville. To protect and regulate trade according to mercantilistic philosophy there were fixed routes of trade. In theory two fleets sailed from Spain each year. One, the Tierra Firma fleet, sailed to northern South America, stopping at Cartagena and Nombre de Dios, and was frequently referred to as the *galeones;* the other, the New Spain fleet, sailed to Veracruz and was known as the *flota.* Veracruz dominated the trade of Mexico, and, coupled with Acapulco and the Manila galleon, was an important link in communications with the Philippines; Cartagena was northern South America's most important port; and Nombre de Dios (Portobello at the end of the century) was the Atlantic port through which Peru's commerce flowed. A vital land link in the established routes of commerce was across the narrow Isthmus of Panama. On the backs of mule trains plodding across this isthmus would be carried more bullion than across any comparable forty-mile stretch in the world. The *galeones* and *flota,* after calling at the New World ports and after the trade fairs were over, assembled at Havana for the return voyage.

From Havana the treasure fleet sailed to Seville, which was sixty miles inland on the Guadalquivir River and the hub of Spain's colonial commerce. Seville had been an important manufacturing and commercial center from the earliest times, but with the development of the Spanish American empire in the sixteenth century Seville embarked on its greatest period of prosperity and was rivaled by no other Spanish city. In this century no port in Spain or in Europe played a greater role in American commerce, though whenever possible, Cádiz, Puerto de Santa María, and other Andalusian ports near the mouth of the Guadalquivir River tried to encroach on Seville's monopoly. From Seville the Casa de Contratación or House of Trade regulated all American commerce in minute detail; it also exercised widespread judicial powers and licensed and trained pilots.

It had a large warehouse for storing merchandise, and, for violators of commercial regulations, a prison—a prison which Englishmen became well acquainted with over the centuries. Seville's American counterparts were Portobello (or Nombre de Dios) and Veracruz, and in the sixteenth century no other American ports were more important or better fortified.

Spain was genuinely concerned about the spiritual salvation and material well being of the Indians but was even more solicitous over exploiting America's mineral and agricultural resources and maintaining a profitable trade between the colonies and the mother country. The latter presented basic problems, for obviously this commerce had to be reciprocal. There was a variety of exports from Spanish America—gold, silver, cacao, dyes, hides, and so on—and in turn there was a brisk American demand for textiles, hardware, and Negro slaves. Spain's fundamental problem was how to satisfy this American demand within a mercantilist framework. Even in the sixteenth century she was not able to supply enough goods for the American market, and this is why thousands of eager foreign merchants swarmed to Seville. At the heart of many Anglo-Spanish New World disputes was England's mounting determination to satisfy, either indirectly through Spain or directly to America and either legally or illegally, the Spanish-American demand for foreign wares.[22]

As the American conquest progressed, Spain formed two viceroyalties out of her New World possessions. Generally speaking the Viceroyalty of Peru was all of South America except Brazil, and the Viceroyalty of New Spain was all of North America—or at least that portion controlled by Spaniards. But this varied: sometimes part of South America, such as Venezuela, was included in New Spain, or sometimes part of North America, such as Panama, the key to Peru's commercial life line, was not. In addition, usually West Indian Islands and the Philippines were part of New Spain. But whatever the changing boundaries happened to be, New Spain's capital always remained the same as during the Aztec period—at Tenochtitlán, renamed Mexico City. Here the King's personal representative, the viceroy, resided and had varying political and military control over this extensive area which at first roughly corresponded to North America. The viceroy's control, never exclusive to begin with and shared with the captains-general and the *audiencias* (legal and administrative councils), was gradually undermined as time went on. Though parts of the viceroyalty became almost independent of the viceroy in Mexico City (particularly the Captaincy-General of Guatemala and the Audiencia of Santo Domingo—Florida was subject to the latter), nevertheless, the viceroy was responsible in an undefined way for the defense of the entire viceroyalty and supervised military measures in times of crisis.[23]

There were many crises. In the first part of the sixteenth century during a period of great national prosperity and expansion Spain had had little competition from other European nations in exploring and exploiting the New World. But as the century progressed, there appeared numerous competitors—France, the Netherlands, and an increasingly aggressive England—all of whom were spurred on by reports of the fabulous wealth in the Indies which was doubling the amount of European gold and silver. In this century the majority of Spaniards scattered throughout New Spain were primarily concerned with establishing government in recently conquered areas, with developing the mines and agriculture, with making sure that the Indians furnished labor under the *encomienda* or some other system, with administering justice to Spaniards and Indians alike, and with handling countless minor details of founding cities and granting lands. A high percentage of the population, Spanish, Mestizo, and Indian alike, lived in the interior or in remote areas and was relatively isolated from the world. The main foreign contacts occurred in coastal ports which were vital for Spanish-American commerce but were usually not major population centers. Nevertheless, the inhabitants and officials who did live in these several ports, in a variety of ways were increasingly reminded of the mounting foreign threat. In the New World and in the Old, Spain was hard pressed to maintain her exclusive claim to America, and this was obvious not only in key coastal ports but also in those areas like Florida which were sparsely inhabited and weakly controlled.

English Intrusions

Chapter 2

England did not become a major contender in the New World until Queen Elizabeth's reign, but even in Columbus's time she displayed a transitory interest in American exploration. There is a reasonable possibility that Bristol fishermen actually reached America a decade before Columbus.[1] Certainly a few years after his voyages, Henry VII, vitally concerned with expanding foreign trade and with strengthening the English marine, granted a patent to John Cabot authorizing him to take possession of any lands not heretofore discovered by a Christian prince.[2] This adventurous mariner and his eighteen-man crew left Bristol in 1497 aboard their tiny vessel, and, following a course which today cannot be precisely determined, they at length sighted a bleak and rocky shore, perhaps Cape Breton Island or Labrador. Here Cabot landed, planted the English standard, and then returned to England where news that he had discovered the island of Brazil, the Seven Cities, and the Kingdom of the Grand Khan excited the greatest wonderment. He was acclaimed, outfitted in silk, and styled the "grand admiral." The next year he made another voyage to this "new-found-land," accompanied this time by his son, the ubiquitous Sebastian; and they probably coasted as far south as Chesapeake Bay, or possibly even to the Florida peninsula.[3] These voyages of discovery proved to be the basis of England's claim to much of North America, though at the time there was disagreement as to whether Cabot had reached the fringes of Cathay or some new land. There had been similar confusion, of course, about Columbus's discoveries.

Immediately Spain asserted that the Cabot voyages and the planting of the English flag in North America violated the papal bulls of 1493 and infringed upon the Treaty of Tordesillas of 1494 which extended the papal line of demarcation two hundred and seventy leagues westward. The provisions of this treaty were expected to be confirmed in the near future by still another papal bull. Henry usually respected spiritual papal edicts, though not necessarily secular ones. But the treaty itself provided convenient loopholes. True, the globe had been partitioned from pole to pole: all lands to the west of the demarcation line "which had been discovered by the . . . King and Queen of Castile, Aragon, etc." [4] belonged to Spain. But were Cabot's northern discoveries contiguous with those of the Spaniards to the south? On which side of the line were these English discoveries? Or, for that matter, exactly where was the line? It was not until 1506 that the Pope issued a new bull embracing the terms of the Treaty of Tordesillas, and until then England was not bound by the provisions of a bilateral agreement between Spain and Portugal. Henry VII, in sending out Cabot, had disregarded the papal bulls; but Spain and Portugal also had ignored the Pope and his original bulls when they negotiated the Treaty of Tordesillas. In short, until 1506 Spain's legal opposition to the Cabot or other English voyages rested on a shaky foundation, because Spanish officials regarded the treaty with Portugal as their most valid claim to the Indies. In 1506, however, the Pope issued his new bull, but only a generation later England broke with Rome. Then papal decrees, spiritual or temporal, were of little significance.

In discussing these papal bulls it must be borne in mind that even if the English rulers had remained Catholic they would not have been bound by these papal pronouncements any more than was Catholic France. No new, powerful monarch of the sixteenth century was likely to have "to go to Canossa" for disobeying a bull of demarcation. The primary influence of the papal bulls was within the Spanish empire itself: they commissioned Spain to bring Christianity to the Indians, authorized her, upon occasion, to wage war and take over Indian lands, and provided a legal basis for her to regulate the varied religious, social, and economic aspects of Indian lives. Outside the Spanish empire, however, the bulls were of little consequence.[5]

Because of contradictions between the Treaty of Tordesillas and the papal bulls of 1493, because of obscure geographical conceptions, and because of Henry's disinclination to obey the Pope in secular matters, the English monarch paid scant heed to the Spanish ambassador's remonstrances that Cabot's "new-found-land" lay in Spanish domains.[6] Verbal protests proving vain, the Spanish monarchs ordered Alonso de Ojeda to follow up his recent Caribbean discoveries and to continue northward toward the region where the English had been.[7] Not only were Cabot's discoveries, plotted by the efficient Spanish cartographer, Juan de la Cosa, on his famous world map of 1500, disturbing, but also Ojeda in his first voyage to the Indies had surprised an unknown English vessel in the vicinity of Coquibacoa.[8] This explorer was instructed to sail northward and to plant the arms of Castile along the way, thereby officially claiming this territory for Spain and forestalling any English advance there.[9] But hostile natives in the West Indies and disputes among his subordinates caused the complete failure of this expedition.

Apparently it made little difference, because for the next half century England played a relatively passive role in the New World. Some Bristol mariners followed Cabot's wake to the "new-found-land" to search for the Northwest Passage, to trade, or even to establish a settlement, but usually they came to fish. In 1527 an English vessel, probably the one commanded by John Rut who was seeking the Northwest Passage, or perhaps merely an unrecorded ship, went first to Newfoundland and then either by accident or design ended up in the West Indies. Claiming that their pilot was dead and that they were lost, the English sailors sought aid at Santo Domingo. Spanish officials, suspecting illegal trading, were hostile and frightened the ship away. An English vessel in the West Indies was "a thing not heretofore experienced in those parts." [10] It was several decades before illegal English trading and freebooting became the rule rather than the exception. Foreign vessels were not uncommon in the Indies in the first part of the sixteenth century, but they were normally French ones, extending the Habsburg-Valois rivalry to the New World, rather than English ships.[11]

During the reign of Henry vii, most of the reign of Henry viii, and even later, it had not been necessary for English ships to risk trading directly in the Indies, because New World commerce, channeled through Seville or nearby ports and theoretically regulated by the Casa de Contratación, was frequently legal and, legitimate or not, was profitable. English trade with the Indies via Spain was only one aspect of the complex, widespread Anglo-Spanish commerce. Within the extensive Habsburg empire England traded primarily with the Basque ports of northern Spain, with Seville and lesser Andalusian ports, with the Canary Islands, with the Netherlands, and indirectly with the Indies. From the Iberian peninsula came iron, oil, and alum, the latter commodities so necessary for cloth manufacture. Textiles were the chief export of the Netherlands—this ancient trade had existed long before a Habsburg inherited the Low Countries. The Canary Islands exported wine, fish and foodstuffs and soon became a focal point for contraband within the Spanish empire. At first bullion was the most notable export from Spanish America though agricultural commodities and forest products soon assumed importance. Britain exported raw wool to the Netherlands and woolen textiles to the rest of the Spanish empire. By the early sixteenth century, however, England was using most of her wool at home to manufacture textiles rather than shipping the bulk of it to the Netherlands. As the century progressed England manufactured more and more, and this, coupled with a drastic decline of the Spanish textile industry and the revolt of the Low Countries, had a profound effect on the entire Anglo-Spanish commerce. The Iberian peninsula was less able to supply the Spanish American demand for manufactures, and England, with her increased output, in one fashion or another began fulfilling part of these Spanish-American needs.

The delicate European political situation during the early Tudor period stimulated Anglo-Spanish trade. The two most powerful continental powers were France and the widespread Habsburg empire, of which Spain and the Holy Roman Empire were the major components. For over a half century the Habsburgs were almost constantly at war with Valois France. There were many reasons why Charles v wanted an English alliance, not the least of which was that an English ally would aid him in his struggle against France, and open English support or friendly neutrality in the Channel would help maintain vulnerable sea communications between Spain and the Netherlands. The Habsburgs and the early Tudors, mutually recognizing the advantages of cooperation, negotiated many treaties.

The first and one of the most important was the Treaty of Medina del Campo in 1489 which provided for reciprocal commercial concessions and arranged for Arthur, heir to the English throne, to marry Catherine of Aragon, daughter of Ferdinand and Isabella.[12]

There were provisions in this and subsequent treaties to stimulate commerce, and for penurious Henry VII, anxious to expand trade and to increase customs revenue, these were of paramount importance. Part of this overall commerce was England's indirect trade with the Indies. From an early date it was apparent that Spanish manufactures could not meet the many New World demands, and foreign merchants eagerly came to Spain to help fulfill American needs. The most numerous who swarmed to Seville and elsewhere in Andalusia were the Genoese, Flemings, and Portuguese. Though less numerous, the English were represented, particularly at Sanlúcar at the mouth of the Guadalquivir, and in various ways, not all of which the Casa sanctioned, they siphoned off part of the bullion returning from the New World.

There were several ways in which foreigners participated in the American trade. As a general rule Spain did not allow them to go directly to the Indies, but there were always exceptions, particularly under Charles V. There were at least a few Englishmen in America as factors of their merchant compatriots in Spain. A reasonably legal way for foreigners to participate in American commerce was by obtaining a special license or by becoming a naturalized Spaniard, which was possible if one had a Spanish wife and had lived in Spain for fifteen or twenty years. Another way of tapping the wealth returning from the Indies—perhaps the most prevalent for foreigners and Spaniards alike—was by fraud and deception, avoiding the many duties and restrictions placed on this commerce. Spain's detailed commercial regulations were one thing in theory and quite another thing in practice. Countless vessels went to and from the Indies with two sets of papers, only one of which was for the Casa.

Until well into Elizabeth's reign there was a considerable Anglo-Spanish trade, of which commerce with the Indies was only one aspect. This facet of the overall trade was profitable for the English merchants involved, though native Spaniards and other foreigners had a far larger stake in the overall lucrative Indian commerce. English trade to the Indies such as it was, legitimate or not, was channeled through the Iberian peninsula. Significant developments, however, were taking place in Europe which affected all Anglo-Spanish commerce. First Henry VIII broke with Rome, and in the future Protestant English merchants had more and more unpleasant contacts with the Inquisition. Later in 1559 France and Spain made their peace, and for Spain there was now less need of an English alliance and less reason to make commercial concessions. In the latter part of the sixteenth century English merchants resident in Spain were increasingly harried for both religious and political reasons. Indirect English trade with the Indies via Spain was becoming precarious. Some English merchants in Spain, and especially others in England, began to surmise that direct trade with Spanish America or plundering excursions to the Spanish Main, though hazardous, might be more rewarding than the existing indirect trade to America. As the century progressed there was a shift from legitimate merchant in Spain to open contrabandist and freebooter in the Indies.[13]

Under the Tudors England was interested in two distinct areas in the New World: to the south there was trade via Spain with Spanish-American settlements; to the north there was fishing off the Grand Banks of Newfoundland which teemed with cod. At least since the Cabot voyages English vessels from Devon and Cornwall had been attracted to this lucrative fishery—valuable both for its fish and for building up a merchant marine and training sailors—and more and more vessels appeared on the scene each decade. Many nations—England, Spain, Portugal, and France—shared the fishery during the sixteenth century. It was an uphill struggle, lasting centuries, that finally resulted in English supremacy in this profitable, strategic region.[14]

After the death of Henry VIII England's relations with Spain fluctuated, influenced both by the status of the Protestant Reformation sweeping England, and by how badly Spain needed English support in the war against France. Relations worsened under the ultra-Protestant Edward VI; next there was a *volte-face* when Catholic Mary, future wife of Philip II, assumed the throne; then there was a compromise when the youthful Elizabeth began her memorable reign. But regardless of whether a Protestant or a Catholic was on the throne, some Englishmen, with or without Spanish approval, showed a mounting concern in New World affairs. At least one accompanied Coronado in his expedition to the southwestern part of the United States.[15] Others, such as Roger Barlow, Robert Thorne, and Sebastian Cabot, either participated in or financially backed a Spanish expedition to Brazil in the 1520s. Cabot and Barlow eventually returned to England and around mid-century urged that England send a large force up the Amazon to seize Peru or perhaps even strike at part of North America.[16]

Mary's reign at mid-century, though brief and unhappy, cannot be ignored. English merchants unsuccessfully petitioned Philip II, husband of their new Queen, to throw open the doors to the American trade. Philip's refusal to grant any commercial concessions insured that Englishmen would not become partners with the Spaniards in exploiting the New World's resources. And Mary's premature death without an heir helped insure that England would not be sucked into the sprawling Habsburg empire. It was also during Mary's reign that Calais was lost. Considered a disaster at the time, its loss proved to be a blessing by severing England's last continental link. England never became as involved on the continent as Spain and in the future England was better able to utilize her resources in expanding her colonial empire.

Possibly because Mary's husband was Philip II and for a combination of other reasons the Tudor monarchs never backed the hostile projects of Barlow, Thorne, and Cabot against Spanish America, yet the spectacular riches of the New World still acted as a powerful magnet to many Englishmen. John Hawkins was the most conspicuous example of a merchant who was unwilling to run the religious and political risks of trading indirectly with America via Spain, and instead determined to trade directly with the New World. Son of William Hawkins, an authorized slave trader and merchant to the Indies in the first part of the sixteenth century, John far outshone his father in the scope of his operations. The fact that Spain normally prohibited foreigners, certainly Protestant ones, from going to the New World only slightly hindered Hawkins. Because of the mounting demand for slaves in Spanish possessions which Spain was unable to meet, Hawkins had little difficulty smuggling in his cargo, though at times his cannon paved the way.

Increased Spanish awareness and defiance made his 1567 voyage less rewarding. Extensive storm damage to his seven ships forced him to seek refuge at Veracruz, New Spain's chief port. It was an awkward situation: Hawkins needed time to refit his squadron; yet the Spanish *flota* was expected imminently. It arrived. To guard against any eventuality Hawkins fortified the island of San Juan de Ulloa which dominated the port. At first the Spanish admiral was conciliatory, hostages were exchanged, and then he was allowed to enter his own port. The short-lived truce ended abruptly when the Spaniards attacked the English vessels, killing many crewmen, capturing more, and allowing only two smaller vessels to escape, Hawkins aboard one and Francis Drake on the other.[17] Lack of provisions compelled Hawkins to leave about one hundred men ashore near Tampico where most eventually were captured and sent to Mexico City. At first the Spaniards parcelled out these and subsequent English prisoners as slaves. After the Inquisition was firmly established in Mexico in 1571 many of these heretics were again brought to Mexico City, tried, and given various sentences—imprisonment, a number of years in the galleys, even burning at the stake. Even after the turn of the century, the Inquisition was still hounding one of Hawkins's crewmen.[18] Some of them, primarily those captured in the fighting at San Juan de Ulloa, had been sent directly to the Casa in Seville, but fagots and oars were equally available in Old Spain. David Ingram, one of Hawkins's starving crewmen set ashore near Tampico, escaped the Inquisition. He made an astounding eleven-month, two-thousand-mile overland journey from the Gulf to Newfoundland where he was picked up by a French fishing vessel. Unfortunately, the narrative of his experiences is unreliable, because his description of the Indians and the terrain, at least in part, is based solely on his imagination.[19]

Hawkins, half-starved, returned to England, fuming to retaliate. He assembled fifteen hundred men and prepared to take his vengeance in America by seizing the Straits of Magellan or some likely spot in New Spain.[20] Elizabeth, unsteady on her throne and concerned about risking a break with Spain by sending so large an expedition, stayed his voyage. Not so for Drake, who, without royal authority, and with less than a hundred well-equipped men, sailed to Panama in 1572, captured Nombre de Dios, and aided by the *cimarrones* and a few French adventurers later succeeded in the quest of corsairs of all ages by surprising the heavily-laden, though weakly defended, mule train bearing silver from Peru across the Isthmus.[21] Drake and Hawkins were ushering in a new era, though their methods were somewhat different. Hawkins was primarily a merchant bent on opening a direct, and if possible, legitimate trade between England and Spanish America. Drake seldom carried merchandise in his vessels and was normally concerned with conquest and plunder.

Deteriorating relations between England and Spain encouraged

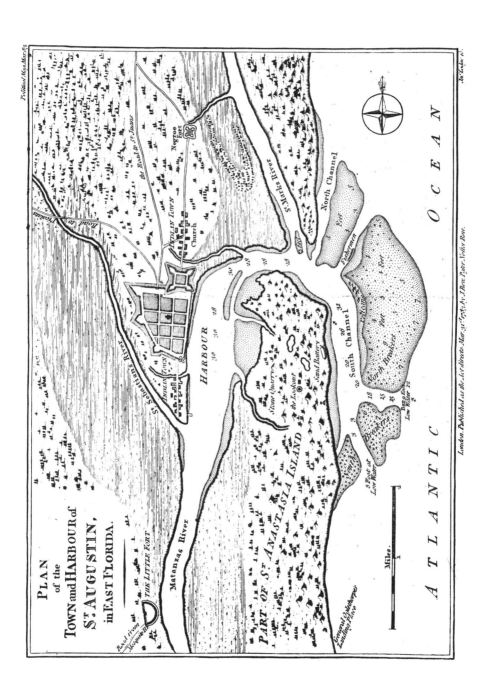

PLAN
of the
TOWN and HARBOUR of
St AUGUSTIN,
in EAST FLORIDA.

THE LITTLE FORT

Road from Jacquin R.

Road to Picolata

S. Sebastian's River

Matanzas River

INDIAN FORT

Church

INDIAN TOWN

Negroe Fort

the Road to St Juans

S.t Marks River

HARBOUR

28

30

30

30

28

28

28

30

32

26

20

20

20

18

15

9

8

3

3

Stone Quarry

the Lookout

Sand Battery

North Breakers

South Channel

North Channel

Fishermen

Feet

Feet

Feet

feet

feet

Feet

Deep Bank at Low Water 24

Breakers

S.t Foot at Low Water

Anvil

General Oglethorpes Landing Place

PART OF S.t ANASTASIA ISLAND

OCEAN

ATLANTIC

Miles
1

London. Published as the Act directs, Mar. 31.st 1763. by T. Jefferys Engraver to the King near Charing Cross.

Jn. Lodge f.

Publish'd Mag. Mar. 1763.

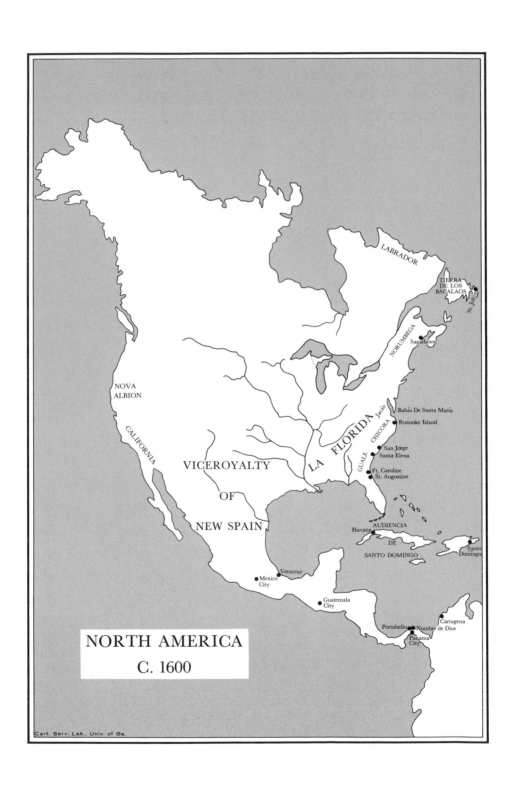

LABRADOR

TIERRA
DE LOS
BACALAOS

St. John's

NORUMBEGA

Sagadahoc

NOVA
ALBION

Bahía De Santa María

Jacán

Roanoke Island

LA FLORIDA

CHICORA

San Jorge
Santa Elena

GUALE

CALIFORNIA

VICEROYALTY

Ft. Caroline
St. Augustine

OF

NEW SPAIN

AUDIENCIA

Havana

DE

SANTO DOMINGO

Santo
Domingo

Veracruz

Mexico
City

Guatemala
City

Cartagena

Portobello

Nombre de Dios

Panama
City

NORTH AMERICA

C. 1600

Cart. Serv. Lab., Univ. of Ga.

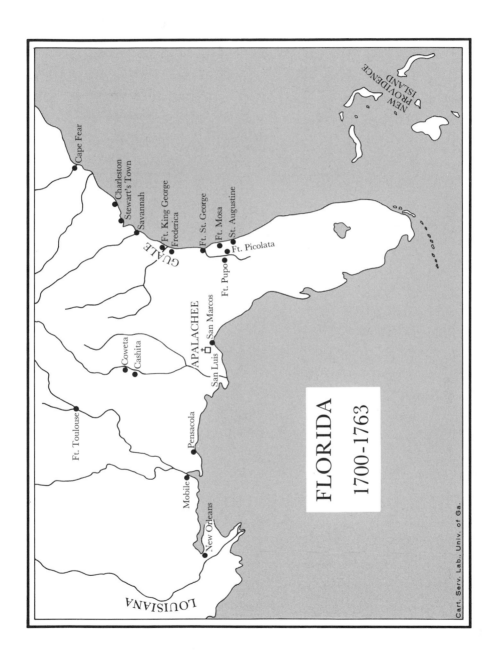

FLORIDA
1700-1763

New Providence Island

Cape Fear
Charleston
Stewart's Town
Savannah
Ft. King George
Frederica
GUALE
Ft. St. George
Ft. Mosa
St. Augustine
Ft. Picolata
Ft. Pupo
APALACHEE
San Marcos
San Luis
Coweta
Cashita
Ft. Toulouse
Pensacola
Mobile
New Orleans
LOUISIANA

Cart. Serv. Lab., Univ. of Ga.

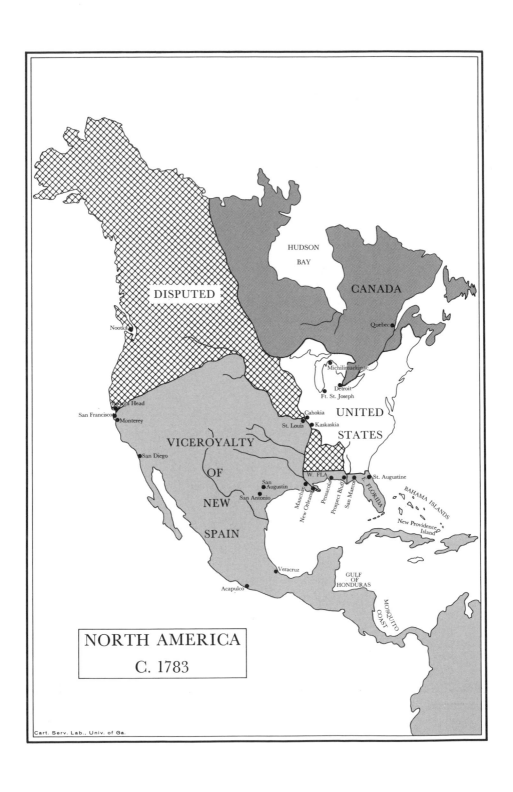

HUDSON BAY

CANADA

DISPUTED

Nootka

Quebec

Michilimackinac

Detroit
Ft. St. Joseph

Trinidad Head

San Francisco
Monterey

Cahokia
St. Louis
Kaskaskia

UNITED STATES

San Diego

VICEROYALTY

OF

NEW

SPAIN

San Antonio

San Augustin

W. FLA.
New Orleans
Manchac
Pensacola
Prospect Bluff
San Marcos
E. FLORIDA

St. Augustine

BAHAMA ISLANDS

New Providence Island

Veracruz

Acapulco

GULF OF HONDURAS

MOSQUITO COAST

NORTH AMERICA

C. 1783

Cart. Serv. Lab., Univ. of Ga.

England to send larger expeditions to the Indies. Drake, on a semi-official mission, was back in the New World in 1578, and this time he sailed through the Straits of Magellan, ravaged the Pacific Coast, forced the alarmed viceroys of New Spain and Peru to rush troops to threatened areas along the extended coastline, and at last sailed to England by circumnavigating the globe. This knighted corsair, now armed with a royal commission, again returned to the New World in 1585, heading the largest English New World expedition of the century, and endeavored to capture key cities protecting Spanish trade routes—Cartagena, Panama, Nombre de Dios, Havana —and pave the way for English domination of the Indies. Though he sacked the ancient West Indian capital of Santo Domingo, Cartagena, and St. Augustine, guardian of the Bahama Channel, his fever-ridden troops were in no position to garrison any major tropical city, and Drake sailed back to England.

During the mid-1580s England and Spain were rapidly drifting into war, and this was manifest both in Europe and in America. Drake's 1585 expedition was but one example. In this same year Elizabeth openly sent troops to the Netherlands; Philip retaliated by seizing English ships and sailors in Spanish ports and hoped the damage to English commerce would make it impossible for England to finance so many hostile projects; Elizabeth countered in America by commissioning Francis Drake to go to the West Indies, by ordering his cousin, Bernard Drake, to Newfoundland to prey on Spanish ships, and by encouraging Raleigh to establish his colony at Roanoke. In retrospect it becomes apparent that Drake's ambitious expedition was the most formidable Elizabethan assault against Spanish America. There were obvious conclusions to be drawn from his failure: Spain after only several generations was surprisingly well entrenched in America and had done a thorough job of her New World conquest; and tropical campaigns waged by Europeans, even when meticulously planned, were fraught with perils. Despite Drake's failure, England nevertheless had supplanted France as Spain's most dangerous New World rival.

During the 1580s there was developing a full scale war in the New World which was spreading to the Old, and soon there would be no peace on either side of the line.[22] Relations with Spain were strained to the breaking point. She considered England the center of Protestantism and was aware of the aid dispatched to the rebellious Hollanders and Huguenots. Philip delayed openly declaring war, hoping that domestic intrigue would place Catholic Mary Stuart on the English throne. In 1587 Elizabeth executed Mary. 1588 was the year of the Armada.

Increasing hostility with Spain culminating in this actual break had disastrous effects on Anglo-Spanish commerce, which included trade not only with Spain proper but also with the Netherlands and indirectly with Spanish America. Philip II in various ways harassed this trade or, anticipating Napoleon's continental system, threatened to cut it off entirely. At times he made good this threat, frequently to further political or religious rather than commercial ends. English merchants in Spain always operated in an air of uncertainty. Would their merchandise be confiscated in retaliation for Hawkins's and Drake's raids? Or, instead, would Spain continue to allow and close-ly supervise this commerce—as valuable and necessary to her as to England—and hope that Britain by having an extensive stake in this trade would be kept on good behavior in America and else-where? [23] Or perhaps Spain would open the door to American com-merce in return for England's successfully mediating the Nether-lands revolt.[24] Theoretically the Spanish inquisition existed only to combat heresy, but whether the Inquisitors were concerned with domestic heretics or with Protestant English merchants might vary in relation to how well English Catholics were treated in England, to whether Dutch privateers were allowed to use English ports or whether the rebellious beggars were abetted in other ways, and to how active English privateers were in the Indies.

Philip II's interfering with English trade to further political and religious objectives was a two-edged sword, because his meddling with this commerce affected his own merchants in the Spanish em-pire as well. Cutting off England's important trade with Antwerp was a powerful weapon in Philip's hand; it also increased distress in the Netherlands and intensified the Dutch will to revolt. In time the Dutch rebels closed the Scheldt, and the decision was no longer Philip's to make. Whenever Philip tampered with English trade he was likely to affect adversely customs duties and funds for the royal exchequer. It was one thing to cut off English trade and hope the ensuing depression would trigger unrest and revolt resulting in Mary Stuart's being placed on the throne; it was something else to find enough money to underwrite Philip's many ambitious projects. Spanish soldiers in the Netherlands and elsewhere had the annoying habit of mutinying whenever they were not paid. English merchants likewise were quick to point out that if Philip stayed commerce with Spain, then English merchants who were able to traffic indirectly with the Indies might be forced to dispatch their vessels directly to Spanish America.[25] Spain soon realized this point was well taken.

There was a sharp contrast between English trade to the Indies in the first part of the sixteenth century and that of the latter part. In the first part of the century England still was Catholic and even after Henry's break with Rome, Spain was likely to court England's favor as an anti-French ally. Toward the end of the century the Anglican Church moved further from Rome, and Spain made peace with her ancient French antagonist which in turn was wracked by civil war. Now there was less reason to court England's favor, to grant her merchants freedom of access to the Indies, freedom of religion in Spain, and other impertinent trifles. Small wonder— particularly after 1585 when England sent troops to the Netherlands and Spain cut off all English trade and confiscated English merchants' property—that these merchants began to give even more consideration to completely by-passing Spain and instead to going directly to the Indies, bent on trade, plunder, or a combination of them both.

But whether the mother countries were technically at peace or at war made little difference in the New World. English seamen had harried Spanish possessions before the final break in 1588, and now they continued their attacks. In the decade of the 1590s and until peace was made after the turn of the century, they assaulted countless Spanish ports in the Gulf of Mexico and Caribbean. In spite of undeniable successes, they inflicted no lethal blow upon the Spanish Indies. One reason is that both the English and French had exposed Spanish weakness in the past, and Spain had begun to strengthen and fortify her exposed vital ports and to better organize and protect the sailings of her fleets. With few exceptions the cities which the English took toward the end of the century were not the most important ones.

And at no time did England make permanent inroads in the Pacific. Since the 1570s she had considered fortifying the Straits of Magellan; Drake, Hawkins and Richard Grenville all toyed with the idea,[26] but neither they nor anyone else succeeded. Drake wreaked havoc along the South American coast, frightened officials in New Spain, and, in order to return home safely with his enormous booty, continued sailing along the North American coast probably searching for the Straits of Anian which could lead him to safety in the North Atlantic. He could not find the elusive passageway and decided to refit the *Golden Hind* before attempting to circumnavigate the globe. Anchoring on the California coast, the English admiral and his party went ashore, where the natives, dancing wildly and scratching themselves with their fingernails, welcomed the white visitors as gods. Treating these animated Indians kindly and taking possession of "Nova Albion" for Her Majesty, Drake spent over a month on the California coast. But transporting his treasure to England, not establishing a colony, was his objective, and soon the *Golden Hind* began to trail the sinking sun.[27] Several years later Thomas Cavendish likewise sailed through the Straits of Magellan, up the Pacific coast and succeeded where Drake failed by capturing the Manila galleon.[28] This vessel, sailing from Manila to Acapulco laden with silks and spices from the East, was one of the most sought after prizes afloat.

Drake's and Cavendish's voyages and mounting English eagerness to find the Northwest Passage alarmed officials of New Spain, who periodically believed that the search for the "English Strait" had been successful and that England had settled "Nova Albion." [29] There was little reason for concern. It was many years before England seriously asserted her claim to "Nova Albion," and she never found the Northwest Passage. That there was no reason for concern was not immediately obvious, however. It was largely alarm over Drake's intrusion into the Pacific that induced Spain to construct and maintain a separate fleet of galleys there.[30]

English interest in fortifying near the Straits of Magellan and on the California coast was apparently part of the larger scheme of opening up a water communication with the Orient via America. Partly because no Northwest Passage or Straits of Anian were discovered, the English began to realize, as the Portuguese well knew, that the best route to India was via the Cape of Good Hope. "Nova Albion" which could be a way station on an all-water route to the East lost much, but never all, of its appeal.

La Florida

Chapter 3

English attacks on both the west and east coasts of New Spain were annoying and at times severely destructive, but never was Spain's hold seriously shaken. England neither colonized "Nova Albion" nor permanently ousted Spain from any port or area on either coast. Time would show that one of the most serious menaces to Spain's exclusive North American claim was directed against the weakly held, apparently barren northeastern part of New Spain, *la Florida*, where enterprising Englishmen were examining the entire Atlantic Coast and contemplating settlements.

The first Englishman seriously to undertake colonization here was Thomas Stucley. Born in England, possibly an illegitimate son of Henry VIII, Stucley served England, France, Spain, and the Pope during his lifetime. In the early 1560s his fortune was depleted, and he was alert for some scheme to replenish his barren coffers.[1] Providentially just at this time the Huguenot adventurer and one of France's foremost mariners, Jean Ribault,[2] was returning to Europe from recently erected Charlesfort at Port Royal Sound on the South Carolina coast. He rendered glowing accounts of *la Florida*'s fertility and affluence, described the excellent harbor at Port Royal, and pointed out its nearness to the Spanish Indies and to the return route of the Spanish treasure fleets. The Protestant-Catholic struggle had rendered France almost prostrate, and upon returning Ribault

landed in England and looked to Elizabeth, who was openly col-
laborating with the Huguenots, rather than to his former mentor,
Admiral Coligny, leader of the hard-pressed French Protestants.

Stucley probably had been in France with English troops aiding
the Huguenots in 1562. Ribault had prepared his expedition in Le
Havre, and Stucley doubtless followed the Florida enterprise with
interest. When Ribault landed in England, Stucley hurriedly made
contact with him and with the Queen, and they soon formulated a
plan to supply Charlesfort the next year. It would be a joint venture: Stucley to supply two ships; Ribault, one; the Queen, one;
and one to be chartered.[3] Elizabeth offered to pay, and possibly
Ribault accepted, a handsome subsidy to turn Charlesfort over to
England. In time, either because of jealousy and distrust of Stucley
or probably, for nationalistic reasons, since the Huguenots and
French Catholics had reconciled their differences, Ribault and three
of his pilots became dissatisfied and attempted to flee to France.
They were apprehended, however. The impulsive Ribault was imprisoned, and his three pilots were placed in chains aboard Stucley's
ships.[4] The expedition continued without Ribault.

Elizabeth subsidized Ribault and supplied Stucley in order to
colonize Florida and gain a foothold in the Indies. Apparently she
expected this foothold to be a fortified port rather than an agricultural colony of farmers with their women and children. Occupying
Florida began to take second place to European privateering in
Stucley's inventive mind, though naturally either course was detri-
mental to Spain. Always alert for a better bargain, the intriguing
Stucley kept the Spanish ambassador informed of the whole project,
expressing devotion to Philip II and intimating that the whole fleet
might be turned over to Spain for a price.[5] Stucley never openly
stated his price, but license to trade directly with the Indies doubtless would have bought him and his associates. Until he could get a
reply from Philip, Stucley maintained he was boring holes in his
ships and delaying the enterprise.[6] Spanish officials wisely decided
to rely on force rather than Stucley's word to insure Florida's safety.
Although the Spanish ambassador complained to Elizabeth, he was
put off by assertions that this voyage was in no way prejudicial to
Spanish interests.

Stucley's fleet sailed from England in 1563, but the vessels of
"lusty Stucley" never reached Florida. Piracy in home waters had
proved more alluring. Elizabeth realized she had wasted royal funds

and with reluctance commissioned ships to overtake Stucley.[7] Eventually he was captured off Ireland, brought to trial in London, but, through the influence of powerful friends, not convicted. Thus the Queen's first colonization attempt in the New World was a fiasco. Early in her reign Elizabeth was primarily concerned with consolidating her power and dared not risk an open break with Spain. It was one thing if Stucley, ostensibly on his own, went to remote Florida which was a region that England could claim by the Cabot voyages. Should it later become necessary the Queen could disavow his actions. But Stucley's sailing from an English port and subsequent piracy off the Spanish coast were another matter. Not at least making a show of prosecuting him upon his return involved more serious risks. Nevertheless, it may be that Elizabeth herself was one of the influential persons responsible for his acquittal.

Ribault's colony at Port Royal, his English account of Florida, and Stucley's activities all revived interest in the North American Atlantic Coast. Charlesfort had failed, but in 1564 René de Laudonnière established another French colony on the St. Johns River. There are indications that had he not gotten there first, Hawkins—now making his second grand trading sweep of the Indies—would have built an English fort himself. The Spanish ambassador in London incorrectly assumed that Hawkins had done just this.[8] Even so, Hawkins, en route home, sought out the new French fort on the St. Johns. Here the English visitors found the colony disorganized, almost devoid of provisions, and threatened with mutiny. Despite Hawkins's readily supplying bread and wine and the outward cordiality between Hawkins and Laudonnière, there was mutual distrust. Ostensibly because of the colony's critical state, Hawkins offered to take all the survivors back to France. The French leader thanked him profusely, but was concerned lest this be a ruse to substitute Anglo-Saxons for Frenchmen in Florida. Instead they agreed that the hard-pressed colonists would purchase a ship and provisions from Hawkins, and then shortly after he had gone, they too would follow.[9] After the English ships sailed but before the French colonists departed, Ribault arrived with supplies from France. Since the massacre of most of these Frenchmen by the audacious Spanish captain, Menéndez de Avilés, has been so well publicized, it is usually overlooked that, because of the many rumors caused by Stucley's preparations in 1563 and because Hawkins actually had been at Fort Caroline in 1565, Menéndez was uncertain whether he would have to deal with Frenchmen, Englishmen, or both until he actually landed in Florida.

When Hawkins returned to England he reported to the Queen that he had examined much of *la Florida* and that it was an exceptionally promising region.[10] Although there were no advanced Indian civilizations or silver mines as in Mexico and Peru, significant quantities of precious metals and pearls had washed and no doubt would continue to wash upon Florida's gently sloping beaches from Spanish galleons wrecked in the treacherous Bahama Channel. Aside from this, the enterprising trader pointed out how easy it would be to cultivate grapes and maize, how quickly cattle would multiply, and how the Queen herself should exploit this fertile region—a region assuredly larger than any Christian nation could maintain.[11] In any discussion of Florida it was obvious to the experienced Hawkins, as it was to Elizabeth, Stucley, Ribault, and Admiral Coligny, that this province commanded the return route of the Spanish treasure fleets.

While Stucley and, to a much lesser degree, Hawkins concentrated on *la Florida,* other Englishmen focused their attention further north. Ever since the Cabot voyages England had been seeking the Northwest Passage. In the 1570s, however, the tempo of the search quickened, and a host of English mariners soon were unsuccessfully probing the rocky northern shores. Among the first was Martin Frobisher, for whom a search for the Northwest Passage was only a secondary mission in his series of voyages to the north of Labrador from 1576 to 1578. His main object was to find gold in the north as Spain had found it in the south. To get reliable first-hand reports on Frobisher's progress, the Spanish ambassador, Bernadino de Mendoza, sent along a secret agent as he had done previously on the Hawkins voyages.[12] Accounts of the ore brought home by Frobisher after his first voyage were highly favorable, actually almost unbelievable, and in 1577 he shipped home two hundred and forty additional tons. Mendoza was relieved when he discovered that there was no Potosí near Labrador and that Frobisher or his backers apparently had fraudulently magnified the content of the ore to insure backing for subsequent voyages. Nevertheless the Ambassador sent a sample of this ore to Spain to be assayed—just in case.[13] On his third voyage Frobisher planned to leave behind one hundred men to garrison a wooden fort which would provide a permanent base to seek out valuable ores and the strait to the South Sea, and which would ward off foreign intruders. Shipwreck of supplies, cold Arctic blasts, and reluctance of the garrison to spend a frigid winter there forced abandonment of this project.[14]

Though Frobisher failed in extracting gold from the New World and in finding a Northwest Passage, another immediately tried to succeed where he had failed. Humphrey Gilbert had been fascinated by the Atlantic Coast since the days of Stucley and Hawkins and envisioned founding a colony here to serve many ends: it could be used as a base to raid the West Indies, to attack the Spanish Newfoundland fishing fleet, or to discover the Northwest Passage.[15] Gilbert's design of fortifying Newfoundland was not unique; Menéndez only a little earlier had urged the Spanish Crown to do the same thing for similar reasons. In 1578 Gilbert received a typical patent authorizing him to discover and occupy lands not possessed by a Christian prince. Little is known of this 1578 voyage—accompanied by Mendoza's agent[16] and probably directed primarily against the Spanish Newfoundland fishing fleet—except that it failed.

Undaunted, Gilbert outfitted another expedition. Persecuted Catholics, assured liberty of conscience and other concessions, were enlisted as colonists. Mendoza used his influence to prevent their going, asserting that this was against the wishes of the Pope and Philip, that only Ribault's fate awaited if they went, and that by leaving England they would drain "the small remnant of good blood [from] this sick body." A majority heeded the Ambassador's words; a few "reckless and useless ones" did not.[17]

Initially Mendoza thought the Englishmen's destination was lower Florida or Cuba where first Gilbert would erect a fort and later reinforce it with ten thousand men from the Queen.[18] Soon the Ambassador discerned that the true objective was Norumbega (southern Canada and New England). In the summer of 1583 Gilbert arrived at St. Johns Harbor, Newfoundland. Mounting a hill overlooking the harbor dotted with English and Portuguese vessels, he took possession for the Queen "by digging of a Turffe and receiving the same with an Hassell wand." [19] Shortly afterwards the main supply vessel was lost and the expedition was abandoned, though all the vessels did not reach England safely. Gilbert, himself, was last seen calmly reading aboard the diminutive ten-ton *Squirrel*.

Gilbert's half brother, the talented, egotistical, many-sided Walter Raleigh, had been identified with both the 1578 and the unlucky 1583 expeditions and at once began to take over where his half brother left off. Raleigh's settlement in that part of *la Florida* to be known as Virginia was part of the overall anti-Spanish policy. Elizabeth's advisors considered that a settlement on the mid-Atlantic Coast would play an important role in reducing Spain's power in the Indies. At least in the beginning the colony would be little more than a fortified port, allowing English corsairs to prey more easily on the treasure fleets, providing them a year round base in the New World, and reimbursing the backers with "King Phillippe's purse." This was only one of several blows aimed at Spain's empire in the Indies. In conjunction with this colony the tempo of English attacks on the Spaniards in Peru, New Spain, and Newfoundland increased.[20] If the valuable stream of American bullion did not regularly reach Spain, Philip II would have to curtail his European ambitions which were usually a menace to England.

Raleigh obtained his patent in 1584 and outfitted Richard Grenville to occupy Roanoke Island. With his fleet of seven vessels, Grenville escorted the one-hundred-odd settlers to Roanoke. In the West Indies they stopped at Hispaniola and Puerto Rico, replenishing their water casks and securing horses and cattle. Spanish officials here became suspicious of English designs on *la Florida*.[21] After reaching Roanoke Grenville left Ralph Lane in charge, then returned to England for supplies, capturing a rich Spanish vessel en route.[22]

Accounts of the first year at Roanoke are meagre, but one thing is certain: summer was fast approaching and Grenville had not returned with the much-needed provisions. He was on his way, but another fleet, Drake's, dropped anchor at Roanoke first. Drake was returning from his devastating West Indian voyage in which he sacked Santo Domingo and Cartagena. After threatening Havana, he next entered the Bahama Channel, and shortly his twenty-nine ships appeared menacingly off St. Augustine. At once he put artillery ashore to batter the crude wooden fort. The Spanish force here was outnumbered many times, and the fort's garrison, "through the thoughtfulness of our General," fled to the woods.[23] Surrender or death were the alternatives.

St. Augustine suffered proportionally more than the other cities ravaged by Drake. The English assaulters found about two hundred and fifty houses in the town, "but we left not one of them standing." [24] Next they put the fort and a caravel in the harbor to the torch. Only the small vessels, miscellaneous hardware, and other supplies possibly needed by the Roanoke colony were saved.[25] After finishing their work, Drake's men departed for the Spanish fort at Santa Elena (Port Royal) contemplating a repetition of St. Augustine's fate. Fortunately for this second Florida garrison, the English admiral either refused to risk navigating the treacherous shoals without a pilot, or, according to Spanish reports, could not even find it.[26] Whatever the reason, Drake by-passed Santa Elena and finally dropped anchor off Roanoke Island. It is probable that he ravaged St. Augustine so completely—only fortune saved Santa Elena from the same treatment—in order to better insure the safety of Raleigh's colony.

Lane and his compatriots were overjoyed at the arrival of this English fleet. Drake agreed to provide a vessel and stores, among which we must assume were the hardware and small craft from St. Augustine and the two hundred and fifty Negro slaves captured at Santo Domingo and Cartagena. A sudden, severe storm wrecked Lane's ship and supplies, while Drake's vessels barely weathered gale winds and a heavy sea in the poor haven off Roanoke. Rather than remain with skimpy provisions, Lane and his followers decided to return with Drake. After they reached England, the indefatigable Richard Hakluyt eagerly sought out and examined two of the Spanish prisoners captured at St. Augustine,[27] while the Spanish ambassador just as eagerly sought out and interviewed one of Drake's captured Negroes.[28] Events proved that Lane should have remained at Roanoke, because Grenville's fleet arrived only to find the colony deserted. Nevertheless, one fact now was obvious: there was no harbor at Roanoke which would serve as a suitable base to raid the Spanish Indies.

Undaunted by this setback, Raleigh immediately outfitted another expedition, and this second colony, headed by John White, was back in Virginia in 1587, though again at Roanoke rather than the more promising Chesapeake as had been planned. Raleigh was not as directly involved in this latter undertaking, because, for a consideration, he allowed White and other associates to settle in Viriginia. White's colony, which included women and children, was to be the basis of a growing, permanent colony rather than merely a fortified port for privateers envisioned by Raleigh. The mystery surrounding the fate of the lost colony is well known. White himself returned to England for supplies. The Spanish Armada and perhaps Raleigh's neglect delayed White's return for three years, and by then the colonists had vanished.

Spain had received many indications of Raleigh's designs. The vessels bound for Roanoke had passed through the West Indies, and the Spanish ambassador had sent disturbing reports from London. While Drake was sacking St. Augustine, several of his Negro prisoners escaped, disclosing that they were to be used as laborers in the new English colony.[29] There was no dearth of signs that there was an English settlement in *la Florida*. But where was it? What was its strength? These were questions asked by Florida governors for the next fifteen years and never answered definitely until Jamestown was founded.

At first after Drake's attack, Menéndez Marqués, now governor at St. Augustine, had more than he could do just to provide for his destitute garrison. "We are all left with the clothes we stood in [and] are without food of any sort except six hogsheads of flour which will last twenty days." [30] Marqués had had no choice when he fled before Drake's onslaught. But to provide for a more effective defense in the future he consolidated the garrison at Santa Elena with that at St. Augustine.[31] Experience had shown, with disastrous results, that they were too far apart to be mutually supporting. At this time Spanish officials were even considering abandoning all of Florida or perhaps maintaining only a single fort near the Keys to pick up shipwrecked seamen.[32]

As soon as Marqués sufficiently recovered from Drake's raid he sent out vessels to locate the English colony. One, commanded by Vicente González, accidentally stumbled upon signs of Raleigh's abandoned colony—a shipyard, barrels, and other debris. Now for the first time there was definite proof of an attempted English settlement.[33] Through information supplied by González, by an English seaman who had been with Grenville and later wrecked in the West Indies, and by a Spanish sailor who had been captured by Grenville and later escaped, the Spaniards gradually pieced together the story of the Roanoke failure.[34] Definitely there was no settlement here. But whether Raleigh's colony was at a new location or whether England had founded other settlements, Marqués was unable to answer with any degree of certainty.

The Anglo-Spanish War did not end with the Armada but continued relentlessly until 1604. English corsairs, individually or in small groups, and Drake and Hawkins in their disastrous 1595 expedition, were active in the West Indies, and there were repeated clashes with Spanish ships in Newfoundland. After the Armada and especially after the 1595 expedition, the Anglo-Spanish conflict was largely confined to Europe. On several occasions Philip equipped subsequent flotillas to invade England; Spain encouraged and sent troops to the rebelling Irish; and she regained Calais and threatened to send the Duke of Parma's army across the narrow Strait of Dover. Elizabeth, in turn, continued to aid the Dutch and to be tied down in Ireland, and, rather than risk her navy in America, concentrated on destroying potential armadas in Spanish ports and on interrupting Spanish-American commerce from the European end. Spain's commerce with the Indies would have suffered as much if England had permanently occupied Cádiz or the Azores as if Drake had gotten a foothold on the Isthmus of Panama.

After the deaths of Philip II and Elizabeth and after France made her peace with Spain, England made more serious efforts to negotiate peace. She demanded the right to trade freely in the Indies and to discover and colonize lands there not occupied by Spaniards. Spain denied these demands and refuted the earlier writings of the Spanish theologian, Francisco de Vitoria, which supported the English position and which English statesmen were quick to cite.[35] Both Philip II and Philip III recognized that trade to the East and West Indies held the key to "all ye power and might of ye kingdoms of Spain" and were determined to retain exclusive control over it.[36] English merchants with Spanish commercial connections were aware that imports of American bullion were at an all time high, that the sagging Spanish industry was not able to supply all the New World wants, and that a right to trade legitimately with the Indies would be infinitely more valuable than any temporary triumph of the corsairs. The English government was sympathetic to the merchants' position, but it was not yet ready to forget the exploits of the Elizabethan Sea Dogs, and clearly recognize that trade was more rewarding than privateering.

War ceased in 1604 when the belligerents signed a compromise, ambiguous peace treaty. Spain agreed to condone any trade which had been allowed before the war, which to Spain meant that Englishmen had no right to be anywhere in the New World without Spanish permission—permission they were not likely to get.[37] To England the treaty meant that future commerce with Spaniards in the New World would probably be clandestine as it had been in the recent past. The treaty made no mention of England's right to claim unoccupied lands, and in spite of Raleigh's and Gilbert's failures, preparations in England were underway for new ventures.

Virginia

Chapter 4

During the latter part of the sixteenth century France, the Netherlands, and England had contested by force of arms the imperious policies of Philip II. By their successes it was obvious in the early 1600s that Spanish hegemony in Europe was a thing of the past. And these same three nations were responsible for the destruction of Spanish hegemony in the Indies. Their inroads on Spanish colonies in the sixteenth century usually had been confined to raiding and privateering; in the seventeenth century they shifted emphasis to colonization and exploitation.

Before or shortly after the turn of the century Spain grudgingly signed peace treaties with her opponents one by one, including the ambiguous 1604 treaty with England. Immediately after the proclamation of this treaty, if not earlier, Englishmen, vigorously searching for new sources of raw materials and markets, were busy formulating a multitude of New World enterprises in North and South America and the West Indies. Among the first was a scheme in 1605 by the Earl of Southampton and Sir Thomas Arundel to provide a Catholic refuge in the northern part of Virginia, an undertaking in many respects similar to Gilbert's of 1583. The West Country of England for the past several decades had had a strong connection with the Maine-Nova Scotia-Newfoundland region, and the present desire to establish a colony here and to take advantage of this territory was but another, albeit more ambitious, attempt. The promoters ordered Captain George Weymouth, an experienced New World mariner, to make a reconnaissance and to select an appropriate site for a settlement. After examining the Maine shores, he returned to England, taking several of the natives with him.[1]

Glowing accounts by these Indians revived the attraction and romance of Virginia which had sagged since Raleigh's Roanoke endeavors. The fact that there was peace, the terms of which—at least by the English interpretation—sanctioned such settlements, and the fact that English commercial and manufacturing interests were concerned with America not only as a source of bullion, or as a foothold to continue search for the Northwest Passage, or as an anti-Spanish privateering base, but also as the site of future populous colonies which would be an end in themselves by producing valuable naval stores, wines, and iron, likewise stimulated interest in relatively uninhabited and otherwise unattractive Virginia. Two groups of backers, one in London, the other in Plymouth, organized a typical joint-stock company, the Virginia Company. The royal charter provided that the boundaries would be between thirty-four degrees (Cape Fear) on the south and forty-five degrees (central Maine) on the north. Two settlements would be made within these bounds provided they were not in territory "actually possessed by a Christian prince." [2] Prior English voyages, the writings of the Richard Hakluyts, and translations of classic Spanish works about the New World all made it plain that Spain had no settlements north of Cape Fear. The Spanish ambassador, Pedro de Zúñiga, ironically observed that though the charter specified that the two settlements would not be within one hundred miles of each other, it made no mention "of the distance at which they are bound to be from your majesty's subjects." [3]

The Plymouth Company's colony was to be in the northern part of Virginia near the region favorably described by Weymouth's Indians and in the region with which for some time Plymouth merchants and fishermen had shown an interest. Taking the traditional route through the West Indies, the *Richard of Plymouth*, with two of these Indians aboard and commanded by Captain Henry Challons, set out in the summer of 1606 to reconnoitre the coast. One morning when the fog lifted in the Caribbean the *Richard* found herself in the midst of eight Spanish sail. The Spaniards seized the crew, divided them among the eight ships, and Seville, not Sagadohoc, was their destination—"the discoverie of our newe found coun-trey hath unhappelie bin Crost by our good friends the spaniards." [4] Both the Casa de Contratación and the Inquisition questioned the prisoners intensively, ordered them to draw charts, and then sent many either to jail or to the galleys.[5] Vigorous protests by the Eng-lish ambassador that these mariners were not bent on any harm to the Spanish Indies and had not violated the recent peace treaty, coupled with the mounting desire of Spain to cultivate English friendship in Europe, eventually secured the release of at least the principal leaders.[6]

Undaunted, but aware "that whosoever goes from England to America must provide goe stronger; for if they be taken, they are to expect noe Remission," [7] the Plymouth Company sent out another vessel the following year, this time with more success. The colonists established a settlement and built Fort St. George on the Sagadahoc River. It did not take Zúñiga long to obtain a plan of this fort and to forward it to Philip III.[8] It is hard to believe that the tem-peramental, unruly, poorly-supplied settlers ever built the well-constructed fort in Zúñiga's drawing, but it made no difference be-cause they abandoned the fort after only a year.

Ventures in the southern part of Virginia proved more fortunate. In 1607 the London Company sent out three small vessels and one hundred forty-four settlers to found a colony. Because of the unfavorable experience at Roanoke Island they by-passed Albemarle and Pamlico Sounds and instead established themselves on the more navigable Chesapeake Bay. Keeping Menéndez's surprise of the French in mind, they spent some time looking for a suitable site. The Jamestown peninsula finally selected offered many advantages: a good harbor, ease of defense from the Indians by land, and time for ample warning of an attack by sea. At once they fortified Point Com-fort at the mouth of the James to give warning to settlements up river. George Percy's experienced eye quickly recognized that had the James been discovered during the Spanish War, "it would have been a great annoyance to our enemies." [9]

The privations, internal quarrels, governmental reorganizations, Indian hostility, and ultimate success of the colony are well known. At first, under the dictatorial leadership of John Smith the colony enjoyed a moderate degree of success. Then after his departure the colony's fortunes dipped to their lowest ebb during the "starving time." The few surviving colonists hung on, and with continual reinforcements from England, the tide began to turn. John Rolfe, through his marriage to Pocahontas, established friendly relations with the Indians and, through his importation of tobacco seeds from the Spanish Indies and his improved method of curing tobacco, gave the colony a substitute for gold or silver. In time the settlers erected new fortifications at Cape Henry and Cape Charles and concluded defensive alliances with the Indians[10] to prevent "that all devouring Spaniard from laying his ravenous hands upon these gold shewing mountains." [11]

Spain's attitude toward this new English plantation was the same shown toward Ribault and Laudonnière in Florida, Raleigh at Roanoke, and recent English designs on Maine. There had been a cloud of secrecy surrounding Raleigh's Roanoke enterprises during wartime, but the plans and progress of the Virginia Company were well-publicized: at once the Spanish people had their "hearts and their eyes fixed much upon" Virginia.[12] Zúñiga vainly protested to James I that this company was usurping provinces of *la Florida,* and at the same time he kept Madrid informed of Jamestown's fortunes.

For over a decade after 1607 the Spanish Council of War, denying England's right to settle here and doggedly insisting that this colony violated the recent treaty, considered sending a one-thousand, two-thousand, or even five-thousand-man expedition, organized in either New or Old Spain, to expel the Jamestown intruders. The danger, direct and indirect, to the Spanish Indies was painfully obvious. Not only was the Chesapeake athwart the return route of the treasure fleet, but given time this "gran cancer" might flourish, expand, and even threaten the heart of New Spain. For a variety of reasons—though not because the council felt exterminating the Virginia settlement would violate the peace treaty—none of its proposals were put into effect. There was a perennial lack of funds, and during the "starving time" when the settlers were reduced to eating vermin and, at least in one case, a fellow colonist, it appeared that Jamestown would succumb by itself as had Sagadahoc and Roanoke.[13] Also it was quickly obvious that the metal which the Englishmen brought from Virigina was "not as rich as had been thought." [14] In fact, it was worthless. By the time Spain realized this colony was permanent, rival and more immediately dangerous ones were appearing in various parts of the New World.

The intricate, rapidly changing European situation was another reason why Jamestown was spared. Tensions were building up to eventually explode in the Thirty Years War, and at once both England and Spain were involved. Spain resumed hostilities in the Netherlands, and Spanish troops supported the designs of the Austrian Habsburg emperor in Germany. English troops were never directly committed in Germany, but James I's Protestant nephew, Frederick V, Elector Palatine, was in the thick of the fighting, and in short order this Winter King lost his domain to imperial forces. Both before and after the actual outbreak of hostilities in 1618, negotiations were underway for an Anglo-Spanish alliance—an alliance appealing more to James I than to many of his subjects. James expected Spain to use her influence with the Austrian Habsburgs to uphold the interests of his nephew in the Empire. Spain, on the other hand, appreciated the value of English neutrality or even open support in the war on the continent. Should there be a formal alliance, it would be buttressed by a marriage of James's son to the Spanish infanta. Even though the alliance and marriage never took place, Spanish theologians during most of James's reign wrestled with the intricacies of a Protestant-Catholic union. The possibility of an alliance and the Spanish desire for England at least to remain neutral on the continent was a consideration that weighed heavily when the Spanish King refused the belligerent advice of his council of war concerning Virginia.[15]

Prior to the colonizing activities of the Virginia Company, Spain had considered abandoning St. Augustine, removing the Christian Indians to Hispaniola, and erecting a new, smaller fort along the peninsula to rescue shipwrecked mariners.[16] After Jamestown she quickly abandoned these ideas. Fortunately her position in Florida was stronger now than it had been for two decades. Zealous Franciscan efforts had paid rich dividends in harmonious Indian relations, and the presidio at St. Augustine had been repaired so that the triangular wooden structure could truly be called a fort rather than a beehive.[17] In addition, the Florida governor ordered Indians living along the coast to capture any Europeans who came ashore for wood and water.[18] It was problematical whether or not the Indians would obey this order because of their numerous prior contacts with English and French ship captains. But it was an unfortunate corsair or colonist who, by whatever means, fell into Spanish hands. A sentence to the galleys was the best fate to be hoped for. At almost the same time that Virginia colonists were stepping ashore at Cape Henry, Spanish soldiers captured a band of French and English "pirates" and took them to St. Augustine. The governor "used the proper treatment toward them" and converted ten to the faith. Then all were hanged as Christians.[19]

The Spanish position in Florida was steadily improving, but there was little the three-hundred-man garrison could do about Jamestown. There was even less that the distant frontier outposts in northeastern Mexico could do, although officials at both places advanced projects to expel the English.[20] The first threat to Virginia came not from St. Augustine, or from Mexico, or from Spain, but rather from Spanish agents within the Jamestown colony itself—at least indications strongly suggest this. In the past half century Spanish confidants had accompanied most of the English colonization voyages to North America, and it would be illogical to think that none were passengers to Virginia in 1607. The Jamestown colonists were not a carefully screened group, and it would have been easy for the Spanish ambassador to include one or more sympathetic Catholics—this is precisely what he did with subsequent voyages. In any case, during the early critical years there were sputterings, grumblings, plots, and intrigues. Many were directed toward Smith and the autocratic manner in which he governed. In turn, he usually charged his antagonists with being Spanish agents. Doubtless most of them committed no offense except to oppose Smith; even so, there is probably at least some foundation for his allegations.

Scarcity of provisions in 1609 forced some of the colonists to split up into groups and to live with and off neighboring Indians. According to Smith there was a Spanish-inspired design, headed by "the Dutchman and one Bently" to incite the Indians to massacre the Englishmen while they were in such a precarious position. Smith sent William Volda to apprehend these two conspirators, but instead of taking them prisoner he joined in their insidious plot. Smith apparently defeated this scheme by executing the major participants.[21]

About this same time a blacksmith was condemned to be hanged for an undisclosed crime. Before going to the gallows, no doubt hoping to avoid the trip entirely, he accused Captain George Kendall, one of the original councilors, of fomenting a dangerous Spanish conspiracy. Though the exact nature of these charges has not been preserved, it is likely there was some basis for them. In the recent past apparently Kendall had been a soldier and an English spy in the Netherlands and could easily have made arrangements to betray the colony into Spanish hands. In any case he was immediately tried, convicted, and shot.[22] There are few first-hand accounts of the early years at Jamestown not written by Smith himself, and it is difficult to determine in what degree all or any of these plots were influenced by Spain.

It is likely that there were Englishmen in Virginia in Spanish employ who worked to overthrow the colony. It is definite that at least some Englishmen did just this at home. Authorities seized a Captain Waiman in an English port when he secretly attempted to flee to Spain to show the Spaniards how best to destroy the new English colony.[23] Another Englishman, the widely-traveled, crafty Anthony Shirley, who in the past had made privateering expeditions to the Spanish Main but now was out of favor at home and was attempting to ingratiate himself at Madrid, vividly pointed out the dangers of Virginia and offered to use his influence with his brother-in-law, the debt-ridden Governor De la Warr, to cause Jamestown's downfall—all for suitable compensation of course; that is, being allowed to send one or more ships to trade with the Spanish Indies. Shirley's machinations were "not of strength enough to draw money out of a dry [Spanish] purse," though Spain pensioned him for other services.[24]

The first Spaniards definitely known to have visited Virginia came not surreptitiously as spies but openly on a Spanish vessel whose mission was to determine the exact state of the English plantation. The Spanish Council of War, which was considering the best method of dealing with this threat to the Indies, dispatched them. The Council ordered Governor Pedro de Ibarra at St. Augustine to make a reconnaissance to discover the precise location of the English settlements and the best route to attack them.

Accordingly, Ibarra outfitted Captain Francisco Fernández de Ecija with a pinnace, twenty-five men, and the Indian wife of a Spanish soldier as interpreter.[25] Ecija, a long-time resident of St. Augustine, and commander of an infantry company, was well qualified for this mission. In 1605 he had commanded an expedition which captured French corsairs on the Savannah River and later that same year had made a reconnaissance as far north as Cape Romain.[26] Now his superiors ordered him to sail to Chesapeake Bay and, if by chance the English colony there had failed, to continue northward to ascertain Champlain's activities in Canada. His first stop was at the Jordan River (Cape Fear) where Indians gave eye-witness ac-

counts of how the whites had built a fort on the Jamestown peninsula, how they had secured it with heavy armaments, how numerous
vessels traded there, and how others guarded the harbor. At the
Jordan he rescued a Frenchman from the Indians. Though he had
lived among them for many years and had almost forgotten his native
tongue, in a short time he was able to confirm and elaborate their
reports.

Ecija sailed for Jacán, as the Spaniards called Virginia, to see for
himself. After passing through the capes at the entrance of the
Chesapeake, he saw that the Indians had told the truth. A ship, a
large one with two topsails and a great banner at its masthead, was
on guard in the bay. It sailed in the opposite direction, and Ecija
became suspicious. Was it purposely enticing him further into the
bay? Not to be outdone, Ecija too sailed in the opposite direction—
back through the capes and down to the North Carolina coast. Here
perhaps he contemplated checking Roanoke Island for signs of
renewed English activity, or possibly he actually examined the island.
But foul weather off the treacherous Carolina coast forced him to
seek refuge in the Jordan where he requestioned the Indians before
finally returning to St. Augustine. His detailed report about the
English in Jacán added little to information obtained long ago by
the Spanish ambassador in London.[27]

To get a more accurate picture of conditions and specific settlements Spain increased her efforts to smuggle spies into Virginia.[28]
At the same time Philip III ordered another vessel to visit Jacán. In
April 1611 the *Nuestra Señora del Rosario* cleared Lisbon. Aboard
were Captain Diego de Molina, Ensign Antonio Pérez, and the pilot,
Francis Lymbry. Molina and Pérez were native Spaniards, while
Lymbry was an Englishman who lived in Madrid with his Spanish
wife. Their official commission authorized them to search along the
coast of *la Florida* for a wrecked Spanish man-of-war and to salvage
its artillery. But this was merely an excuse to spy out the Virginia
colony.[29]

Molina and his confederates touched at Havana and St. Augustine
before sailing boldly into the Chesapeake. Quickly they detected
signs of English activity at Point Comfort, and squads of Englishmen
emerged from the forest to greet Molina as he stepped ashore from
his longboat. The Spanish Captain patiently explained that he
desired only to continue searching for the shipwrecked vessel. His
English hosts warily replied that they would have to report this to

their governor thirty miles up river at Jamestown. Meanwhile why
not place the Spanish vessel in safety behind Point Comfort? Molina,
Pérez, and Lymbry remained ashore, while John Clark returned with
the other Spaniards to the *Nuestra Señora* to pilot her in the strange
waters. Smouldering suspicion now broke into open flame. The
Englishmen refused to let Molina and his two companions return
to their ship. At the same time, the remaining Spaniards, becoming
alarmed, refused to take shelter behind Point Comfort or to release
the pilot Clark. The *Nuestra Señora* beat up and down before Point
Comfort but, because Molina failed to give the prearranged signal,
did not land. Fearing for their safety, the Spaniards fled the Chesapeake with the unwilling English pilot aboard.[30]

The three Spaniards were taken to Jamestown and interrogated
thoroughly. Though prisoners and watched closely, their treatment
seems to have been no harsher than was made necessary by the
rigorous conditions at Jamestown. Pérez died in 1612 "more from
hunger than from sickness," [31] but such a fate was not reserved only
for Spaniards.

Two years later, Lymbry, the "confidential" Englishman, supposedly encouraged five colonists to desert Jamestown in a small
bark and to head for Spanish Florida. At once Thomas Dale, now
in charge of the colony, hired Indians to track them down. English
reports had it that the five fugitives were overtaken and "receive[d]
their desserts," [32] though Molina contended this was only a false
rumor to prevent similar attempts in the future.[33] Lymbry did not
know whether the fugitives made good their escape or not. He did
know that it was likely he would soon die. In addition to being involved with the escapees, it came to light that he had been an English
pilot in the Spanish Armada of 1588. Sentenced to death, he temporarily saved his life by confessing that there were several Spanish
ships bound for Virginia to ferret out the state of the colony. This
reprieve proved short-lived, however. He was aboard ship when the
stern Marshal Dale returned to England in 1616, and for an undisclosed reason Lymbry was hanged en route.[34]

Molina fared better than his two companions. Until 1616 he remained in Virginia where he was able to smuggle letters back to
England between the soles of a Venetian's shoe and in other ingeni-
ous ways. These letters told how the colonists were almost destitute,
how a Spanish fleet would be welcomed "to release them from this
misery," [35] and how Samuel Argall had overcome a weak French

colony in Canada and had the reckless idea of doing the same thing to the Spaniards in Florida.[36] Molina was at last shipped to London —a passenger aboard the same vessel that carried Rolfe and his Indian bride Pocahontas—and was turned over to the Spanish ambassador.[37] Ultimately Molina secured his release and returned to his native Spain.

John Clark had made a similar enforced odyssey. From Jamestown he was taken to Havana where Spanish officials recorded voluminous pages of his testimony concerning particulars of the colony, the outpost at Point Comfort, the main fort at Jamestown, the number of able-bodied men, the "pirates" that used Jamestown as a base, and a myriad of other details. From Havana Clark went to Madrid and, either because of expediency or religious conviction, became a Catholic en route. Once in Spain he was imprisoned, questioned, and finally released in exchange for Molina.[38] Clark returned to London and piloted other ships to Virginia, including the *Mayflower* which landed at Plymouth in 1620. [39]

Ever since the organization of the Virginia Company, Spain had protested against the English plantation and had threatened to use force. She subjected the English ambassador in Madrid to frequent "hot disputes" over this illegal settlement.[40] She quickly realized, however, that verbal remonstrances were useless and instead prepared elaborate plans to expel these venturous Englishmen. This is why Ecija and Molina made their reconnaissances. But Spain never sent an expedition: she was almost bankrupt and her decaying navy was overextended; there was the advantage of maintaining the friendship of England to keep her from openly committing herself to the Protestant cause in the Thirty Years War; and during and after the "starving time" it appeared that the colony would fail without Spanish interference.

Jamestown's location was partly responsible for its protection. It was adjacent to the return sailing route to Europe which for Spanish naval commanders presented difficulties. A logical force to use against Virginia were the galleons which were in the West Indies awaiting to convoy the merchant ships to Europe. Supposedly while these merchantmen were protected at Portobello, Veracruz, and other ports and the trade fairs were in progress, the galleons could pay Jamestown a visit. Because of the prevailing winds and currents it was easy to sail from the West Indies to Jamestown, but it was difficult to return. Should the galleons not get back to the

West Indies in time to convoy the treasure fleet it would be disastrous. Theoretically the galleons could detour and stop at Jamestown while escorting the treasure fleet to Europe, but this was risky and never seriously considered. Had Jamestown been in the West Indies within easy reach of the galleons or been founded a half century earlier when the Spanish navy was stronger and the mother country not so exhausted from wars, then the English would have suffered Ribault's fate. Stucley, who had been associated with Ribault and Queen Elizabeth, may have been wiser than most realized when he took to piracy rather than colonizing Florida in 1563.

Nevertheless rumors circulated throughout Europe that a powerful Spanish armada had departed for Virginia, that the galleons of the treasure fleet had paid Jamestown a visit before returning to Spain, or that Spain had actually destroyed the infant colony.[41] These reports were still prevalent two decades after Jamestown's founding. In 1620 John Rolfe received supposedly reliable word of a forthcoming attack in the spring. With no place of strength to retreat to, few experienced soldiers, and poor ordnance, this news was disheartening.[42] Five years later England and Spain were at war, after all efforts to bring about a Spanish marriage collapsed, and the anti-Spanish Parliament at last had its way. The colonists, almost prostrate after the recent Indian massacre, braced themselves and hoarded their powder for the expected Spanish descent.[43] Fortunately Spain was deeply committed in Germany, in defending Cádiz from a mismanaged English expedition, and in warding off the Dutch elsewhere in America; and this threat to Virginia, like every other, failed to materialize.

In spite of famine, internal discord, and Indian hostility, the budding English colony survived and in time prospered. Meanwhile other English colonies were founded, and Spain could ill afford the luxury of venting her spleen exclusively on this one. Governor Gates en route to Virginia in 1609 was shipwrecked on the tiny dot of Bermuda in the North Atlantic. The Virginia Company established a colony here and for several years after the "starving time" considered it a more promising one than Jamestown, while the Spaniards considered it a more dangerous one.[44] Less than a decade later the desperate Raleigh was actively searching for El Dorado in Guiana and attempting to carve out an empire along the Orinoco. He failed, and lost his head for doing so, but his South American enterprises, closer to the heart of the Spanish Indies, were of more immediate concern to Spain than either Bermuda or Jamestown.[45] These other English colonization attempts diverted attention from Jamestown and helped insure its success. Equally important in diverting attention from Jamestown were the exploits of the Dutch who were founding the New Netherlands in North America, taking over much of Brazil in South America, raiding Spanish possessions in all quarters of the New World, and in one year (1628) even capturing the entire Spanish treasure fleet.

Spain was on the defensive in the West Indies and in *la Florida* and was almost excluded from her lucrative share of the Newfoundland fishery. This fishery was valuable not only for codfish but also for stimulating a nation's merchant marine and training seamen—important for both peace and war. It had been galling to Spain to see the Virginia Company successfully settle Jamestown and Bermuda and at the same time to see English men-of-war exclude Spanish vessels from the fishery.[46] Philip II never recovered from the blows struck by Bernard Drake and Raleigh in 1585 when both in Newfoundland and in European waters they captured many Spanish or Portuguese vessels; equally ruinous was the fact that even before the Armada the entire Spanish fishing industry, along with Spanish industrial life in general, was in a state of decline from various causes. During the wars with England, France, and the Netherlands, Spain impressed large numbers of Biscayan seamen to man her warships. After the turn of the century, when at least quasi-peaceful conditions existed, England and France for all practical purposes had divided the fishery; Spain now was forced to import fish from one or both of these nations; and there was little Philip III, whose marine was weakened by the recent wars, could do. A few Biscayans still fished at Bacalaos, but gone were the days when one or even two hundred Spanish vessels visited the fishery annually. When war again broke out in 1625 after the unorthodox wooing of the Spanish infanta by impulsive Prince Charles and all attempts at a Spanish marriage had broken down, it was reported that Spain had prepared a one-hundred-and-forty sail armada to capture the English fishing fleet.[47] This project came to naught, and Biscayans contented themselves with sending a dozen or so vessels to the Channel to intercept English ships returning from Newfoundland.[48]

Though Spain was excluded from the fishery and rival European settlements were popping up with alarming frequency in the Indies, Spain did not forget Virginia. Indeed she could not. Virginia never became the nest of pirates that Spain feared, but there were always enough to merit attention. Ralph Bingley, one of the earliest Virginia settlers, was charged with commanding a vessel which seized Spanish ships off Spain. That he was acquitted and his captures made in European waters did not remove from Spanish minds the close association between piracy and Virginia.[49] After 1610 Robert Rich outfitted a number of vessels which frequently carried secret commissions from foreign countries to prey on Spanish commerce. Several of his ships were readily provisioned and allowed to trade at Jamestown, particularly when Samuel Argall was governor.[50] The founding of Puritan New England in 1620 considerably enlarged the pirates' nest in Spanish eyes, when periodically "divine Providence" directed Spanish booty to Boston and Plymouth.[51] Had Raleigh or someone else successfully founded a settlement on the Chesapeake during the war against Philip II, then Spain would have had far more to fear from Virginia privateers.

The garrison at St. Augustine had had no direct and little indirect contact with the Jamestown colonists. After 1607 at least the common soldiers were more concerned with whether the *situado* would arrive and with submitting petitions for relief and for permission to leave than with the Englishmen in distant Jacán.[52] Nearby friendly Indians furnished little information about the English because of distance and the language barrier with the Algonquin Indians who lived near Jamestown. Occasionally prospective Virginia colonists were wrecked on the Florida coast.[53] If they escaped death at the hands of the Indians, they would find comparative safety at St. Augustine and would tell something of Virginia. One pauses to wonder, though, whether the tedious, minute, repetitious questioning by Spanish officials was less painful than remaining with the Indians.

Florida governors were more worried about English penetration in the West Indies than about English settlements in the northern part of *la Florida*. English colonies in the Lesser Antilles and in Old Providence were bad enough, but they were only a prelude to what Oliver Cromwell contrived. His Western Design envisioned capturing major Spanish centers in the New World and in time wresting the entire Indies from Spain. The first attack by Admiral William Penn on Santo Domingo in 1655 was a failure, and uninviting, almost undefended, Jamaica seemed a poor compensation at the time. Spain had not known where Penn would strike and had considered

St. Augustine one of several likely targets.[54] Bitter memories of Drake stimulated the undermanned garrison here to redouble its defensive efforts. Thus in the 1650s the Englishmen in distant Jacán seemed not so serious a threat as their rapid expansion in the West Indies. All this changed abruptly when they settled at San Jorge, a far more southerly province of *la Florida*.

Carolina
Controversy

Chapter 5

Spain was alarmed but not surprised when foreigners usurped fertile, inviting, and unoccupied Chicora—later called San Jorge, Santa Elena, and Carolina.[1] The English settlements here in the 1660s were not the first attempt to exploit this region. Ayllón, Ribault, and Raleigh had all been forerunners and had all met disaster. Menéndez established temporary Spanish control of this area when he built Fort San Felipe at Port Royal and constructed blockhouses in the interior, but within about a decade these blockhouses were abandoned, and Drake's devastating raid in 1586 forced the Port Royal garrison to withdraw to St. Augustine. Later the northernmost province of *la Florida* occupied by Spain would be Guale or Georgia, though at times Santa Elena in southern South Carolina should also be included. Here enterprising Franciscans dotted the coastal islands and nearby mainland with numerous missions.

Spain and England both claimed Carolina: Spain by the papal bulls and first discovery, and England by the Cabot voyages. Not legalistic theorizing, however, but effective occupation settled this dispute, and other similar ones, in England's favor. To the north both Sweden and the Netherlands had claims on part of North America, and both followed up their claims by establishing colonies. Ultimately New Sweden capitulated to the Dutch in 1655, and in turn England conquered the New Netherlands in 1664. If these two countries had been unable to make good their North American claims by actual colonization, what chance was there that largely uninhabited Carolina would remain under even nominal Spanish control?

In the seventeenth century Spain was in an unfavorable position to contest the Atlantic Coast with England and other powers. From an early date England had asserted that she had the right to explore and occupy lands not actually settled by the Spaniards, and in this century there was little likelihood that Spain would settle the Atlantic Seaboard. At home her economy was in a miserable condition; her leading manufacturing and commercial centers were decaying; her navy was shattered; her population was decreasing; and the immigrants who continued to go to the Indies in fairly large numbers still went instead to Mexico and to Central and South America, where there was an established government and society, where the Indians had been largely subdued, where there was economic opportunity, and where there was relative safety from foreign attack.

English conditions in the seventeenth century were entirely different. Although there were periodic depressions, her economy prospered and expanded; there was a marked increase in her population and, at least in the first part of the century, supposedly she was overpopulated. Colonies were an ideal vent for this apparent surplus population, and, as has been seen, one area where England was determined to plant these colonists was on the North American Atlantic Coast. With a mounting surge of settlers streaming across the Atlantic, England could well afford to uphold the doctrine of effective occupation in Virginia, in New England, or now in Carolina. This doctrine, which England had been advocating since the sixteenth century, affirmed that Christian European countries had the legal right to occupy territory and the moral duty to convert the heathen in any part of America not actually colonized by Christians.

It is difficult, if not impossible, to say exactly when England began to settle Carolina. In the early 1630s when Maryland was becoming a Catholic refuge and New England was becoming a Puritan retreat, plans were underfoot to have Carolina become in part a Huguenot haven under English auspices. French Huguenots, harassed at home, were fleeing to England in increasing numbers. Several of their leaders proposed that they and Protestant Englishmen jointly settle Carolina, claiming it for England and thereby aiding her in the war with Spain. Charles I in 1629 granted to his influential advisor, Attorney General Sir Robert Heath, all of Carolina between the thirty-first and thirty-sixth degree latitude, which provided a legal basis for the Protestant colonists to go to Carolina.[2] A goodly number prepared to leave England; some actually left and got as far as Virginia; a few made explorations along the coast; but none, or possibly only a trickle, ever reached their destinations.[3]

Because England made peace with Spain in 1630 and because Charles I revived negotiations for a Spanish alliance and for opening the American trade, the English monarch lost interest in Carolina colonization. This did not apply to all of his subjects, as in the case of the governor of Barbados who intimated he was going to settle Carolina,[4] or in the case of other Englishmen who, perhaps excited by Heath's activities, continuously eyed Carolina. During the Cromwellian period England became more aggressive in the New World, and apparently part of the Lord Protector's unsuccessful Western Design to control key areas was to capture St. Augustine and the adjoining coastal region dominating the return sailing route to Europe.[5] The promotional tracts published in the early 1650s are one example of heightened Puritan concern for Carolina, which, among other advantages, afforded a dumping ground for paupers, orphans, royalists and other undesirables.[6] Early in the following decade adventurous New Englanders formed a fleeting, ineffectual colony on the Cape Fear River.[7] But with the exception of scattered, irregular settlements on Albemarle and Pamlico Sounds by colonists who had drifted southward from Virginia, there still was no permanent English colony in Carolina.

Since the founding of Jamestown and the establishment of English colonies in the West Indies, Spain had realized that England was or soon would be covetous of Carolina. But Spain, having more serious problems with the Dutch in the New World and plagued by a decaying navy and an empty treasury, was not able to oppose English ambitions effectively or to strengthen her own position materially in northern Florida. But there were exceptions. The Franciscan missions in Timucua, Guale and Santa Elena, despite numerous setbacks, extended their influence over additional Indians and enjoyed a steady growth.[8] The constant rumors before 1660, some of which were true, that Englishmen were in Carolina and even had built a fort there, caused the Florida governor to send out periodic military expeditions along the coast.[9] During the war with Cromwell's Protectorate, Spain nurtured the idea of regaining Virginia or at least of limiting its southern boundary,[10] but she was fortunate to lose nothing more than Jamaica in the New World and some of her returning treasure vessels before they reached safety in Cádiz or Seville. As in the past, there were the usual complaints that Florida's garrison was "perishing of hunger," and nothing altered the basic fact that Spain's hold on Florida was a tenuous one.

It was not until after the English Restoration when Charles II adopted a more aggressive imperial policy that Spain had serious cause for alarm. At their suggestion, he rewarded and reimbursed his faithful supporters during the barren years of the Interregnum with extensive New World grants. It was in this manner that in 1663 the eight Lords Proprietors of Carolina received a charter to the territory formerly granted Heath. Two years later the crown extended the boundaries to thirty-six degrees thirty minutes on the north, which included most of the settlers around the Chowan River, and to twenty-nine degrees on the south, which included the extensive missions in Guale, the presidio at St. Augustine, and not an insignificant part of New Spain itself. The primary reason for extending the southern boundary was to include the northern Gulf Coast which had only a few more whites now than in de Soto's day. Heath's charter of 1629 stipulated that he could occupy only territory not inhabited by the subjects of any Christian prince. It was no oversight when Charles II omitted this provision from his charters.[11]

The Lords Proprietors confidently expected to secure colonists from New England, Virginia, the West Indies, and particularly from overcrowded Barbados where political and economic conditions favored such a move. Leading planters here dispatched Captain William Hilton in 1663 to select a desirable site for the new plantation. This experienced Massachusetts mariner, who had explored the Cape Fear region the preceding year for a group of New England entrepreneurs, sailed from Barbados in the *Adventure* and by late August was off Carolina, just north of Port Royal. Indians poured forth out of the dense forest to greet this strange vessel, and Hilton bartered trinkets for information. They related that not long ago an English vessel was wrecked here and that some of the crew were still alive, prisoners in nearby Indian villages. Using bribery, threats, and coercion, Hilton rescued some and was bargaining for the remainder when a canoe with an Indian "standing up and holding a paper in a cleft stick," approached the *Adventure*.[12] The mysterious paper was a letter from a Spanish officer announcing that the remaining Englishmen were Indian prisoners at Santa Elena. He claimed he would arrange their exchange for Hilton's Indian hostages and suitable presents, if only the *Adventure* would put in at Santa Elena.[13] Hilton, his suspicions aroused, replied that he could not read the Spanish letter, that his only concern was to rescue the Englishmen, and that "at present [I have no] business with you." [14] Because the Indians ashore became increasingly hostile, Hilton decided to abandon the remaining prisoners altogether.

Before leaving Port Royal he saw signs of prior Spanish influence —a deserted mission with a large cross still before it, and the ruins and entrenchments of an abandoned fort. These probably were the remains of one of the two Spanish forts erected on Parris Island, or possibly even the vestiges of Ribault's Charlesfort.[15] From Port Royal Hilton headed north, intently scrutinizing the Carolina coast until he finally reached the Cape Fear River which he had mapped in detail the previous year. Here there were cattle running about and a letter nailed to a post by New England settlers giving a disparaging account of the colony's brief existence. Undaunted by this unfavorable account and his reception at Port Royal, Hilton returned to Barbados and, as he had done in his 1662 relation, again painted glowing pictures of "pleasant and delightful" Carolina where "the ayr is clear and sweet," and "the lands are laden with large tall oaks, walnuts, and bayes." [16]

Influenced by Hilton's favorable description of his two voyages, Barbadian settlers founded a colony at Cape Fear in 1664. Colonel Robert Sanford explored southward for desirable sites for future settlements, and in his detailed examination of the coast he concurred with Hilton as to the desirability of Port Royal with its excellent harbor and fertile soil. Fortunately the Indians with whom he came into contact were much friendlier than those encountered by Hilton. One cacique even insisted that his son join the English, and, in return, a member of Sanford's party, the youthful doctor, Henry Woodward, provided with an Indian maid to care for his every need, volunteered to remain with the Indians to learn their language and customs.[17] Sanford returned to Cape Fear where a combination of misfortunes soon brought about the colony's downfall. His voyage, however, like Hilton's before, pointed out the many advantages of southern Carolina, even though it was "in the very chops of the Spaniards." [18] It was here that the Lords Proprietors determined to plant their next colony, and it was here that for the first time they were successful. They selected Port Royal as the most promising spot, but after reaching Carolina the colonists themselves decided the region further north on the Kiawha (Ashley River) was better. In this fashion in 1670 Charleston had its genesis.

Ever since the 1650s Spain had nervously observed the penetration into Carolina by the English. There were endless accounts of their progress from numerous sources—the ambassador in London, English promotional tracts, Spanish patrols sent out from Guale, friendly Indians, and English prisoners. Immediately Spain was cognizant of Charleston, and for the next half century the cardinal policy at St. Augustine was to expel these English intruders. A relatively remote settlement at Jacán was one thing; this new settlement at San Jorge, bordering on Guale and threatening all of *la Florida*, was entirely different, for it was apparent that a successful colony here placed Florida in grave peril.

A more immediate threat, however, and one more severely felt, was a destructive freebooting raid on St. Augustine in 1668 by the notorious Jamaican corsair, Robert Searles. He had captured a Spanish vessel laden with flour bound for St. Augustine. With the cowed Spanish crew at pistol point still manning the ship, Searles and his men, safely hidden below deck, slipped into St. Augustine unnoticed. The pirates who emerged from this floating Trojan horse completely surprised the town. They killed men, women, and children indiscriminately; the governor and part of the garrison escaped to the woods; and a few made it safely to the fort. Though Searles did not have the artillery to overcome the fort, the town itself was at his mercy. Holding the governor's daughter as security, the pirates methodically looted houses, churches, and storehouses. Stripping the sails from vessels in the harbor and vowing to return, they finally departed with their plunder.[19]

Searles took a passenger aboard—not a hapless Spaniard to await ransom, but the enterprising English physician, Henry Woodward. After remaining with the Indians in 1666 and even sharing regal authority with the cacique, Woodward had been rudely dethroned by a Spanish patrol. His captors had taken him to St. Augustine where his treatment appears to have been anything but harsh. Awaiting to be sent to the Casa de Contratación, he served as an interpreter and at the same time observed at first hand the tenuous Spanish hold on Florida, based primarily on the garrison at St. Augustine and the mission system. In the future this cost the Spaniards dearly. For awhile Woodward plied his trade as surgeon in the West Indies, then joined the fleet bringing the original Charleston colonists, and in time became the most effective and influential Indian trader and agent in the southeast.[20]

English expansion in Carolina, possible English designs westward on New Mexico—Diego Dioniso Briceño Peñalosa, a former governor of New Mexico, was in London urging England to take over that province and especially others in the Indies[21]—and above all English depredations in the Caribbean infuriated the Spaniards. To ease these tensions in the New World and others in the Old, England and Spain signed a treaty in 1667 which was broken more often than observed, certainly so by English buccaneers like Searles. England did not want a war with Spain which would ruin Anglo-Spanish commerce to the benefit of the Dutch and French, and correctly felt the shaky Spanish monarchy, menaced on several fronts by Louis XIV, needed English support. Also in 1668 Spain grudgingly admitted the independence of England's ancient ally, Portugal. Conditions, therefore, were favorable for another, more explicit treaty. This new treaty of 1670, appropriately called the American Treaty, had many provisions, though one of the most controversial was the clause asserting that England had the right to "hold and possess forever" all lands she now occupied in America. Clearly this meant that Spain gave up her claim to Jamaica and recognized English settlements in Virginia and to the north. But what of fringe areas in the New World recently occupied by Englishmen, such as remote spots on the Yucatán peninsula where valuable logwood trees grew, or Charleston? Were Englishmen established in these areas before 1670? Did this give England title to these regions? If so, what were their boundaries? [22] Though these issues attracted little attention in drawing up the treaty, they were soon raised and were not resolved quickly—or, for that matter, ever.

For the Spanish government in Madrid the most dangerous peril was not Charleston, but the hundreds of former buccaneers swarming ashore cutting logwood on the Yucatán peninsula, or those who were not ashore and were still a-roving. But for the Spanish governor at St. Augustine it was a different story. This new English settlement at Charleston, or San Jorge as the Spaniards called it, bordered on the province of Guale, threatened to undermine the extensive mission system there, and in time could wrest Spain's control of St.

Augustine, of the Gulf Coast, and even of the mines of New Spain. At once, and for years to come, there was the unceasing demand at St. Augustine that the English be expelled from Charleston.

Even before news of the signing of the 1670 Treaty of Madrid and with only the limited forces at St. Augustine, Governor Manuel de Condoya launched an abortive attack. Disturbing reports at Charleston that a menacing Spanish and Indian force was hovering south of the infant settlement threw its inhabitants into consternation. A timely relief vessel scurried into Charleston, and, according to Dr. Woodward, the Spaniards were afraid to try anything against the well-supplied, resolute Charleston defenders.[23] A sudden storm scattered the Spanish craft and was equally important in forcing them to withdraw to St. Augustine.[24]

After signing the Treaty of Madrid of 1670 and after one unsuccessful venture, Condoya contemplated a second attack, even though he believed such an attack would be a treaty violation. For several years Condoya erroneously considered that Port Royal had been settled in 1669 (probably because the Proprietors had shown such an interest here) and that England had a valid claim. But this did not deter the Florida governor. Not overly concerned with the 1670 treaty and confronted with the immediate Carolina menace, he "neglected" to publish the treaty at St. Augustine and continued preparations for a renewed attack[25]—an attack delayed only because of insufficient forces. The home government ordered the viceroy of New Spain to furnish troops, money, and supplies to Florida immediately, while at the same time to strictly obey the American Treaty. Since for some time the viceroy also believed that Carolina was founded in 1669 and an attack would then be a treaty violation, he delayed sending reinforcements until the Spanish crown made clear its policy, which it was not quick to do.[26] In the interval Condoya anxiously watched the small unfortified settlement at Charleston prosper, expand, and strengthen itself. He did not abandon his determination to destroy Charleston, but the forces at St. Augustine first needed reinforcements from other parts of the Indies. This dilemma was as obvious as it was difficult to overcome.

Almost a century earlier the Spaniards in Florida had had the almost impossible task of discovering what, if anything, the English were doing in Jacán. This was never a problem at near-by Charleston. Indian accounts, first-hand reconnaissances by Spanish soldiers, and testimonies of English prisoners or fugitives from Carolina kept St.

Augustine supplied with timely information. The most valuable early accounts came from Englishmen themselves who, for one reason or another, ended up in St. Augustine. Even in 1670 some of the Charleston colonists fell into Spanish hands. During a violent gale, the *Three Brothers* became separated from the rest of the fleet, and, battered and crippled, sought respite at St. Catherines Island in Guale. The outwardly hospitable Indians gladly supplied food and water, and not until a shore party failed to return did the English have cause for alarm. They spent an anxious night aboard the *Three Brothers,* and the following morning their worst suspicions were confirmed. Then "we heard a drume, and presently saw 4 Spaniards armed with muskets and swords" file out of the forest. The Englishmen defiantly refused to surrender and amid "a volley of musket shott and cloud of arrows" hastily departed St. Catherines, abandoning the eleven men and women in the shore party.[27] Next month Governor Joseph West sent a vessel from Charleston to St. Catherines to secure his compatriots' release. The Spaniards not only refused to give up their captives from the *Three Brothers* but also added two more to their catch from this second vessel.[28] The English prisoners not killed by the Indians were taken to St. Augustine where the governor had ways to persuade them to tell all about Charleston.

Not all the Englishmen in Spanish Florida were such unwilling guests. During the first years, conditions at Charleston were rigorous: the virgin forest had to be cleared for crops and houses, and much labor was required to construct even rudimentary defenses against the constant threat of Spanish attack. This prospect of ceaseless toil was one of the reasons that some indentured servants and "noted villains" deserted to Florida.[29] Here they were well received, and their comprehensive, derisive accounts of Carolina were most welcome.

It was this growing English colony, and the destructive, humiliating raid by Searles in 1668, that spurred Spain out of her usual lethargy when Florida was concerned. She sent over a hundred men to supplement the undermanned Florida garrison and began to build a truly formidable fort at St. Augustine. Since Menéndez's day there had been nine different forts, all wooden and none impregnable. Using Indian labor and native stone—soft, workable coquina —and utilizing the ideas of the noted French engineer, Prestre de Vauban, she began work on the new Castillo de San Marcos in 1672. Fifteen years later the imposing fortress was essentially completed.

The effectiveness of its commanding location, its massive coquina walls and wide moat, its dominating four-sided bastions, and its generous allotment of heavy artillery was demonstrated on more than one occasion when it withstood both storm and siege.[30]

Spain not only strengthened St. Augustine itself but also took less successful measures to buttress her control throughout Florida. The Gulf Coast region of Apalachee, included in the Carolina charter, was given prime consideration. As early as 1633 Franciscans extended their missions westward into Apalachee. The center of missionary activity was San Luis (Tallahassee) from which thirteen lesser missions radiated at the high tide of missionary effectiveness around 1675. Because of the English threat in Carolina and the pirate threat to the Gulf Coast, Spain sent troops to San Luis in 1658; shortly afterwards she built Fort San Marcos near the intersection of the St. Marks and Wakulla Rivers.[31]

Since there were only scattered missions and a handful of troops in Apalachee, Spanish control here depended almost exclusively on Indian loyalty—a fact appreciated no less in Charleston than in St. Augustine. Indian allegiance frequently was ephemeral and became even more so with the appearance of Carolina traders. In the late 1670s the Florida governor made frequent but futile pleas that Spanish Canary Island colonists be sent to Apalachee to ward off the aggressive Carolinians and to provide St. Augustine with a dependable food supply.[32] But it was no easier to entice Canary Islanders to Florida than colonists from the Spanish peninsula itself.

Strengthening the presidio at St. Augustine and fortifying and, to a limited degree, colonizing Apalachee were merely passive measures taken to contain the Carolinians. The attack launched from St. Augustine in 1670 had failed, and hoped-for reinforcements from the West Indian Windward Squadron or from Spanish colonies never materialized. Yet perhaps there was another solution: Holland was engaged in a periodic naval war with England. Why could not Spain cooperate with the Dutch to the detriment of their common foe? Already these ancient enemies had submerged their hostility and had drawn together in face of French advances in the Low Countries. Therefore, the Spanish Council of War recommended in 1674 that if the Netherlands would furnish ships and join in a combined attack on Charleston, then they should net the captured booty while Spanish forces would retain possession of the city.[33] But Holland directed her main effort in the New World toward New York, and in a short time the two naval belligerents made peace. Spain's proposed joint attack did not take place; the Spanish navy alone was unable to furnish the warships; and Charleston was spared.

Unencumbered by serious Spanish opposition and aided by the natural fertility of the land, a commanding position among adjacent Indians, and a lucrative fur trade, Carolinians became increasingly aggressive after 1680. In that very year three hundred English-led Indians, supplied with new firearms, descended on the Spanish missions in Guale. The fort and mission of St. Catherines Island, provincial headquarters of Guale, received the worst treatment. In the past it had been contemplated that this island, reinforced like Apalachee by Canary Islanders, would be a bulwark against Carolina inroads.[34] Repeated incursions from the north shattered this dream. To make matters worse, the powerful, warlike Yamasee Indians, resenting the Spaniards and fearing English raids, deserted Guale for new allies in Carolina.

English expansion was not confined to nearby Guale, but extended at least as far west as the Apalachicola River. At the same time that English and French corsair attacks on the Gulf buffeted Apalachee, English traders were rapidly expanding their influence to the north among the Lower Creeks. On more than one occasion the garrison at San Marcos rushed troops northward to punish the aggressive but elusive "John Henry," no other than the ubiquitous Henry Woodward.[35] To forestall English expansion in this area Spain built a fort in 1689 at Coweta, the principal Lower Creek war town on the upper Chattahoochee River. But there were not enough troops to man this fort effectively and at the same time to protect the Gulf Coast. Only two years later the tiny garrison abandoned and burned the fort.[36]

Florida was being battered on all sides—by Carolina-led or inspired attacks in the north, by frequent corsair raids in Apalachee, and by disturbing foreign interest in the entire Gulf Coast. And the region around St. Augustine itself was not spared. In 1683 the enterprising French buccaneer, the Sieur de Grammont, with three English and as many French warships caught the sentinels napping at Matanzas—the back door to St. Augustine—and barely missed surprising the city. Frustrated there, he headed for Guale where he terrorized the missions while refitting his ships.[37] Then the corsairs sailed to Charleston where, despite Governor James Colleton's forceful denials, there is good reason to believe they were well received.[38]

The next year other English corsairs hovered off St. Augustine. They put a twelve-man party ashore north of the city to secure provisions and to spy out the land. Shortly afterwards this group entered the Spanish presidio, not triumphantly leading a storming party, but escorted as prisoners by vigilant Spanish troops. The governor tried all these adventurers for piracy and sentenced their leader, Andrew Ranson, to death by strangulation.

The entire city turned out on the day of execution. The ever-tightening rope relentlessly pinched Ranson's neck. Then suddenly the rope snapped. Murmurings of "miracle" swiftly spread among the surprised onlookers, and before astonished Spanish officials realized what was happening, Franciscan friars had whisked Ranson into the sanctuary of the convent. Now began a squabble lasting many years between the governor and the Franciscans as to Ranson's subsequent fate: was this truly a miracle or should the death sentence be carried out? Ultimately Ranson's life was saved, but the governor received some satisfaction when this "pirate" proved to be a skilled artisan and his talents were put to use in building the new Castillo—and he was neither the first nor the last Englishman to labor on this fort.[39]

Corsairs infesting the islands off the coast of Guale and Carolina-inspired or led Indian attacks were rapidly undermining the extensive Guale mission system. What was worse, Carolinians were pushing their settlements further and further south. While Grammont and his colleagues were terrorizing St. Augustine, adventurous Scots were founding Stewarts Town at Port Royal. Though relatively late comers to the New World, the Scots had been active in colonizing enterprises in Nova Scotia and New Jersey, and in 1671 a Scottish group had received a charter for the island of Dominica and all of the Florida peninsula.[40] This charter was never used, and twelve years later another group had a less formidable task when they secured permission from the Carolina Proprietors to settle around much-heralded Port Royal. In 1683 Henry Erskine, Lord Cardross, a much-persecuted Scottish Presbyterian, personally led the vanguard of thirty-odd colonists to Carolina and founded Stewarts Town.[41] This new settlement under the auspices of the Lords Proprietors was, of course, a violation of the recent Treaty of Madrid, and matters did not improve when the Scots began to encourage the Indians to attack the Spaniards.[42]

Corsair depredations and this latest encroachment at Stewarts

Town were too much for harried Governor Hita Salazar at St. Augustine. He was aware that Cardross's colony was weak, at least temporarily so, and to a certain extent was isolated. Since unquestionably it violated the American Treaty, there was legitimate provocation for attack. And Salazar did not pass up his opportunity. His Spanish-Indian-Mulatto troops had little difficulty in overpowering Stewarts Town, already ravaged by sickness. With Scottish fugitives precipitately flying before them, the Spaniards pressed northward to the Edisto River, ransacking outlying plantations, carrying off Negro slaves, even killing the brother-in-law of the Carolina governor.[43]

Lurid accounts of how the attackers whipped and burned their prisoners threw the Charlestonians into an uproar. They immediately prepared to avenge "all the bloodly insolencys the Spaniards had committed against this colony." A French privateer which "happened" to be in Charleston, her crew reinforced by two hundred Carolina volunteers, prepared to wreak sanguinary vengeance on St. Augustine. Just before it got underway, a new governor arrived, and deeming that Salazar had ample provocation and not wanting to encourage piracy, unequivocally forbade any retaliation.[44] He was aware that an attack would disrupt the contraband trade with St. Augustine, and from the English standpoint, little more had been lost than a few Scottish Presbyterians.

During the 1690s open hostility in the Southeast abated, not because Carolinians were fond of Spaniards, but because England after the Glorious Revolution joined Spain in a coalition against Louis XIV's expansionist policies. Superficially cordial relations existed between Charleston and St. Augustine. Each kept the other informed of the latest French movements, the Carolinians returned a few captured Spanish Indians,[45] Englishmen wrecked on the Florida coast were aided and sent on their way,[46] while the mother countries combined in an ineffectual action against Saint Domingue.[47]

Despite outward signs of amiability, however, there was latent hostility between English Carolina and Spanish Florida. Negro slaves who had been deserting to St. Augustine since the mid-1680s continued to do so and were not returned.[48] Florida officials were more aware now than ever before that the Carolina charter included St. Augustine itself, and made casual reference to this in correspondence with Carolina.[49] At the same time venturous Carolina traders extended their operations far west of the Chattahoochee River, some even reached the Mississippi,[50] and they or their Indian allies continued to capture Spanish Indians for sale as slaves in Barbados and elsewhere.[51] England also was showing more interest in the Gulf Coast, first proposing to occupy it with Spanish consent to forestall France. Later England proposed to occupy it without Spanish consent to forestall both France and Spain.[52]

One of the most active Englishmen in these Gulf Coast projects was Dr. Daniel Coxe who was an experienced New World colonizer and claimed much of *la Florida* by virtue of the Heath patent of 1629. Initially he wanted to colonize Apalachee or Tampa Bay, though he was casting covetous eyes westward. Like Heath before, Coxe arranged with refugee French Huguenots to form the nucleus of his colony and after King William's War sent out two vessels on a preliminary reconnaissance.[53] Competition from foreign nations, however, proved the downfall of Coxe's schemes. Before his ships reached the Gulf, the Sieur d'Iberville fulfilled LaSalle's dream by establishing a Gulf Coast colony at Biloxi. And just before this, Spain, in an effort to ward off France, and to a lesser extent Coxe, fortified Pensacola.[54] Coxe's ships returned from the Gulf, bringing the melancholy news that France and Spain, not England, would take up where Narváez, de Soto, and Luna had left off a century and a half ago.

During King William's War there had been a precarious peace in the Southeast, and to a certain extent imperial aspirations remained dormant. But the forthcoming War of Spanish Succession saw a realignment of European powers, and in America it acted as a catalyst to plunge the entire Southeast into turmoil. Whereas in the past England had gradually undermined Spanish influence in most of Guale and to a lesser extent in Timucua and Apalachee, now she would forcibly attempt to make good the terms of the Carolina charter which included St. Augustine itself. She would imperil the Spanish position in that city and indeed in all of *la Florida*.

Queen Anne's War
and Yamasee Unrest

Chapter 6

Sickly, unimaginative, impotent Charles II of Spain died in 1700. His death came as no surprise; it had been a topic of conversation, speculation, and negotiation for many years. The question of who his successor would be was no abstract genealogical controversy, but a question which affected the destiny of Europe and the New World. Would an Austrian succeed Charles, thereby continuing a Habsburg on the Spanish throne? Or would Louis XIV's kinsman be installed instead, thus upsetting the balance of power and making the House of Bourbon supreme in Western Europe? When, just before his death, Charles willed the entire Spanish domain to Louis XIV's grandson and when Louis XIV disregarded previous treaties and accepted this will, it precipitated a major crisis. William III at once perceived the danger to England and Holland of French troops in the Spanish Netherlands and of a combination of the French and Spanish navies. William's last achievement before his death was the organization of the Grand Alliance—England, Holland, and Austria—to oppose a Bourbon succession to the Spanish throne.

The resulting War of the Spanish Succession saw the audacious Duke of Marlborough winning victories with monotonous regularity in the Low Countries, while a combined English, Dutch, and Portuguese force stumbled and faltered for years in the Iberian peninsula, unsuccessfully trying to install the Habsburg contender. At first, Eng-

land and Holland, two of the foremost naval and commercial powers, had considered seizing Spanish America and in this fashion keeping France out of the lucrative New World commerce. They quickly
shifted emphasis to Europe by wholeheartedly backing the Habsburg
contender, who, if he made good his bid for power, would, and in
fact later actually did, grant liberal commercial concessions to England and Holland but none to France. Or if the English and Dutch
could capture and retain Cádiz, they could control Spanish-
American commerce regardless of whether a Habsburg got the Spanish crown and without the necessity of dispatching expeditions to
America. Unfortunately the French reinforced the Spaniards at
Cádiz, and the Anglo-Dutch attack on this port failed.[1] Nevertheless,
future major military and naval campaigns were still fought in Europe—and for Spanish America this was indeed fortunate—though
naturally hostilities were spread throughout the world.

In America, where the English colonists called the conflict
"Queen Anne's War," the precarious, somewhat paradoxical French-
Spanish alliance undertook to conquer or at least to contain the relentlessly expanding British colonies. Fighting took place in the West
Indies and at each end of the elongated British Atlantic Coast colonies. In the north French Canadians and their Indian allies inces-
santly harassed their Puritan neighbors, while, on more than one
occasion, enterprising New Englanders invaded Canada. In the West
Indies privateers took a heavy toll; English or combined Spanish-
French fleets threatened and at times attacked enemy sugar islands,
while Spain contended with the logwood cutters in Yucatán. In
Florida Carolinians attacked the Spaniards almost at will, even in
the face of French aid from Louisiana. Released from the imposed
friendship of King William's War, the Carolinians considered this
an appropriate time to eradicate the ever-present Spanish threat.
Spurring them on was the possibility that at a moment's notice a
French fleet and French troops might reinforce St. Augustine's three-
hundred-man garrison.[2] Thus a century and a half later perhaps
Ribault's dream would be realized—French control of the Bahama
Channel.

As soon as news of the war's outbreak reached America, there
were rumors in both Florida and Carolina of an imminent attack,
and each colony undertook hurried defensive measures. Governor
José de Zúñiga y Cerda at St. Augustine had the almost impossible
task of guarding an extensive frontier with few troops and of supply-

ing his few friendly Indians with food, presents, and arms. To supplement his scanty supply of powder, shot, and guns, he solicited assistance from the French in their new nearby colonies of Louisiana
and Saint Domingue.[3] And in Carolina Governor James Moore was
not idle. He accelerated work on Charleston's unfinished fort, established scattered outposts and lookouts of Indians and whites as far
south as the Savannah River, and requested the exasperatingly de-
liberate Lords Proprietors to rush munitions to the colony.[4] North
of Charleston, however, there were few effective defenses. The Chesapeake Bay was protected by decaying fortifications and an occasional
guardship; while to the south Albemarle and Pamlico Sounds were
completely exposed—"their poverty [was] their security." [5]

Although Carolina organized elaborate defenses, they were only
a necessary prelude to the main objective—conquest of Florida. Disturbed by reports of French reinforcements, the Carolina Commons
House of Assembly pressed for an attack on St. Augustine, the heart
of Spanish Florida. Who should lead such an important expedition?
Members of the Commons "tur'd [their] Eyes Round about" and
could "find no person so every way capable" as the newly-appointed,
headstrong governor, James Moore.[6] He organized a composite force
of eight hundred Indians and Carolinians and equipped them with
scaling ladders and intrenching tools. It would be a two-pronged attack: Colonel Robert Daniel with five hundred men would march
overland through Guale, while Moore, carrying food and munitions,
sailed with the remainder of the force.[7]

In the autumn of 1702 Moore's sixteen brigantines, sloops, and
smaller vessels ominously anchored at the entrance to St. Augustine's
harbor as Drake's fleet had over a century before. Though Moore's
force was not as large, the effect on the undermanned Spanish garrison was the same. There was one important difference: in 1588
there had been no Castillo de San Marcos. The arrival of the enemy
fleet was no surprise to Zúñiga. Reports from Indian spies and refugees fleeing Daniel's overland march had given ample warning. There
was time to collect corn and other foodstuffs from outlying villages
and time to drive a large herd of cattle under the walls of the fort.
Disheartened missionaries, terrorized Indians, and refugee Spanish
settlers streamed into the city from Guale, Timucua, and any outlying area subject to murderous visitations from Moore's Indian
allies. Many of these fugitives brought only the clothes on their backs
and no food for a prolonged siege.[8] Moore estimated with satisfac-

tion that there were one thousand "eaters" in the fort, though in reality the number was closer to fifteen hundred.[9]

With English ships effectively blockading the harbor, Moore and Daniel had little difficulty in capturing the city, and once again the inhabitants saw their houses burned, churches looted, and public buildings mutilated. But taking the castillo, on which hinged the fate of Spanish Florida, was another matter. At first, Moore contemplated storming San Marcos, but dropped this plan, and instead decided to bombard and besiege the Spanish garrison into submission. Unfortunately there were two flaws in this strategy: the governor did not have the proper artillery—mortars and bombs—to shell the fort advantageously, and he was not able to seal off the Spaniards' outside supplies. While Moore ineffectually bombarded the fort and Zúñiga countered with even less consequence, the siege, never completely effective, dragged out for eight weeks. Zúñiga, in fact, was losing more men from exploding overcharged Spanish cannon than English shells.[10] Moore realized the futility of his siege and sent a vessel to Jamaica for suitable artillery. It was an ill wind and difficult sailing against the Gulf Stream, or possibly reluctance to cruise alone in the Caribbean, that caused this vessel to land at Charleston rather than at Kingston.[11]

This marked the beginning of Moore's bad luck. The day after Christmas he spotted the sails of four vessels on the horizon which brought not the expected munitions from Jamaica but Spanish reinforcements from Cuba. Since these large vessels appeared sufficiently formidable to blockade the small English craft in the harbor, Moore abandoned the siege. Burning his ships and the town as well, and hastily carrying off plunder and captive Indians, Moore and his disheartened, diseased, discontented troops retreated overland to their pirogues on the St. Johns River.[12] From there he made his way back to Carolina with only a few casualties but with a deflated ego and a greatly enlarged public debt.

Zúñiga was elated. The castillo survived, and continued Spanish control of Florida was assured. He had conducted an able defense, and the Spanish Crown heaped honors upon him. But after collecting food, sheltering refugees, and sending urgent requests for aid, there was little he could do during the siege except ration supplies, maintain order and vigilance in overcrowded San Marcos, conduct an occasional sortie, and anxiously await the arrival of reinforcements. He could expect them from either Apalachee, Pensacola, Mobile to the west, or more likely, from Cuba to the south. Even though a Cuban force broke the siege, guns, powder, and flints from Mobile, a few soldiers from the diminutive Pensacola garrison, and six hundred Spaniards and Indians from Apalachee were on the way.[13] Zúñiga was justifiably jubilant about St. Augustine's salvation but had little other cause for rejoicing. Guale's once extensive mission system was now completely destroyed. Drake's attack had forced the withdrawal of the Florida frontier almost to Guale; Carolina expansion and piratical forays made further inroads; and Daniel's most recent incursion snapped the last slender thread of Spanish control north of the St. Johns River. And the worst was yet to come.

Moore and his dissatisfied troops had returned safely to Carolina, but he was chagrined and humiliated by his ignominious defeat and precipitate retreat. Some of the Commons now "tur'd [their] Eyes Round about" and found only incompetence, avarice, and even cowardice in his recent conduct. His detractors intimated that he planned this attack merely to catch Indian slaves, that he sent a relief vessel not for munitions but to dispose of his St. Augustine spoils, and that he unnecessarily cowered and retreated at the sight of the four Spanish ships.[14]

To restore his reputation and to replenish his coffers, Moore decided on another stroke. This time his objective was not St. Augustine with redoubtable San Marcos, but almost undefended Apalachee, strategically located between the main Spanish and French settlements and a prolific territory in which to "go a slave hunting." Destruction of Spanish influence in Apalachee would facilitate the expansion of the lucrative Carolina fur trade, pave the way for Pensacola's capture and a firm foothold on the Gulf of Mexico, and help protect Carolina from Spanish raids. As recently as 1702 Spanish soldiers conducted almost a thousand Apalachees against the Creek Indians which were supplied and led by Carolina traders. The Creeks ambushed the Spanish Indians near the Flint River, however, and killed or captured over three-fourths of them.[15]

In the fall of 1703 Moore, at his own expense, equipped fifty whites and one thousand friendly Indians for his forthcoming expedition. Marching overland from Charleston, first to Savannah Town on the upper Savannah River, then southwest across the Oconee and Ocmulgee Rivers, his force by mid-December was on the outskirts of the Apalachee missions. As the sun slowly rose in the chilly winter morning, Moore struck the unsuspecting village of Ayubale. His forces quickly breeched the mud walls, but a large number of the Indians, swiftly herded by the friars, sought refuge in the church enclosure, and once inside put up a stout defense. Not by choice, the Carolinians bore the brunt of the assault. By afternoon, however, ammunition depleted and church afire, the harassed defenders surrendered unconditionally. The following day Spanish dragoons and Indians from nearby Fort San Luis belatedly arrived. After a fierce half-hour battle Moore routed these would-be rescuers and captured most of them.[16]

In the future he met little resistance. He overpowered other mission villages, and a few, prompted by reports of how captured Spanish friars and Indians were tortured and burned at the stake, surrendered before the invaders were in sight. Completing his mission, Moore began the laborious journey back to Carolina with his extensive booty—silver plate from the missions, four thousand women and children slaves, and thirteen hundred Apalachees who "voluntarily" moved to Savannah Town. With satisfaction he proclaimed that "we have made Carolina as safe as the conquest of Apalatchia can make it," and he had restored both his prestige and his personal fortune.[17] Because Fort San Luis and a handful of missions temporarily survived, the conquest was not entirely complete. But Moore's boast was no idle one: the Apalachees had seen at first hand the price they had to pay for siding with Spain, and it is not surprising so many returned with Moore. Before his raid there were eight thousand Indians in Apalachee; shortly afterward there were not two hundred.[18] Even though the Spaniards wanted to reinforce Apalachee with troops and colonists, it was only a few years before they had to burn the other missions and even Fort San Luis to keep them out of English hands, and the garrison retired to Pensacola.[19] For Zúñiga at St. Augustine the whole affair had been frustrating because he had been aware of Moore's every move but could do nothing. To send troops would seriously underman the Castillo. If Apalachee were lost it would be a setback; but if St. Augustine were lost, so was *la Florida*.[20]

Obviously the English at San Jorge were at the root of all the ills and indignities suffered in Florida. Though they had to be castigated, St. Augustine officials had long realized that they alone were powerless to do it. The viceroy of New Spain considered dispatching the hard-pressed Windward Squadron in the West Indies to their aid, but this squadron could meet only a fraction of the demands placed on it.[21] Fortunately outside help was forthcoming—and none too soon. In 1704 two privateers, one Spanish and one French, put into St. Augustine. Zúñiga persuaded them to fall upon San Jorge, pillage the city, and avenge Apalachee's devastation. For some reason the larger vessel, the Spanish one, never reached her destination; the smaller French ship, with only forty men, arrived at Charleston harbor on schedule. Conspicuously flying the English flag, her crew dressed as English sailors, the privateer boldly signaled for a pilot. An unsuspecting Carolinian was sent out, quickly enticed aboard ship, and just as quickly kicked below deck. He disclosed that most of the inhabitants were on their plantations and that there were barely a hundred Carolinians in the city. This news tempted the Frenchmen to attack, but they decided against so great a risk, contenting themselves with raiding outlying plantations before returning to St. Augustine.[22]

Two years later there was a more serious threat to Carolina. Five French privateers rendezvoused in Havana, and the Spanish governor persuaded them to attack San Jorge. With eight hundred well-armed men they sailed first for St. Augustine where a small number of Spaniards and Indians joined them, and then the combined force continued northward. A terrified Dutch privateer and "five smokes" from the lookout on Sullivan's Island alerted Charleston of the impending attack. The alarm rang out, and the city, already weakened by pestilence, was thrown into turmoil. The authorities proclaimed martial law, mustered the militia, and rushed ships anchored in the harbor to defensive positions. For several days the French and Spanish fleet hovered forbiddingly, threatening to launch an attack against the city at a moment's notice. During the night a strong, alert watch and "lights from every window" were the rule to prevent surprise.

The invaders decided not to hazard a landing in the face of several English vessels in the harbor, including a hastily-improvised fireship, or to risk a direct assault against the town's fortifications with "one hundred choice great guns mounted thereon." Instead they decided that, one by one, they would raid, loot, and put to the torch outlying plantations. Shortly afterwards telltale spirals of smoke on the horizon told their sinister story. Militia rushed to the threatened areas and by "boldly huzaing and fireing" repulsed the raiders, capturing many of them. Nearby alert English ships caught a four-gun French sloop napping and seized her. By now the attackers had had enough; leaving behind over three hundred French, Spanish, and Indian prisoners, their fleet, "like a second Spanish

Armado," retired decisively defeated. In spite of prodding by the Spanish king, there were no more attacks launched against Charleston during the war, nor, in spite of tortuous negotiations with French authorities, was there any subsequent Franco-Spanish expedition.[23]

To relieve the pressure on Spanish Florida it was necessary to crush San Jorge. The 1704 and 1706 privateering raids were a harassment and inconvenience, but little else. In fact, rather than improving, Florida's situation deteriorated. There were no more large scale attacks such as the ones on St. Augustine and Apalachee, but there were constant, insidious, highly destructive Indian incursions throughout Florida from the peninsula to as far west as Pensacola. The collapse of the Franciscan mission system and Spanish reluctance or inability to furnish the natives firearms had proved disastrous. Whereas at the height of Spanish influence Indian converts numbered in the tens of thousands, now only pitifully few remained. And most of these were hard put to ward off the murderous, vengeful, slave-hunting attacks from the north. Even in the Florida peninsula itself, there were few places of safety outside the St. Augustine presidio. Small bands of Yamasees, sometimes accompanied by Carolinians, roamed the peninsula at will almost to the Keys, and then returned to Charleston in triumph with their captured Indian slaves.[24] The Indians still retaining their Spanish allegiance flocked to St. Augustine; indeed many had remained there after Moore's attack. Since it was unsafe to venture beyond the walls to hunt, graze cattle, or get firewood, the Spanish quartermaster had an almost impossible task in trying to feed the city's many inhabitants. Most of the cattle had already been driven off, ending up on the hoof in Carolina for sale, or roasting on a spit over a nearby Yamasee campfire. To make matters worse, the foodstuffs formerly provided by Apalachee were no longer available, and rumors of an English settlement further down the peninsula did little to buoy Spanish spirits.[25]

Conditions were no better in the rest of Florida. Guale, of course, was completely lost, and after Moore's raid Apalachee was abandoned, desolated, and in ruins. Farther west English-led Upper Creeks in 1707 sacked and burned the town of Pensacola and barely missed capturing the newly-built fort. Early warning by French traders, a resolute defense by the tiny Spanish garrison, and reports of French reinforcements from Mobile—which arrived too late—saved the day.[26] After this, Indian attacks became the rule rather than the exception, and the English flag was frequently seen flying over the town's rude wooden houses.[27] The claim was not greatly exaggerated when Thomas Nairne, the daring, energetic highly effective Carolina Indian agent, asserted that through Indian allies "we have firm possession . . . from Charles Town to Mobile Bay, excepting St. Augustine." [28] It was not until the war's end in 1713 that the haggard, battered, frustrated Florida inhabitants received a respite.

The war dragged on until the belligerents negotiated a peace settlement in the Dutch city of Utrecht. Both France and Spain made concessions in America. While France surrendered to England territory and fishing privileges in Canada, Spain, although pressured to cede prominent American ports to Britain, only conceded the *asiento* or monopoly of supplying slaves to the Spanish Indies. English statesmen, recognizing the advantages of legitimate trade over freebooting, for a half century had been trying to win the *asiento*. Jean Colbert's disciples in France had attempted to do the same thing, and when war had broken out in 1702, they prodded the new Spanish king to grant the *asiento* to his French grandfather. To all foreigners this commercial concession appeared attractive. In the latter part of the sixteenth and particularly in the seventeenth century Spanish industry could not approach meeting New World demands, and with the loss of the Portuguese African colonies, she had few areas which could furnish slaves. England could readily supply them from Africa and believed that establishing factors to distribute them would facilitate legitimate trade as well as contraband. Spain promised never to surrender any American territory to France, Britain finally won the *asiento*, and France agreed that her merchants, in spite of the fact that a Bourbon was on the Spanish throne, would not seek preferential treatment. Quite accurately England believed she was well on the way to dominating the Spanish-American market.[29]

Apparently not all the terms regarding Spain's American possessions were unfavorable. The Utrecht treaty reaffirmed prior Anglo-Spanish treaties, including the 1670 American Treaty. In 1670 Spain, as a concession, recognized England's title to all American territory she occupied in that year; reaffirming this article in 1713 ostensibly restricted English expansion into areas which she did not occupy in 1670.[30]

Spain refused to sign the Treaty of Utrecht without a provision protecting her right to fish off Newfoundland—a right little exercised for a century. Philip v, inspired by the French example, was trying to infuse new vitality and strength into the once-powerful Spanish empire. From the sixteenth to the eighteenth centuries major nations adhered to the tenets of mercantilism, which included establishing colonies for self-sufficiency in raw materials and maintaining a large navy to protect these scattered possessions. Spain had a plethora of colonies, but her navy left much to be desired. Over the years the Newfoundland fishery had become highly desirable not only because of the prolific cod, but also as a training ground for sailors. Therefore Spain, trying to revitalize her navy, rebuild her fishing industry, and reduce her dependence on English and French fishermen, doggedly insisted on a provision which would restore to her a share of the fishery. Reluctantly England agreed to the ambiguous article "that all such privileges as the Guipúzcoans and other people of Spain are able to claim by right, shall be allowed and preserved to them." [31] After the conclusion of peace Spain sent out trial vessels to test the effectiveness of this article. English men-of-war had orders to prohibit these ships, "without offering the least violence or insult to them." The result was a foregone conclusion, and Spain failed to reopen the fishery.[32]

While Spain was being politely rebuffed in Newfoundland, developments were more encouraging in *la Florida*. After over a decade of English-conducted or instigated depredations against Florida—depredations which almost snapped Spain's weak hold on this frontier province—the tide unexpectedly changed. The cause was the explosive Yamasee revolt in 1715 which threatened Carolina's very existence. The Yamasees, who had deserted Guale thirty years before and now lived in ten villages just north of the Savannah River, suddenly, in conjunction with other tribes, turned on their English allies. These Indians were alarmed by encroachments on their tribal lands and provoked by the ill-usage and underhanded dealings of the traders. In a matter of days the Indians slaughtered hundreds of Carolinians, and the piercing war whoop reverberated disconcertingly close to Charleston itself. There was a reign of terror for over a year, but finally the militia, reinforced by neighboring colonies and by the powerful Cherokees, quelled the insurrection.[33]

As soon as the revolt erupted, the Yamasees sent emissaries to St. Augustine, where with alacrity they were "restored to the serene and acknowledged [Spanish] authority." [34] Even though Spain in the past had tried to win over these Indians and she did not lament the Carolinians' plight, the often-repeated charge that she stirred up the Yamasees does not appear true. The empire-conscious Virginia governor,

Alexander Spotswood, remonstrated with Governor Francisco de Córcoles y Martínez at St. Augustine for inciting this revolt, supplying arms to the Indians, and breaking the recent peace in numerous other ways. There is no reason, however, to disbelieve Córcoles who replied that he had not prompted or aided the Yamasees and the misconduct of Carolina traders brought on the uprising.[35] The main significance of this spontaneous revolt for Córcoles was that it barely missed accomplishing overnight what Florida governors had been plotting for half a century—destruction of San Jorge. By a narrow margin San Jorge was spared, but there was a resettlement of Indian tribes and a realignment of their allegiances in Spain's favor. English hegemony in the Southeast, which Thomas Nairne so recently boasted stretched almost to Mobile Bay, was shattered. The Yamasees, imbued with a deep-seated hatred of the English and ministered to by the Franciscans, instead of raiding the Florida peninsula, now became the most dependable Spanish allies.

In Apalachee and further west Spain's fortunes also were on the upswing. While the Yamasees were making their hegira to Florida, the Apalachicolas (Lower Creeks) for similar reasons were returning to the Chattahoochee River. Spain, instead of being a negligible rival in this region, once again was a formidable contender. She immediately began to reoccupy abandoned Apalachee, restore the devastated mission system, refortify San Marcos, and especially win over all of the Lower Creeks.[36] Diego Peña, a veteran soldier experienced in Indian affairs, made a series of journeys between 1716 and 1718 to the upper Chattahoochee in an attempt to restore Spanish influence over the Creeks. In spite of Indian inconstancy and of competition and opposition by English traders, Peña won over a number of caciques, and together they returned to St. Augustine, triumphantly entering the city amid salvos of artillery and volleys of musketry.[37] As a result of Peña's successes, in the ensuing decades Carolinians had their work cut out trying to eradicate Spanish influence among the Lower Creeks and eastwardly-expanding French influence among the Upper Creeks.

While England, Spain, and France all were bidding for the capricious Creek allegiance, another drama was being enacted at the tip of the Florida peninsula. Ships of the returning treasure fleet had been wrecked on the Keys, and scores of Spaniards were busy locating and recovering the sunken treasure. They had partially completed their task when Captain Henry Jennings and six hundred of his fellow Jamaicans proffered their assistance. Not only was Jennings "so obliging as to help the Spaniards to fish up their Flota," but also he carried "away what they had fished." Then with the comforting jingle of three hundred and fifty thousand pieces of eight in his hold and a "heavy Clamour" among the Spaniards, Jennings returned to Jamaica.[38]

In Europe the Treaty of Utrecht was rapidly falling to pieces. The ambitions of Philip v, prodded by his aspiring wife, Elizabeth Farnese, and his contriving minister, Cardinal Alberoni, were running headlong into conflict with the Quadruple Alliance—England, France, Holland, and Austria. There was a bungling Spanish attempt to invade Scotland, while in the Mediterranean a supposedly revitalized Spanish fleet suffered a rebuff at the hands of English men-of-war. This war, officially proclaimed in 1718 and primarily caused by intricate, conflicting European aspirations, soon spread to the New World. This time Spain was not allied with France against England, nor with England against France; instead Spain had to face both alone. The prospect was not well received in St. Augustine.

Fortunately the revolt of the Yamasees and their defection to Florida allowed the peninsula to escape the ravages of Queen Anne's War. And an invigorated Spanish marine, using St. Augustine and West Indian ports as bases, preyed on English shipping. Prizes from the Caribbean and the Gulf of Mexico, from the Carolina coast, from within the Virginia Capes, and from as far north as New England were condemned in St. Augustine and other ports. To recoup some of her shipping losses, Virginia sent a vessel to St. Augustine, but neither threat of force nor negotiation was of any avail.[39]

During the entire three years of hostility, Carolina was in a state of alarm. Weakened after the recent uprising, she feverishly reinforced her scattered outposts, repaired and strengthened the diminutive fort at Port Royal (reoccupied after the Stewarts Town fiasco), and expanded Charleston's defenses. At the same time colonial authorities urged the crown to send regulars to safeguard the exposed southern flank of her American colonies.[40] Need for reinforcements was not imaginary. Rumors from English West Indian colonies and from English prisoners in Cuba trickled into Charleston indicating that Spain was outfitting a fleet of fourteen ships and fourteen hundred men in Havana for another descent on San Jorge.[41] The expedition was set to sail at short notice, and only a quirk of fate—news that France had captured Pensacola—prevented its departure.

The French at Mobile, released from their Spanish alliance of Queen Anne's War and not sparing the sensibilities of the new Bourbon dynasty in Madrid, turned on their former ally. The Sieur de Bienville's raw recruits and Indian allies, swiftly moving eastward by land and sea, surprised Pensacola, and in this dramatic fashion informed the Spanish commander of the war's outbreak. The Spanish prisoners sent to Havana arrived with the unpleasant news of Pensacola's fall just before the Carolina expedition was to sail. Cuban authorities reshuffled their plans and ordered the fleet westward to Pensacola rather than northward to San Jorge. Spain dislodged the French; later Bienville returned and captured the city again; and finally after the cessation of hostilities French troops withdrew as provided in the 1721 peace settlement.[42]

Thus the French peril from Louisiana spared Carolina an invasion. Instead of a vigorous Spanish attack, the Carolina-Florida frontier witnessed only occasional harassing raids by both sides. This frontier would not have been so placid, however, had the powerful English Board of Trade had its way. It was urging the conquest of all of Florida which would remove Spain from this quarter and block the eastward French thrust along the Gulf.[43] To execute this design required English regulars who were never made available. After involved negotiations, in which Spain unsuccessfully tried to swap Florida for Gibraltar, peace was proclaimed in 1721, and the frontier lapsed into its traditional semi-peaceful state with the three powers bickering and maneuvering for position among the Indians.[44]

During Queen Anne's War and the brief hostilities of 1718–1721 Spain scored both successes and failures. She made good her claim to Yucatán's west coast by expelling the logwood cutters and by fortifying Carmen Island; she failed, however, to make good her claim to Belize on the east coast or to the Mosquito Shore farther south. She conceded the *asiento*, which gave England a share of New Spain's legitimate commerce over and above the existing large scale contraband trade; however, England made no headway in engineering a Spanish-American Indian revolt. The fact that Philip v, a Bourbon, secured the Spanish throne and that her American colonies remained attached to it, was in itself a Spanish victory. This prevented Holland and Britain from partitioning large parts of Spanish America or from forcing a successful Habsburg contender to make extensive concessions. After 1713 with Bourbon rulers firmly established at Versailles and Madrid, there was a closer connection between the two Latin states which, from the Spanish standpoint, meant that in the future she had a powerful maritime ally, albeit a capricious one, to help defend her empire.

Spain almost lost Florida as a result of Moore's siege; later the Yamasee revolt and Spanish countermeasures put the Carolinians on the defensive. But Spain's respite was short-lived, because soon Carolinians began occupying the "debatable land" of Guale.

Guale Becomes
a Utopia

Chapter 7

Thriving British colonies covered almost all of the Atlantic seaboard between Canada and the Florida peninsula by 1720. But there was one important exception—the level forested region between the Savannah and St. Johns rivers, abandoned by Spain, coveted by Britain, and claimed by both. Though Spain had withdrawn from Guale by 1702, she still professed sovereignty over this province; and in spite of the fact that the 1670 American Treaty apparently restricted Britain to Charleston, she consistently claimed territory as far south as the twenty-ninth parallel by virtue of the charter to the Carolina Proprietors. Neither nation experienced difficulty in amassing documentation to support its title, but, as usual, occupation, not deliberation, was decisive; and it was no more feasible for Spain now to colonize Guale than Carolina or Virginia in the past. Spanish colonists coming to the New World still went to the more stable, less exposed regions farther south.

The Lords Proprietors had long been interested in settling this area, but the destruction of Stewarts Town pointed out the risks of a too rapid southern expansion. After Queen Anne's War, however, Britain, fortified by concessions from Spain and France, showed enthusiasm for any New World project. This was the frenzied period of the South Sea bubble. The South Sea Company, awarded the *asiento* and other valuable concessions, began to reap fabulous paper profits. Many additional schemes, some practical, others preposterous, emerged in the South Sea Company's speculative wake. One was the ambitious project by the Scottish knight, Sir Robert Montgomery, to establish an elaborate dominion in America. He obtained a grant from the Lords Proprietors to all the land between the Savannah and Altamaha rivers to found the margraviate of Azilia—a semi-feudal colony with the margrave's manor in the center, surrounded by the estates of the lesser gentry and the cottages of the tenants.[1] But the bursting of the South Sea bubble in 1720 shattered the fond hopes for Azilia, where investors would reap a fifty-per-cent profit the first year.

Though publication of laudatory tracts advertising Azilia was Montgomery's only concrete achievement, more consequential events were taking place in Carolina itself. An overwhelming majority of the inhabitants, provoked over the long period of negligent, inefficient rule by the Proprietors, revolted in 1719 and proclaimed South Carolina a royal province. The crown, anxious for direct control over this colony, recognized the revolution and sent a new royal governor, Sir Francis Nicholson, to Charleston. Nicholson and other officials manifested keen interest in the territory so recently advertised by Montgomery's promotional literature.

There were many advantages in settling south of the Savannah River: for the former Proprietors (who were still landlords), there was the prospect of quitrents; for the Carolinians, settlement offered protection from Indian raids and less probability of Negro slaves' fleeing to St. Augustine; for prospective colonists, this area represented one of the few uninhabited spots on the Atlantic Coast; and for the crown, occupation would effectively settle the Florida boundary dispute and deny this region to France. Not only were Spaniards vociferously asserting a claim to Guale, but also aspiring Frenchmen, with less fanfare but more effect, were pressing eastward from Mobile. After taking Pensacola (retained for only a short period) and erecting Fort Toulouse at the junction of the Coosa and Tallapoosa rivers, the French appeared bent on reaching the Atlantic.[2] Their insistence during peace negotiations with Spain in 1720 that, in addition to giving up Pensacola, Spain should cede the remainder of the Gulf Coast to Tampa Bay, was as alarming to England as to Spain.[3] It portended a French encirclement of the British colonies from Canada in the north, to the Ohio and Mississippi in the west, to Guale in the south.

It was for a variety of reasons, therefore, that Governor Nicholson decided to occupy Azilia—at first, however, with militia and regulars rather than colonists. These troops would bar the French from the Atlantic and override Florida's claim to Guale. At the same time, they would promote trade with the Indians and help assure their fidelity. For a while Nicholson considered occupying all the major rivers, the Savannah, Ogeechee, and Altamaha, and dotting the Guale coast with British garrisons rather than Franciscan missions.[4] He soon abandoned this plan for the less ambitious, less expensive project of erecting a fort near the mouth of the Altamaha. Thus in 1721 John Barnwell, an experienced Indian fighter and trader, with about thirty unruly frontier scouts began the difficult, unhealthy task of constructing Fort King George and of mounting its five small pieces of artillery deep in the "debatable land" of Guale.[5] This unpretentious structure, one hundred miles from the infant settlement at Port Royal and one hundred and fifty miles from Charleston, maintained a solitary, precarious vigil on the southern frontier.

Spain at once denounced the building of this fort and maintained that it stood on territory claimed by Spain for centuries and was a flagrant violation of the American Treaty. The British Board of Trade was "very much surprised that the Spanish ambassador should make any complaint" because this fort assuredly was within South Carolina,[6] while Governor Nicholson categorically informed Florida officials that this fort "shall be maintained as long as His Majesty" deems necessary.[7] Nevertheless, in a partial attempt to mollify Spain, the Duke of Newcastle, secretary of state for the southern department, suggested that the Carolina and Florida governors work out a common boundary. For this reason Francisco Menéndez Marqués and a small detachment of soldiers set out in a pirogue from St. Augustine, armed with the voluminous correspondence between Newcastle and the Spanish ambassador, optimistically hoping to secure the abandonment of Fort King George. Navigating the intricate inland waterways, they first sailed to the Altamaha River and got a first-hand view of the root of the current dispute, before continuing to Charleston. Their efforts here were completely ineffectual. Nicholson, after lodging his guests in the inhospitable jail, contended he had no authority to negotiate such a weighty matter.[8] Either Newcastle had been too busy borough-mongering to send instructions, or more likely this was an evasion by Nicholson. In any case the

Carolina governor changed the subject to runaway slaves harbored at St. Augustine, and Marqués and his men, frustrated and dejected, "returned home as they came." [9]

Though Marqués did not secure Fort King George's abandonment, unhealthy conditions, administrative incompetence, scarcity of supplies, and a destructive fire achieved what negotiation failed to attain. The commander of this fort was caustic in his criticism of the post, which he contended was as necessary as one "placed in Japan." The three-story cypress structure occupied only one-third of an acre, and part of that was in a marsh. According to the discontented commander, the unhealthy air and lack of fresh provisions had caused the deaths of "130 odd serjeants and private centinells in six years." To make matters worse, a fire broke out in 1726; though not started by the garrison, nevertheless the grumbling troops "were not so active as they might have been" in extinguishing the blaze.[10] This fire and the boldness of Indian raids to the north brought about the garrison's withdrawal to Port Royal.[11] Soon Spain asserted that Britain abandoned this fort because she finally realized it was illegally situated on Spanish soil.[12]

During the 1720s Fort King George was the most vexatious but not the only controversy between St. Augustine and Charleston. Annoying border raids by both sides were becoming more numerous. Deadly forays by small parties of Spaniards, who allegedly paid their Indian or Negro allies for British scalps, kept isolated Carolina settlements in a state of unrest. To protect Port Royal was one of the major reasons for withdrawing Fort King George's garrison, and the fact that these raiders continually prowled around the fort and ambushed unsuspecting soldiers no doubt hastened the withdrawal.[13] To stop these incursions, to profit by a brief period of hostilities with Spain, to further chasten the embittered Yamasees, and to negate their influence among their kinsmen the Lower Creeks (the Yamasees were pressing the Creeks to turn against the Carolinians), Colonel John Palmer, seasoned Yamasee War veteran, in 1728 led a band of whites and Indians southward through Guale right up to the gates of St. Augustine. He destroyed part of the city's newly-built outer defenses and hounded the Yamasees, but failed to take the capital.[14] To the west other Indians made the Spanish reoccupation of Apalachee precarious at best.[15] These English raids would have been more telling had not Carolina merchants traded regularly with the Spaniards and supplied them firearms—the same thing

New Englanders had been doing with the French in Canada.[16] These weapons permitted the Yamasees and other Spanish Indians to better ward off the hostile attacks.

Actually during the late 1720s a number of disputes threatened the peace of Europe and, as has been seen by Palmer's raid, open warfare briefly flared up between Britain and Spain. The causes were the aggressive designs of the Spanish queen to recover Gibraltar, Minorca, and all of Italy; and Spain lent Austria support in establishing the Ostend Company which would trade with the Indies and was a commercial threat to Britain. Spain toyed with supporting James Edward, exiled pretender to the British throne, and opened the trenches against Gibraltar, while Britain blockaded the Spanish coast and dispatched a squadron which unsuccessfully tried to intercept the *galeones* in the West Indies. Even so, this squadron, in spite of an excessively high mortality rate due to tropical sickness, maintained an effective blockade of Portobello and for several crucial years denied Spain use of the Peruvian treasure. In the New World the Carolina boundary, British occupation of New Providence Island, British smuggling and Spanish reprisals, the logwood cutters, and, of course, the Portobello blockade, all had contributed to the rupture. During this short conflict Palmer intimidated St. Augustine; British men-of-war continued to blockade Portobello; Spanish troops unsuccessfully besieged Gibraltar; and Spain again confiscated South Sea Company goods and ships in American ports. Fighting ceased in 1728, and the following year the two nations signed the treaty of Seville. Other than providing for a cessation of hostilities, restoring certain prizes, including the valuable *Prince Frederick* of the South Sea Company, and adjusting commercial matters, the treaty had no provisions directly affecting the New World. Britain's right to all of Carolina and to New Providence Island, the privilege of cutting logwood, and the claim of Spanish Basques to fish off Newfoundland were discreetly by-passed.[17]

For several years there was relative peace on the southern frontier, until once again British expansion embroiled relations with St. Augustine. The new British settlement in Guale, or Azilia, now for the first time called Georgia, was no diminutive garrison on the Altamaha but the nucleus of a flourishing colony. Georgia, a proprietary colony with a grant to the lands between the Savannah and Altamaha rivers, had the same boundaries and would serve the same ends as Azilia by forming a buffer against Spain and France. This border colony immediately assumed a pivotal role in the inflamed triangular struggle for the Southeast.

Philanthropic no less than strategic reasons influenced the Georgia experiment. The plight of British debtors, languishing in overcrowded, unsanitary prisons, attracted the attention of such men as Thomas Bray, Viscount Perceval, and James Oglethorpe. Their ambition was to establish a utopian New World colony where the most unfortunate and worthy debtors could be transported free of charge, where they could exchange Newgate Prison's foul air for the invigorating American climate, and where they could hopefully begin life anew as industrious farmers or artisans. These benefactors considered several locations for their colony, but the region south of the Savannah River, recently brought to public attention by Montgomery and which the crown wanted occupied after the Fort King George debacle, was the most promising.

The 1732 charter provided for a Board of Trustees, composed of leading philanthropists, who, subject only to the crown, had complete authority to establish and govern this new colony.[18] Within a short time the Trustees adopted regulations declaring that with few exceptions the largest farms could be only fifty acres and prohibiting rum and slavery. These Trustees were forerunners of the powerful anti-slavery movement in Britain at the end of the century. Of course, on a mere fifty-acre tract there was no pressing need for slaves.

There was another important reason for prohibiting slavery. Georgia was carved out of Carolina, and at first the affairs of both colonies were closely intermeshed. Whereas in Georgia the Trustees envisioned small farms and no slavery, in Carolina fur trading was giving way to intensively cultivated, highly profitable rice plantations employing many Negroes. At the time Georgia was founded the ratio of Negroes to whites in certain parts of the Carolina low country approached ten to one. The Carolina planter's dread of a spontaneous or Spanish-inspired slave insurrection, or of Negroes' escaping to St. Augustine, was well founded. This new philanthropic colony, a slaveless wedge between Carolina and Florida, would make it more difficult for Negroes to escape or for Spaniards to intrigue among them.[19]

The Trustees commissioned imperious, altruistic James Oglethorpe, one of their members, an outspoken champion in Parliament for prison reform, and a military figure of some repute, to lead the first contingent of colonists to Georgia. Oglethorpe's official position was curious: he was not governor—there was no governor—but he was commander of the Georgia militia which in turn was under control of the South Carolina governor.[20] To further complicate matters, Oglethorpe had the sometimes incongruous tasks of fulfilling British imperial aspirations and of carrying out the Trustees' philanthropic aims. In 1733 Oglethorpe escorted the one-hundred-odd carefully selected colonists to America. After landing at Charleston where they were welcomed and gratuitously furnished with food, seed, cattle, and money, they sailed southward to found their utopia. Sailing into the broad, tranquil Savannah River, they laid out the well-planned city of Savannah in a clearing on a bluff about eighteen miles upstream. Reinforcing the Trustees' title to this area, Oglethorpe concluded a treaty with Tomo-chi-chi, chief of the Yamacraws, which permitted the British to settle here and from the beginning was a basis for friendly relations with these nearby Indians. Soon Oglethorpe sent this chief and other important Georgia Indians to London to be received at court.[21]

Shortly afterward the original Georgia settlers were followed by scores of others—hard-pressed English debtors, persecuted Moravian and Salzburg pietists, discontented Scottish Highlanders, oppressed Jews, and, of couse, the usual Spanish spies.[22] Savannah expanded, smaller settlements appeared up river and in surrounding territory, and another town, comparable only to Savannah, arose. This new town, Frederica, on St. Simons Island at the mouth of the Altamaha River, was on Georgia's southernmost border and was a substitute for burned and deserted Fort King George upstream. And this was only the beginning. To guard the inland water route between Frederica and St. Augustine a fort stood guard at each end of Cumberland Island, while farther south, Fort St. George on the St. Johns River, less than fifty miles from St. Augustine, commanded the mouth of that river. Not since the days of Ribault and Laudonnière had there been a foreign fort so near the Florida capital. Some British statesmen judged that now was the time to press westward to the Gulf of Mexico—included in the Carolina charter—and to take root at Apalachee Bay or Tampa.[23] Though Oglethorpe did not establish outposts here, he did build a number of them south of the Altamaha River, which was in Carolina but outside the Trustees' grant. Imperial expansion was taking precedence over charitable activities.[24]

Spain was disturbed by the rapid colonization and fortification of Georgia. It looked as though the tiny colony established over a century ago in Jacán would continue expanding until by sheer momentum Spain would lose all of *la Florida*. St. Augustine's officials realized that the best way to stop the British was to beat them at their own game—colonization; but Spanish efforts to lure colonists to Florida made little headway. As in Menéndez's day Florida was still little more than a military outpost. The Spaniards were also losing ground in their bid to win over the Lower Creeks. After Queen Anne's War, Florida governors tried to expand or at least to maintain influence among these Indians in order to stem British advances. In distant Coweta and Kashita on the upper Chattahoochee River each nation's agents vied to outbid and outmaneuver the other. Though Spaniards like Diego Peña had considerable success and Creek caciques continued to be lavishly entertained at St. Augustine, nevertheless the tide steadily turned in Britain's favor.[25] And Apalachee, which Spain reoccupied and refortified, though not on the same scale as before Moore's attack, again was periodically raided by British-led Indians. Captured Indians from here and other parts of *la Florida* graced the slave markets of Charleston and Jamaica.[26]

From the beginning Spain's ambassador denounced the founding of Savannah and Frederica. Spain could recover Guale either by negotiation or force, and she considered both alternatives. Oglethorpe's most irritating action was building Fort St. George at the mouth of the St. Johns River—a gateway into Florida's interior and to the rear of St. Augustine. Oglethorpe blandly asserted that this "defensive" fort existed merely to bar the Creeks from crossing into Florida and molesting his good friends the Spaniards.[27] Eventually, however, he and the Spanish governor, Francisco del Moral Sánchez, began negotiations to relieve mounting tension. The ex-soldier of fortune, Captain Charles Dempsey, an Irish Catholic resident of Georgia with a brother in the Spanish army, shuttled back and forth between Frederica and St. Augustine and laid the groundwork for a Georgia-Florida treaty.[28] At the same time Antonio de Arredondo sailed from St. Augustine to confer personally with Oglethorpe. As a result, the two extreme positions—British claim to the twenty-ninth parallel and Spain's insistence that Britain evacuate all settlements south of Charleston—were ambiguously compromised. Each side would restrain its Indian allies, and Britain would abandon Fort St. George, though she would retain title to the St. Johns River "as if the said garrison had never been withdrawn." Each side agreed not to occupy the disputed area until the mother countries made a definitive boundary settlement.[29] Though Oglethorpe withdrew the exasperating St. George garrison, a victory for Sánchez, nevertheless, Spanish authorities, skeptical about this agreement which possibly conceded Britain's right to the St. Johns River, disavowed the treaty. They asserted that Sánchez had no authority to imply such sweeping concessions and recalled the imprudent governor.[30] In addition to this treaty, Sánchez was charged with illegally trading with the British and allowing armed groups of their sailors to freely roam St. Augustine's streets "as if they were in London." [31]

Instead of making new territorial concessions, Spain demanded that Britain give up Georgia, New Providence Island, Old Providence Island, San Andres Island, the Virgin Islands, and the logwood settlements in the Gulf of Honduras, all violations of the American and subsequent treaties.[32] At the same time Spain redoubled her efforts to strengthen what remained of *la Florida*. This is why the Cuban governor's favorite, Antonio de Arredondo, an outstanding military engineer, who helped negotiate the ill-received treaty, was in Florida. He made widespread recommendations, many of which were later adopted, that Spain build several strategically located outlying forts to better protect St. Augustine, that she provide more troops, and that she furnish colonists for new settlements at the St. Johns River, at Ays (Indian River), and in Apalachee.[33] In addition, Arredondo made a detailed map of the Georgia coast, indicating the location of new British fortifications, their strength, and the best routes of approach.[34] He went to Frederica primarily to secure information for his map rather than to negotiate. Justly suspicious, Oglethorpe offered to transport Arredondo on a speedy Royal Navy sloop to protect him from the "pernicious airs," [35] but the Spanish engineer graciously refused, preferring a shallow draft Spanish vessel which permitted close inspection of Oglethorpe's string of forts.[36] Even though the Georgians billeted Arredondo and his party separately in tents at St. Simons Island, the visitors gleaned much detailed information.

Spain had need of an exact map, because she had ambitious plans of recovering Guale by force rather than negotiation. At the root of this scheme was the "very Gay and Brisk" soldier-of-fortune, John Savy, alias Don Miguel Wall.[37] Savy had lived in both Carolina and Georgia and, before his precipitous return to Europe in 1735, had contracted embarrassing debts and was even implicated in a murder charge. After arriving in Europe, he revealed to the Spanish crown that he had an intimate knowledge of Oglethorpe's colony and proposed that he head a Spanish force to reclaim it. The Council of the Indies, already entertaining such an attack, accepted his offer. Savy then sailed for Cuba where the island's officials royally entertained him and preparations began to collect men and supplies. The Florida governor assisted by impressing a Carolina ship captain and bustling him off to Havana to help pilot the expedition.[38] But before long Savy's grandiose scheme ran into snags. The allotted amount of shipping, troops, and money failed to materialize, while the Spaniards began to question both the competence and the reliability of the erstwhile Georgian. It was not difficult for the South Sea Company's factor in Santiago, Cuba, to invite Savy—who "loved his Glass"—to dinner and in the course of the evening to ferret out the essential outline of his project.[39] Savy's numerous indiscreet remarks and incessant boasting, mounting Spanish skepticism over his strategy of having the attacking troops march overland to Georgia carrying all of their food and equipment, failure in obtaining sufficient men and supplies, and the fact that Britain was conscious of what was going on caused Spain to abandon this design in 1737. [40] With the collapse of his scheme, Savy returned to Spain, secretly boarded a vessel for London where he disclosed the entire Spanish design, and, being so well versed in affairs in that quarter of the globe, felt that he was best qualified to lead a British expedition against St. Augustine or Havana.[41]

Savy's conduct in Spain and Cuba and visible preparations in Havana frightened the Southern colonies. They accelerated work on their unfinished and undermanned fortifications, dispatched swift vessels to watch the harbors of St. Augustine and Havana—perhaps they could contact the South Sea Company factor at the latter city[42] —and maintained a strict vigil to bar Spanish spies from entering either colony. It was well that they did all this, because, even though Spain dropped Savy, she did not abandon the idea of attacking Georgia, and she continued preparations for a descent the following spring.[43] In London the Trustees petitioned for regulars to safeguard their utopian experiment, and fortunately their plea did not go unheeded. The crown commissioned Oglethorpe, now in London, to return with a seven-hundred-man regiment—a regiment which would no longer glare down at the Spaniards from the Rock of

Gibraltar but instead across swampy savannahs in the New World. Oglethorpe employed these troops not only in Georgia, but also in various forts and outposts south of the Altamaha River, which, of course, was part of South Carolina. For this reason the crown commissioned him commander-in-chief of both colonies, which made Spain more nervous than ever.[44] The British troops began arriving in Georgia in 1738 and soon had their work cut out for them.

Relations with Spain were reaching the breaking point, and the turbulent Florida boundary was only one of several virulent American disputes. Another, more acrimonious one, was the conduct of the *guarda costa*. Spain, in an effort to restore her native industry and marine, was determined to stop the widespread contraband, and strengthening the swift, light draft *guarda costa*, which patrolled the Caribbean, Gulf of Mexico, and Bahama Channel, was an effective way to do this. They were likely to seize any British vessels carrying Spanish coin or products, or to condemn British vessels which were not on a direct course from one British colony to another. From Britain's standpoint this was bad enough, but some of the self-styled *guard costa* were commanded by nothing more than pirates who regularly carried British prizes, and sometimes even Spanish ones, into Cuba, Puerto Rico, and other Spanish harbors. The seizure of British vessels, whatever the pretext, became a mounting controversy during the 1720s and 1730s. [45]

Closely associated with West Indian commerce was the South Sea Company. After the South Sea bubble burst, the British crown severed its close connection with Company finances, but the Company continued to supply slaves and to trade with Spanish colonies, and to employ factors in the principal Spanish-American ports. Since the Company's formation there had been continual bickering with the Spanish crown over the size of the Company's ships, when and where they would sail, the price and condition of the Negroes, and the amount the Company owed the crown. The Company regularly intrigued in Spanish politics and used its influence and money to secure the appointment of friendly officials in key positions.[46] When war broke out, as in 1718 and 1727, Spain impounded the Company's effects in American ports which gave rise to endless disputes after the war was over. The differences between Spain and the Company were as involved and heated in the 1730s as ever before.

And then there was the issue of the logwood cutters. Though Spain recently had expelled them from the western part of Yucatán, soon they were back in force on the peninsula's eastern coast and at other areas bordering the Bay of Honduras. They were scattered out all along the rivers and inlets of the Bay, but their chief resort was the old pirate rendezvous of Belize. Spain during the 1720s and 1730s was bringing to bear both diplomatic and military pressure to force the logwood cutters out of their new haunts. The perseverance of the logwood cutters, the wrangles and intrigues of the South Sea Company, the seizures by the *guarda costa*, and the controversial Florida boundary, all were disputes paving the road to war in the late 1730s.

The British prime minister, Robert Walpole, eager to keep Britain at peace and himself in power, signed a convention with Spain providing that commissioners would meet in the immediate future to settle the Florida boundary and to adjust outstanding commercial claims.[47] Though Spain wanted all of Oglethorpe's forts destroyed before signing the convention, there was merely a stipulation that neither side would erect new fortifications until they reached a final settlement.[48] Agreeing to adjust outstanding differences was one thing; reaching accord was another. Walpole's opposition in Parliament, either determined on a Spanish war to uphold British honor or bent on hostilities as a means of overthrowing the prime minister himself, daily gathered momentum, and the commissioners were severely handicapped from the beginning. Walpole admitted that Oglethorpe might have occupied too much territory and probably was willing to concede part of the region south of the Altamaha River or, as his critics charged, all of Georgia, because war was likely unless Britain made concessions.[49] But imperious William Pitt and his Boy Patriots, London merchants demanding direct access to Spanish-American markets rather than facing effective French competition in Andalusia, as well as aggressive colonial officials, would have no compromise and, citing the Carolina charter, questioned Spain's "unjust Pretensions to St. Augustine itself." [50] They asserted that violations of the American Treaty by the *guarda costa* rendered it null and void.

While the futile, protracted negotiations were in progress in Europe, in America both sides prepared for what appeared to be an inevitable rupture. Enterprising Governor Manuel de Montiano at St. Augustine, chagrined at the cancellation of the 1737 and subsequent attacks, was energetically adopting some of Arredondo's proposals for strengthening Florida. He increased the number of his troops, improved the castillo, occupied abandoned Fort St. George on the St. Johns River, and encouraged Carolina slaves to desert to St. Augustine. At the same time Montiano employed friendly Indians, deserters from Oglethorpe's regiment, and "a German physician" to determine the exact location, strength, and condition of the Georgia forces.[51] In London the Spanish ambassador, alarmed by Oglethorpe's regiment, insisted that Britain honor the provision regarding new fortifications, and that she recall the imperialistic Don Diego Oglethorpe.[52]

But Oglethorpe was neither recalled nor idle. He had just returned from London where he had been among the leading members of the Parliamentary opposition. Once back in Georgia he devoted his time to the details of situating, quartering, and provisioning his regiment. He billeted the main body at Frederica and maintained smaller garrisons on coastal islands to the south and at strategic locations in the interior. Dissatisfaction over living conditions, arrears of pay, and prompting by Spaniards who openly visited Cumberland Island, caused part of that garrison to mutiny. Though shot "between wig and cheek," Oglethorpe quickly restored discipline after some of the mutineers had escaped to St. Augustine.[53]

When it appeared early in 1739 that the next sail might bring news of war, Oglethorpe, hampered by recurring fever attacks, made a flying three-hundred-mile trip to Coweta, the principal Lower Creek town, in order to reaffirm Indian friendship. With the tribal chieftains assembled about the great square, and "having drank black drink together, according to the ancient custom," Oglethorpe concluded a treaty which reasserted the Georgians' right to settle in Creek territory, provided that the Creeks would have no dealings with Spaniards or Frenchmen, and stipulated that they would apprehend runaway slaves.[54] This treaty clearly signified that Spanish attempts, which had been intensified since the Yamasee revolt, to secure allegiance of the Lower Creeks had failed. Neither Britain's hold over these warlike Indians nor the presence of Admiral Vernon's squadron in the West Indies contributed to the Florida governor's peaceful slumber.

Jenkins's Ear

Chapter 8

Captain Robert Jenkins, appearing before a tense House of Commons in 1738, exhibited to the hushed members a severed ear in a remarkable state of preservation. He maintained that he had lost this ear seven years before at the hands of barbarous Spaniards in the West Indies while on a legitimate trading mission. Whether his mission was legitimate or whether Jenkins was an interloper is debatable, but his appearance before Parliament proved a rallying point for imperialists and merchants who were concerned with *guarda costa* "depredations" in the New World.[1] Jenkins had failed to elude their vigilant eyes. A Spanish captain captured Jenkins, dangled him by a rope to make him tell where his money was hidden, then bound him to the mast where the captain "took hold of his left ear and slit it down with his cutlask." [2] Jenkins asserted to the Commons that in this precarious condition he committed "his soul to God and his cause to his country." [3] The opposition in Parliament, unyielding South Sea Company directors, and a vociferous public, all decrying the insult to national honor and spoiling for a fight with Spain, triumphed over Walpole's delaying tactics and forced a war declaration the following year. The commissioners meeting in Madrid to fix the Florida boundary, regulate the log-wood cutters, and adjust claims of the South Sea Company and *guarda costa* seizures, discontinued their futile negotiations. Hostilities initially involved only Britian and Spain but soon spread until they engulfed most of Europe. The inextricable question of the Austrian succession expanded the British-Spanish conflict so that in a few years Austria, Prussia, and France all were drawn into a general European war.

It was lucky for Spain that France came into the conflict. The Spanish navy, under José Patiño and other reforming ministers, was more formidable than in the latter part of the seventeenth century, but it was still only one-quarter the size of the British navy. Even the combined Franco-Spanish Bourbon navies, on paper about equal to Britain, were neither as well manned nor as effective. Viewing her exposed American possessions and the fact that she could not necessarily count on French aid, it was perilous for Spain to take on Britain. British statesmen and particularly British merchants, not satisfied with existing trade with South America, largely illegal, appreciated the Spanish dilemma and felt that now was the hour to strike and expel Spain from much or all of America. The channel of limited legitimate trade via the South Sea Company had lost most of its appeal years before; now, should Spain be expelled, British merchants would no longer have to ship goods first to Cádiz and then by subterfuge to America or risk them in contraband trade directly in America itself. Instead, these merchants could look forward to dominating the vast American market without reference to Andalusia, which would enrich Britain at the expense of her Bourbon rivals. Fortunately for Spanish America the Bourbon alliance grew tighter and France came more openly into the war against Britain.

Since France did not officially enter the war until 1744, New World hostilities at first centered around British and Spanish possessions. One was the fringe area of Florida where Oglethorpe was preparing to resolve the boundary dispute by force; a vastly more important area was Mexico and Peru. After war broke out in 1739 Britain worked to oust Spain both from Florida and, with the support of discontented Indians and Creoles, from Mexico and Peru. Then Britain could either take over these colonies or monopolize the trade of the grateful, newly-independent American nations. Her first move was to gain control of the Panamanian Isthmus, for as Drake, Cromwell, the buccaneers, and the Spaniards all knew, whoever controlled this region dominated the commerce of Peru.

Britain directed her initial stroke against Portobello which was the unhealthy Atlantic terminus of the Isthmian trade route, the site of an annual trade fair, and one of the favorite *guarda costa* ports. Admiral Edward Vernon, a veteran naval officer with West Indian experience and one of Walpole's most outspoken critics in Parliament, demanded that a squadron be sent to the West Indies to avenge *guarda costa* insults. In his diatribes he insisted that with a mere six ships he could take Portobello. Soon Vernon had his way. Even before the war's outbreak the government ordered him to the West Indies to intercept the galleons on their return from Cartagena and Portobello, to destroy Spanish shipping wherever possible, to prevent any descent on Carolina, and to "commit all Sorts of Hostilities against the Spaniards in such Manner as you shall judge the most proper." [4] Vernon could not make contact with the elusive galleons, and he returned his attention to Portobello, considering its destruction a service that would be "most proper."

After several weeks at Jamaica, Vernon, in November 1739 with six ships-of-the-line and a marine detachment, set sail for Portobello. His objective was to neutralize the city's fortifications, to capture or destroy the *guarda costa* and merchant vessels in the harbor, and to occupy the city—at least temporarily. On all counts he succeeded brilliantly. His squadron sailed boldly into the harbor, and within a short time the audacious admiral made himself master of Portobello and of its valuable booty.[5] The capture of this city and the subsequent destruction of its fortifications, coming within a month of the declaration of war, took London by storm. Vernon was the hero of the hour, and dozens of medals were struck in his honor. His early success verified the impression that the war would be short and glorious and that Panama, Havana, Cartagena, and Mexico City would soon suffer Portobello's fate. The administration began raising a large army and outfitting new ships and were confident that they would succeed where Drake and Cromwell had failed and that New Spain and Peru, like the New Netherlands earlier, would soon have another name.

After Vernon's spectacular triumph and while he was at Jamaica refitting his ships damaged by a storm and awaiting reinforcements, the scene of action temporarily shifted northward to Florida. The Spanish rupture had not surprised Oglethorpe. Just before the war's outbreak he had been in London where he had listened to Vernon's speeches and had seen at firsthand the rising temper of Parliament, and upon arrival in Georgia he worked assiduously to establish his regiment and to improve Indian relations. Already he had concluded his favorable treaty with the Lower Creeks, and when a Rhode Island privateer brought news of war, Oglethorpe was at Fort Augusta on the Savannah River negotiating a similar treaty with the Cherokees and Chickasaws.[6] His success in winning Indian friendship and the presence of his regiment made Georgians more confident than they had been for several years. They at once sent a war party into Florida, while hundreds of additional Cherokee and Creek warriors promised to fight the Spaniards.[7]

Oglethorpe, determined to strike St. Augustine, hoped to succeed where Moore had failed forty years before. Times were propitious bcause Vernon's cruisers were blockading Havana and minimizing the possibility that Spain might reinforce Florida. Coordinating the attack from his headquarters at Frederica, Oglethorpe communicated with the scattered Georgia garrisons, friendly Indians, British warships on the North American Station, and other American colonies.[8] The crown, in addition to furnishing supplies for the expedition, provided six twenty-gun men-of-war and two sloops.[9] Cooperating with this naval force was Oglethorpe's regiment, Georgia and South Carolina militia, and numerous Indian allies.

While the General was busy organizing his expedition, frontier clashes became more numerous. Late in 1739 the enemy raided his southernmost outpost at Amelia Island which was only fifteen miles off the mouth of the St. Johns River and guarded by a small Jacobite Highlander detachment. A Spanish-Indian war party surprised a group of the Highlanders, killed two, and allegedly fled with the victims' heads.[10] With less success the Spaniards also intensified their efforts to win over the Lower Creeks.[11] To curb the increasing tempo of Spanish incursions, Oglethorpe assumed the offensive and, with only part of his Georgia troops and Indian allies, swept down into Florida and easily captured the undermanned outposts of San Francisco de Pupo and Picolata on the St. Johns River. After taking a few prisoners, burning Picolata, and in other ways annoying the Spaniards, Oglethorpe hastened back to Georgia to put the final touches on his St. Augustine expedition.[12]

He worked closely and harmoniously with South Carolina officials. Initially he contemplated a traditional siege by encircling the city, cutting off its food supply, and finally forcing the famished, overcrowded garrison to capitulate. This plan required a large, well-equipped force: South Carolina's allotment alone was six hundred infantrymen, eight hundred Negro pioneers, one hundred rangers, and two thousand Indians.[13] Recalling the burdensome increase in the public debt after Moore's attack, South Carolina was reluctant to pay for such a large force. Another drawback was denuding the colony of so many whites, because recently the colony had experienced a savage slave uprising. Oglethorpe continued to haggle with the Carolinians but in the end modified his plan. He would still capture St. Augustine but now by direct assault, which supposedly required fewer men and less money. Quickly South Carolina voted to furnish a four-hundred-man regiment and to equip five hundred Indians with guns, hatchets, blankets, and corn.[14]

Governor Manuel de Montiano, who replaced the hapless Sánchez at St. Augustine, was aware of Oglethorpe's resolve and diligently prepared the presidio for any eventuality. Oglethorpe had hopes of surprising the Spanish garrison—a salient feature of his revised strategy—but the enemy had been at the walls of the castillo during the wars of 1702 and 1728 and there was every reason to expect them again. Moreover, Oglethorpe's capture and destruction of the Florida border posts in January of 1740 did not make Montiano more complacent. Because there were only five hundred regulars and another hundred free Negroes in Florida available for service, Montiano appealed to Havana and even to Louisiana for reinforcements, food, and munitions.[15] At this time there were a mere fifty Indians serving under him, though he could enlist others if he could furnish them arms and presents.[16] But even if he did, Oglethorpe's effective Indian policy placed Montiano at a disadvantage. The harried Yamasees, who did not command the same respect as before, and the inconstant Yuchis, who wavered in their allegiance, furnished the bulk of Montiano's Indian allies. He could expect additional support from Florida's free Negroes, the majority of whom had been slaves in Carolina. The policy at St. Augustine—and in Central America and the West Indies—was to encourage British slaves to desert, to grant them freedom, supplies, and small plots of land when they reached Spanish territory, and to accept them into the Catholic Church. Most of them in Florida settled north of St. Augustine at Fort Mosa, which was astride the main route from the St. Johns River mouth to the Florida capital and soon was called the Negro Fort.

By the spring of 1740 Oglethorpe was ready to descend on Florida with his heterogeneous two-thousand-man force. He easily captured

Picolata and San Francisco de Pupo (reoccupied by the Spaniards) and entered Fort Mosa on the city's outskirts, which had been abandoned at his approach. Now only the castillo and the entrenchments surrounding the presidio barred his way to complete success. After hurried last minute consultations with Commodore Pearse of the British squadron, the stage was set for the assault. Supported by naval gunfire, the infantry would breech the city's defenses, allowing the soldiers and hundreds of Indians to swoop in on the hapless defenders. There was one obstacle, however. Six half-galleys bringing reinforcements had eluded Vernon's cruisers at Havana and recently arrived, and now these armed vessels rode anchor at the foot of the castillo, complicating any joint land-sea operation. It was the job of the British men-of-war to neutralize these vessels. Oglethorpe meticulously deployed his forces and then gave the prearranged signal for the British squadron to advance—but there was only an awful silence. As the minutes slowly ticked by, Oglethorpe hastily sent a messenger to the fleet, and he soon returned with an explanation: a shallow bar and the half-galleys prevented the men-of-war from moving into range and fulfilling their crucial role. Reluctantly Oglethorpe called off the attack.[17]

The alternative was a siege. He encircled St. Augustine, established a supposedly tight naval blockade, and moved heavy, long-range guns into position. But conditions in the Spanish capital were far different in 1740 from what they had been in 1702. Whereas Moore had crowded fifteen hundred "eaters" into the castillo and had looted the city, now entrenchments ringed St. Augustine and the twenty-four hundred inhabitants and refugees lived relatively unmolested in the city's houses, while Oglethorpe's men daily became more diseased and discontented. What was worse, they grew careless. During the night three hundred Spaniards quietly slipped out of the city and surprised the disorganized Highlanders and Carolina militia at the Negro Fort, killing or capturing seventy, forcing the remainder, many wounded and half clothed, to flee.[18] The fort's recapture partially opened up land communications with the rest of Florida. Then a few days later one of the blockading warships left its post at the Matanzas inlet; reinforcements from Havana leaped at this opportunity and were soon under the castillo's protective guns. To make matters worse Commodore Pearse disclosed that he would have to leave soon because the hurricane season was rapidly approaching.[19]

With the blockade broken and the Spaniards reinforced, dissatisfaction became rampant among the besieging forces. The Indians sulked and grew restless, the Carolinians denounced Oglethorpe and many returned home, and the high rate of sickness did not improve conditions. Oglethorpe had no choice but to call off the unsuccessful eight-week siege and return crestfallen to Frederica. Both his high hopes and Georgia-South Carolina equanimity had been shattered. It is debatable whether the expedition failed because of Oglethorpe's leadership, Colonel Vanderdussen's allegedly partisan, inefficient handling of the Carolina troops, Commodore Pearse's unwillingness to cooperate, or because of the presidio's inherent strength. Regardless of where the blame lay, the initial close harmony betwen Georgia and South Carolina was destroyed, and in the future each colony assailed the other's conduct during the campaign. More alarming than this rift was the probability that the Spaniards would assume the offensive against the disorganized, dismayed Georgians. They were apprehensive upon learning that the Spaniards had been "reinforced, the General's army harassed and weakened, and the Indians provoked and discontented." [20]

Fortunately the southern colonies secured a temporary reprieve from Spanish wrath because large-scale reinforcements began reaching Vernon at Jamaica. Wondering where he would strike first, the Spaniards everywhere in the Indies were on the defensive. His strategy was primarily maritime—neutralize and possibly occupy Spanish West Indian ports, destroy the Spanish navy, and by firmly controlling the sea lanes, dominate the New World's commerce. The home government, which was bent on occupying Spanish territory, partially overruled him, and in addition to twenty ships-of-the-line, eight thousand men commanded by General Wentworth began arriving at Jamaica in January 1741. Jubilant over Vernon's success at Portobello, the government was intent first on capturing and holding the Isthmus of Panama, then the important Spanish West Indian ports, and finally, aided by dissatisfied Creoles and Indians, parts or all of Mexico, Guatemala, New Granada, and Peru.[21] The ministry urged Vernon to march overland on the *camino real* and duplicate Henry Morgan's feat by capturing Panama and hopefully the Peruvian treasure fleet in the harbor;[22] it was enthusiastic when the Admiral sailed into the Chagres River, bombarded the castillo at its mouth, forced the commander to raise the white flag, and then leveled the port's fortifications;[23] it directed Vernon to cultivate the friendship of the Mosquito and Darien Indians, who along with nearby Creoles, would be of inestimable value in forthcoming campaigns;[24] and it dispatched still another squadron to the New World.

But this new squadron was not to reinforce Vernon. Commanded by George Anson, it was ordered to the Pacific to set upon Spanish ports and shipping, incite the discontented Peruvian Indians to revolt, and cooperate with Vernon in gaining control of the Isthmus. Though Anson wreaked devastation on Spanish shipping and is famous in British naval annals, he reached the Pacific too late to render effective aid.[25]

Vernon and Wentworth, who were not able to await Anson's arrival in the Pacific, realized that "soldiers, no more than other people, cannot do anything when they are dead, and that will be their fate if they stay too long in Jamaica." [26] With Anson unable to cooperate, their first objective was Cartagena rather than the Isthmus. This city was the most important port in northern South America, and through it and Portobello flowed most of the commerce between the mother country and South America. Cartagena, however, had ample warning of an impending attack, and Spain had repaired its fortifications and reinforced the garrison. Determined Spanish resistance, sickness incapacitating over half the British soldiers, and vitriolic bickering between Vernon and Wentworth caused the attack to fail. With disease rampant and everyone in bad humor, the expedition returned to Jamaica. Subsequently joint attacks by the remaining healthy forces against Santiago, Cuba in the summer and fall of 1741 and against the Isthmus early in 1742 met with even less success and even more feuding between the two commanders.[27]

After the unfortunate Panama expedition returned to Jamaica in 1742, most of the fleet and the army sailed to Europe—"too late to stop at Augustine, tho' if that could have been done it would have been of very great service to . . . Carolina." [28] In London the testy commanders defended their actions and explained their failures to a disappointed Parliament and nation. Britain scored few successes in the Spanish West Indies after the initial triumph at Portobello, and no Privy Council committee had to wrangle over a substitute name for New Spain and Peru.

With the recall of Vernon and Wentworth, with France coming more openly into the war, and with heavy Spanish reinforcements arriving at Havana, the dormant Spanish threat against Georgia became active. Spain realized that Britain's North American colonies were in a weakened condition: the northern and central ones had furnished troops for the unsuccessful Cartagena expedition, while the southern ones had dissipated their strength before St. Augustine. Now, with most of Vernon's fleet in Europe, was the ideal time to strike, and the Cuban governor, Juan Francisco de Güemes y Horcasitas, began assembling a powerful force. He would avenge the St. Augustine siege by "sacking and burning all the towns, posts, plantations, and settlements of the enemy" up to Port Royal.[29] Instead of the "very Gay and Brisk" John Savy, the Cuban governor commissioned intrepid Governor Montiano, because of his St. Augustine defense and intimate knowledge of the terrain, to lead the expedition.

Montiano carefully laid his plans. Shipping, veteran regulars, and militia from Cuba would augment the enlarged forces at St. Augustine.[30] While these preparations were under way, the Florida governor intensified his efforts to induce a slave revolt in Carolina and sent out Spainsh Negroes, speaking the various African dialects, to urge the slaves to rise, massacre their masters, and flee to Florida where freedom and land beckoned.[31] In the early summer of 1742 the Cuban contingent arrived at St. Augustine. A storm and high winds caused almost a week's delay, but finally "at the beat of the drum" the almost four thousand troops boarded their ships.[32] Included among the thirty-six-odd vessels were a frigate, a galley, and the familiar six half-galleys, and it was reported that "one Paris, belonging to Port Royal" piloted the armada.[33] Though the number of these vessels was formidable, their strength was not: the largest man-of-war was only a twenty-gun frigate.[34]

Oglethorpe realized that, given the opportunity, the Spaniards would renew their projected attack of 1737, and he was fully cognizant of Montiano's designs. Ever since the unsuccessful siege, Carolina Indians had watched and annoyed the Spaniards right up to St. Augustine's walls. At the same time Oglethorpe further strengthened his chain of forts stretching southward from Frederica. He repaired old batteries, erected new ones, and improved the intricate system of interlocking communications by adding watch towers, scout boats, prearranged signals, and even a canal. His sentinels soon observed Montiano's fleet, and it was no surprise when on July 4, 1742, the large Spanish flotilla appeared off St. Simon's Island convoying a force over four times larger than any in Georgia.[35]

Montiano planned to capture Frederica and to beat Oglethorpe decisively, thereby cutting his communications and destroying the only Georgia force capable of serious opposition. As soon as the Spanish fleet came within sight of the southernmost tip of St. Simons —easily recognizable because of the "lofty wooden tower" at Fort St. Simons—Montiano raised the British ensign. He hoped to deceive the garrison here long enough to allow his ships to proceed upriver to Frederica.[36] But the expectant Georgians were not misled. They hotly contested Spanish passage up the Frederica River, and it was only after a fierce four-hour bombardment that Montiano silenced the fort's batteries. Next he put his troops ashore several miles below Frederica in preparation for the final assault.

The inhabitants of St. Simons and the surrounding territory were petrified, as well they might be, by these four thousand invaders. Oglethorpe, undaunted and displaying capable military leadership, deployed his regulars, organized the militia, called for men-of-war at Charleston, and solicited Indian support. Even so, his total force was less than seven hundred. To defend Frederica succesfully against such odds was problematical. Instead he decided to ambush the Spaniards in the tangled, low-lying area covered with live oaks and festooned with Spanish moss, which the enemy had to cross before reaching Frederica. As far as it went, this strategy was markedly successful. In a muddled, confused battle known as Bloody Marsh, Oglethorpe routed the Spanish advance guard. Then, through the artifice of a forged dispatch, he tried to convince Montiano, who had remained with the main body in the rear, that he was greatly outnumbered. Apparently deceived, the Spaniards hastily re-embarked, leaving behind guns, supplies, and booty.[37] But it was not this misleading dispatch nor even the minor skirmish at Bloody Marsh involving only a small fraction of Montiano's force, which caused this precipitate departure; instead it was the probability that British warships would soon bottle up the Spanish armada in the Frederica River. Already Montiano had sighted a few men-of-war, and Oglethorpe now was primarily concerned lest the Spaniards escape before the remainder of the British warships arrived.[38] Crestfallen, Montiano returned to St. Augustine, berating "the All Powerful [who] brought to naught" this ambitious project.[39]

Shortly after the Spanish fleet left St. Simons, the men-of-war which alarmed Montiano arrived from Carolina, headed by two of His Majesty's frigates, and they cruised southward in pursuit of straggling enemy ships. Though they had no success, a short time later Rhode Island privateers captured three of the smaller enemy vessels.[40] Since by and large Montiano made good his escape, and since the threat to Georgia had abated, the Carolinians soon returned to Charleston and, according to partisan Georgian authorities, received resounding huzzas for their brilliant victory over the Spaniards.[41] But it had not been a solidly united Georgia which resisted the invasion; in fact, terror had been so great that the rapid desertion of the militia almost depopulated some areas.[42] As one New England journalist describing the battle reported: "They both did meet, they both did fight, they both did run away; they both did strive to meet again, the quite contrary way!" [43]

After Montiano retreated to St. Augustine the Spanish peril subsided, but did not disappear. Oglethorpe intensified his efforts to protect his exposed colony by repairing damage incurred during the attack, obtaining reinforcements from Virginia, and maintaining Indian war parties on St. Augustine's outskirts. Later that year thirteen British warships appeared off the bar at St. Augustine and for several days made half-hearted attempts to enter the harbor. The six half-galleys, now back at their anchorage, had little difficulty in warding off this attack, and a hurricane soon dispersed the British squadron.[44] The next year Montiano made a hostile overland demonstration toward the St. Johns River; Oglethorpe rushed southward with part of his regiment, Virginia reinforcements, and Creek allies, forcing the Spaniards to retreat. Since "the usual terror took them and they retired within the walls of St. Augustine" and Oglethorpe was unable to lure them into the open, the general, once again frustrated before the Florida capital, returned to Frederica.[45] Also during this period Oglethorpe was intriguing with Mexican agents whereby Britain would lend support to expel Spain from Mexico and would get favorable commercial advantages for doing so. But the project of setting up an independent republic in New Spain with Oglethorpe's aid was no more successful than similar projects of Vernon, Anson, and the Jamaica governor.[46] Because of charges levied against Oglethorpe by Carolinians in regard to the St. Augustine expedition and allegations of misuse of army funds made by a subordinate officer, the general in 1743, like Vernon and Wentworth the preceding year, returned to London to clear his name. Oglethorpe never saw Georgia again.

Meanwhile the conflict which had broken out between Britain and

Spain in 1739 was rapidly developing into a general war with Spain, France, and Prussia pitted against Britain, Austria, and Holland. The French and Spanish Bourbon monarchies renewed the family compact, agreeing to work in concert to dislodge the British from Georgia and "any other fortified place which they have constructed in territory of his Catholic majesty." [47] On the American mainland, Spain interpreted this to mean Honduras and the Mosquito Coast. Even before France's official entry into the war in 1744, the Bourbon powers worked closely together both in Europe and in America. For a while it appeared that a French man-of-war would accompany Montiano's fleet in 1742,[48] and before the war's outbreak French Louisiana furnished food and munitions to the hard-pressed Florida garrison. With France definitely in the war, known in the British colonies as King George's War, there were fresh rumors of a Georgia-bound fleet outfitting in Havana, and the tempo of border incidents quickened. Spanish Indians boldly raided St. Simons Island and captured several prisoners; in turn Georgia troops with their Indian allies rushed southward and ambushed these over-confident invaders as they prepared to recross the St. Johns River.[49] And the fact that France was now openly in the war offered little comfort. "The Slowness of the Spaniards, which always discovers, and often defeats, their Designs, has in a great measure, proved our safety;" the same could not be expected from the French.[50]

In spite of persistent rumors of either a French or a Spanish invasion, and in spite of Indian forays and privateer clashes at sea, the scene of major fighting shifted to the north, climaxed by the New Englanders' capture of Louisburg on Cape Breton Island. In the West Indies weak, ineffectual expeditions were sent out from Jamaica against Cuba and Venezuela, both sides constantly threatened enemy sugar islands, and there were several major naval engagements at sea. Meanwhile the disheartened Montiano in Florida, receiving little support from either Havana or Louisiana, had his hands full in repairing damage done by Oglethorpe and in securing the bare necessities for his garrison. Shortage of food and of Indian presents became so acute because of the disruption of normal routes of trade that it was necessary to trade illicitly with British vessels. The clandestine trade between St. Augustine and Charleston or New York flourished to a remarkable degree during the latter years of the war, and Montiano could boast that he was well supplied with all necessities.[51] The crown could not denounce this illegal commerce when, at the same time and for similar reasons, it allowed British merchants to trade with Portobello, Panama, and Cartagena.[52] Aided in part by British merchandise the Spaniards strengthened San Marcos in Apalachee and by 1747 won the allegiance of the nearby Yuchi Indians.[53] The only serious threat to St. Augustine came not from Georgia, but from remote Cape Breton Island. In devising her strategy for 1746, Britain considered reinforcing the New England troops at Cape Breton and attacking Quebec; or if the winter season were too far advanced and the St. Lawrence frozen over before plans were coordinated, then temperate St. Augustine would be an ideal objective. Spanish agents got wind of these plans and Montiano grew uneasy, but because of herculean French efforts to retake Louisburg, Britain needed all available troops at Cape Breton, and her projected attack never took place.[54] Now that France was in the war, and since Britain was usually fully committed in America to taking over French colonies or defending her own, St. Augustine and most other Spanish colonies were spared in 1746.

The limited fighting in the south shifted from Florida and the "debatable land" of Georgia to frequent naval encounters by British and Spanish privateers. *Guarda costa* depredations had been a primary cause of the war, and maritime hostilities continued unabated. At first New England vessels preyed on Spanish commerce, but before long others were sent out from the southern ports of Charleston, Savannah, and Frederica. Captain Caleb Davis, a former merchant, outfitted a twenty-gun brig at Savannah, and for the remainder of the war each of his voyages netted one or more Spanish prizes.[55] Another Georgia vessel—this one equipped by Oglethorpe himself—snatched a prize right from under Spanish noses. Early in 1742 a long-awaited supply ship laden with munitions and provisions arrived off the bar at St. Augustine. The Spaniards fired the castillo's cannon and lit bonfires, but before high tide permitted entrance into the harbor, Oglethorpe's sloop captured the relief vessel.[56] Later in the war a British privateer made off with the forty-seven thousand pesos dispatched to pay the Florida garrison.[57] It was probable that any Negro, free or not, captured on a Spanish prize, would be sold in Newport, New York, or another British port.[58]

British vessels came to Spanish ports like St. Augustine not only to make captures but also to trade. This was particularly true during the latter stages of the war when the scarcity of European manufactures was more acute in Spanish colonies. One way for Britain to exploit this situation and to trade with the Spaniards was to make a formal agreement to traffic in non-military commodities. Another method was to continue contraband traffic in the usual fashion, while still another solution centered around prisoner exchange. It was common practice during wartime to exchange prisoners, and it was just as common practice for the British vessels bringing prisoners to Spanish ports to have their holds laden with merchandise. Prisoner exchange and contraband trade were almost synonymous in both Spanish and British eyes. By whatever means, British goods in large volume continued reaching Spanish New World markets during the war as they had in the past, and this took much of the sting out of Spanish reprisals on the effects of the South Sea Company and out of the fact that during the war few British merchants were allowed in Andalusia.

Not all privateers flew the Union Jack. A renaissance had taken place in the Spanish navy and merchant marine under Philip v, and between 1739 and 1741 alone over fifty privateers carried at least three hundred prizes to Spanish ports, with some thirty going to St. Augustine.[59] From St. Augustine, Havana, Veracruz, Portobello, and other West Indian ports, these privateers ranged from the Caribbean to New England. North of the Virginia Capes they confined themselves to lying off the coast and seizing unsuspecting merchantmen. The Carolinas were not so fortunate. Heavily armed, small draft Spanish "row galleys" infested the Carolina sounds and inland waterways, intercepting incoming ships and ravaging surrounding territory. Throughout the war both the Carolinas rushed construction on corresponding "row galleys" which could pursue the Spaniards into shallow water and meet them on equal terms. The Carolinians did not build enough, because the Spaniards sacked Beaufort and neighboring towns and snatched prizes out of their harbors near the war's end.[60]

Meanwhile in Europe the wearied combatants concluded the treaty of Aix-la-Chapelle—an indecisive document providing for the *status quo ante bellum*, and conveniently by-passing or relegating to a vague future settlement the right of search by *guarda costa* crews, the Florida boundary, and British monetary claims. In America neither Spain nor Britain surrendered any territory or made any major concessions.[61] British mismanagement of tropical campaigns, coupled with French aid and internal reforms in the Spanish empire, allowed Spain's colonies to emerge relatively unscathed from the conflict.

Bourbon
Blunders

Chapter 9

In the decade after Aix-la-Chapelle there was a surprising improvement in British-Spanish relations manifest both in Europe and in America. This novel amity was not a result of any provision in the inconclusive peace treaty, but instead was a result of the world-wide struggle between Britain and France which had been waged intermittently for decades and now was approaching a climax. In America and in distant India Frenchmen vied with Britons, regardless of whether their countries were at peace or war, always conscious that an empire was the prize. The stakes were high, and the combatants were evenly matched; each sought some advantage which might tip the balance. Though Spain was not the commanding power she had been under Charles I and Philip II, her influence could not be discounted: the Spanish fleet, the third largest afloat, was growing yearly, and Spanish possessions in Europe and abroad made her a force with which to be reckoned. If the bonds of the Bourbon family compact drew tighter or even remained in effect, then perhaps France would win the duel for empire. If, on the other hand, Spain could be weaned from the close relationship with her Bourbon neighbor, then possibly the tide would turn in England's favor. In order to win over Spain, Britain had to abandon her contemptuous attitude displayed before and during the recent war and be willing to make concessions. For awhile Britain was willing to do this, and with one dangerous exception, the period immediately after Aix-la-Chapelle was more tranquil than any for half a century. Of course there still were outstanding New World disputes—the continual seizures by *guarda costa*, the Florida boundary, the compensation for damages claimed by the South Sea Company, the Spanish right to fish off Newfoundland, and the British liberty to cut logwood—but some were settled and, excepting the problem of the logwood cutters, the others remained in the background.[1]

In America the discretion of the *guarda costa* crews in exercising their right of search and the removal of Oglethorpe's regiment from Georgia both were assuaging influences. After the war, Henry Pelham, the British prime minister, enacted sweeping economies which forced the discharge of thousands of soldiers, and Oglethorpe's unit, like many others, suffered heavily. Over loud Georgian protests the regiment disbanded, though three independent companies remained to guard the southern frontier. But by 1750 even these companies were transferred from Georgia to South Carolina.[2] Most of the forts erected by Oglethorpe were either abandoned and left to decay or were manned by only skeleton forces. Fort William at the southern tip of Cumberland Island was the southernmost post still occupied, and a mere corporal and six privates garrisoned it.[3] For all intents and purposes there were no British settlements south of the Altamaha River. Though Spain still regarded Frederica at that river's mouth a usurpation, at least British troops were not within fifty miles of St. Augustine on the St. Johns River.

While tensions were easing on the Georgia-Florida frontier, the mother countries were drawing closer together, largely because of British concessions. In the 1750 Treaty of Madrid, Britain agreed to relinquish the vexatious *asiento* for a monetary consideration, and outstanding financial claims on both sides were wiped out.[4] Much had been made over the *asiento* and annual ship which was allowed to trade in goods other than slaves, and British merchants had hoped that here was an opening to begin widespread legitimate commerce with Spanish America. Frequent wars resulting in the impounding of South Sea Company goods and haggling over interpretations of numerous provisions had resulted in the *asiento* and annual ship's being of little profit.

In the post-war period Florida's Governor Melchor de Navarrete repaired the damage suffered during the war and tried to win the friendship of more Indians. Though food, material, and labor were scarce, he rebuilt and reoccupied forts Diego, Picolata, and Mosa, which were all within a twenty-mile radius of St. Augustine. And more important, Spain, disturbed over the ease with which all of Florida except the presidio had been overrun in the past and determined to maintain her post on the Bahama Channel, at long last sent colonists to Florida. When they began arriving, Navarrete expected to send some two hundred and fifty Canary Island immigrants westward to Apalachee or northward to the St. Johns River as Arredondo had urged.[5] At the same time he gave land to fugitive slaves from Carolina and Georgia, organized them into an independent company, and added them to the Negro Fort's garrison.[6]

Georgians were concerned about the improvements in Florida's defenses and especially about the new influx of colonists. Reports in Savannah indicated that Spanish families had established themselves not only on the St. Johns River, but even farther north on Amelia Island—the site of one of Oglethorpe's abandoned outposts. Georgia officials commissioned a scout boat to determine as discreetly as possible how much of the "debatable land" Spain had reoccupied. The disturbing rumors at Savannah proved exaggerated: there was neither a settlement on Amelia Island nor one on the St. Johns River.[7] Indian hostility had restricted the Canary Islanders to the vicinity of St. Augustine. The Creeks and, more often than not, the Yuchis, inspired by Georgians or incensed by some Spanish action, made life unbearable for unprotected and dispersed farming communities.[8] Soldiers guarded such ones as existed around St. Augustine, Fort San Marcos in Apalachee, and Pensacola, and there were no extra troops to protect exposed settlements on the St. Johns River. The mother country had encouraged and partly underwritten the locating of Canary Island colonists in Florida. Even though many of them were dissatisfied at home, they, like most Spanish immigrants, had a low opinion of Florida and would not have gone there without prodding by the crown. Subsequent conditions in Florida did little to change their opinion of this province. Spanish officials were anxious to populate new areas in Florida not only as a buffer to Georgia, but also to render the land productive. It was just as true and as galling after the war as during recent hostilities that English merchants furnished much of St. Augustine's food.[9] Immediately after Aix-la-Chapelle most of the contested territory from the Altamaha River almost down to the Florida capital remained unoccupied; each side closely watched the other's movements, and each hoped that it would be the first to colonize part, if not all, of this deserted region.

In spite of the fact that Britain tried to conciliate Spain in the post-war period, their differences did not all disappear. Negroes, mulattoes, and Indians captured aboard Spanish ships during the war had been imprisoned in New York. Unable to prove to the satisfaction of local authorities that they were free, many were sold as slaves. Long after the cessation of hostilities, these former prisoners still were slaves, and Spain still was trying to free them.[10] In turn Negroes from Carolina and, for the first time, from Georgia, which now permitted slavery, continued to abscond to Florida where they were still welcomed. Another point of contention arose in 1750 when a Spanish treasure fleet bound from Cuba to Spain encountered a storm off the American coast, and the surviving vessels, battered and mastless, reached safety in various North American harbors. Most of them outfitted again in Norfolk or some other Chesapeake Bay port;[11] others less fortunate had been wrecked off the North Carolina coast and had their cargoes stolen by contriving Carolinians.[12]

Added to these minor controversies was the aggravating presence of logwood cutters and traders at Honduras and on the Mosquito Shore—a condition which almost led to war. During the recent conflict Britain had occupied and fortified Roatán and had sent troops to the Mosquito Shore. In turn Spain had tried to expel Britain from all Central America, and Spanish attacks were fairly successful at Belize. The peace treaty stipulated that all captured territory must be returned. Britain had occupied Roatán during the war and was forced to evacuate it—but not Honduras and the Mosquito Shore. Britons had been here for years and could claim one or both by right of effective occupation, cession from the natives, or European peace settlements ranging from the American Treaty to Aix-la-Chapelle. After the war Britain was determined to maintain her position in the Bay of Honduras and to at least the northern part of the Mosquito Shore. And Spain was resolved to force Britain out of every part of Central America. These disputes involving the logwood cutters remained the chief threat to the precarious British-Spanish *rapprochement*.

This was the state of affairs when in 1756 France and Britain openly resumed their temporarily suspended conflict known as the Seven Years War. At the beginning Britain suffered nothing but humiliating defeats: in Europe her allies underwent severe reverses; she lost Minorca in the Mediterranean; in India it was the time of the "Black Hole of Calcutta"; and in America another attempt to capture Louisburg (returned to France in 1748) was a failure. Two years before war was even declared, the youthful, strong-willed George Washington and his Virginia militia capitulated to a larger French and Indian force in the Ohio country; and the next year this defeat was followed by the rout of General Braddock's regulars in the same region. While Britain's fortunes were at such a low ebb it seemed more necessary than ever to keep the family compact inactive and to maintain quiet in America.[13] William Pitt, now directing the war effort and foreign policy, was angling for a Spanish alliance, but the indiscretions of British privateers and the continuing presence of logwood cutters and troops in Honduras and the Mosquito Shore prevented the two countries from becoming formal allies.

Nevertheless, in an attempt to win Spain's favor, Pitt tried to prohibit American privateers from preying on Spanish commerce.[14] In addition, he forbade Georgians from moving south of the Altamaha River lest they, like Oglethorpe two decades before, stir up a hornet's nest on the southern frontier. In the past colonists fleeing their creditors had established themselves in the "debatable land," but though Pitt conscientiously tried to have them returned, he could no more do this than he could make them pay their debts.[15] Moreover, the extensive trade carried on between British colonies and Spanish Florida continued in spite of the fact that French privateers based at St. Augustine might use these provisions. Food and merchandise from New York, flour, beef, and pork from Maryland, and herds of cattle driven overland from Georgia—all helped sustain the troops and new colonists in Florida.[16] Because the war disrupted commerce, the Spaniards here faced starvation on several occasions, and eventually the Florida governor had to promise to bar French privateers from St. Augustine and to return all runaway slaves.[17] As a good will gesture, the Georgians returned Spanish prisoners captured by the Indians.[18] In a further attempt to win over Spain, Pitt offered to restore Gibraltar and to surrender all claims in Honduras and the Mosquito Shore, and at the same time he appointed a governor in Jamaica who was more acceptable to Spain.[19] Pitt never got a formal alliance, but his conciliatory moves helped keep Spain neutral during the critical early years of the war.

The tide of battle, which first favored France, turned in Britain's favor. The brilliant, imperious, perhaps mentally unbalanced Pitt took over the reins of government in 1756 and at once proceeded to shape victory out of defeat. He replaced older incompetent officers who held high rank merely because of wealth and position with young military leaders of proven ability, and soon London's bells wearied tolling the victories. Britain began to force France out of India; Britain and her allies won battles on the continent—or at least Frederick the Great was not overcome by France, Austria, and Russia—while the French fleet suffered crippling setbacks at sea; and in America Fort Duquesne on the Ohio, Guadeloupe in the West Indies, Louisburg on Cape Breton Island, and Quebec, the heart of the French empire in America, all fell, the latter to the mortally wounded General Wolfe.

With constant reports of some new victory the need for a Spanish alliance, or even neutrality, rapidly faded, and differences which had remained dormant in the past again assumed an ominous tone. Though at first Pitt tried to make privateers distinguish between French and Spanish vessels, be became less insistent as the war wore on. At first he was willing to make concessions concerning the logwood cutters, or perhaps even to give up Honduras and the Mosquito Shore, but not now. At this same time Spain brought up the disputed Florida boundary and began insisting that she be allowed to participate in the Newfoundland fishery whose importance was appreciated now as never before. Spain sent out several vessels to fish off Newfoundland—perhaps merely an excuse to trade with the beleaguered French forces in Canada—and she was adamant that Britain allow Biscayans their traditional fishing rights. The fact that Spain, even though her navy was greatly enlarged, was finding it impossible to man effectively all, or even a majority of her ships-of-the-line, was a powerful incentive for such a demand.[20] But the imperial-minded Pitt, imbued with the importance of the fishery and determined to make it a closed preserve, was obdurate in his opposition to Spanish demands, and would not permit "the great nursery of Our Seamen, and a principal Basis of the Maritime Power of Great Britain, to be, in any degree, pared off, and divided." [21]

With victorious Britain unwilling to make significant concessions and with France suffering setback after setback and pressing more than ever for a Spanish alliance, the Spanish king, Charles III, began to favor renewing the family compact. Perhaps Spain and France together could command respect from Britain where neither alone had much success. For Spain, however, there was a more important reason. Unless there were a change for the better, France seemed destined to lose her extensive North American possessions. Once France was reduced to an insignificant colonial power, what chance was there that Spanish colonies could withstand the British onslaught? News of Quebec's fall made Charles III's "blood run cold," and the Spanish monarch feared that news of new British conquests might include Florida, parts of Central America, or Mexico.[22] Even the formerly pro-British Spanish ambassador, Ricardo Wall, pointed out that since the British were bent on appropriating Spanish possessions, these colonies might as well be "seized with arms in His Subject's Hands, and not to continue the passive Victim." [23] Spain renewed the family compact in 1761 which provided that each nation would guarantee the other's possessions and that if France did not soon make peace, then Spain would openly enter the war. France did not soon make peace, and after the treasure fleet safely anchored at Cádiz at the end of the year, Spain lost no time in declaring war. At first Spanish troops had some success against a joint Portuguese-British force on the Iberian peninsula, and Charles III was optimistic that the combined Bourbon navies might challenge Britain's almost exclusive control of the sea. In a little over a year it was obvious that he had made a terrible mistake.

This time Georgians launched no formal expedition against Florida, although Indians still preyed upon the Spaniards and Spain prepared to reinforce St. Augustine, Pensacola, and even the hard-pressed French in New Orleans.[24] At the same time both French and Spanish privateers based at St. Augustine ranged the Atlantic seaboard and preyed on British ships as far north as Newfoundland.[25] Indeed other Spanish men-of-war not based at the Florida capital captured Newfoundland fishing vessels and on several occasions put raiding parties ashore.[26] The scarcity of food at St. Augustine was an added incentive for privateers sent out from this port. But even with provisions from captured prizes supplementing the scanty diet of fish and flour, it was necessary to continue trading with British colonies. In spite of the fact that George III strictly forbade this commerce, provisions from Georgia, Charleston, and New York continued reaching the distressed Spaniards in Florida in the same illicit way they had been reaching the beleaguered French in Canada.[27] The Spaniards had other problems besides a precarious diet. Roving bands of Indians harried all of Florida from St. Augustine in the east to Pensacola in the west so that Spaniards hardly dared venture forth for firewood. Recently French agents had been active among the Creeks, and there was danger that these Indians might be won over to the Bourbon cause. But prompt Georgia counter-measures kept the Creeks loyal, and after 1762 they, along with the Yuchis, made life unpleasant for both Spaniards and their Indian allies. It was not uncommon for a Spanish scalp to appear in Savannah.[28] The Florida Indians were hounded so unmercifully that Spain had little choice but to transport some of them to Cuba.[29]

Except for tormenting Indian harassment and lack of provisions, Spanish Florida escaped relatively unscathed from the war. Other Spanish colonies were not so fortunate. In 1762 a powerful fleet and ten thousand men left England bound for the Indies. These troops landed outside of Havana and prepared to besiege supposedly impregnable Fort Morro, key to the city's defenses. Despite a heavy toll taken by sickness and a determined Spanish resistance, the fort capitulated after a seven-week siege and a surprisingly successful assault. A short time later Havana, "Queen of the Indies," surrendered, yielding much booty in silver and stores. Across the Pacific it was the same story over again when British regulars and sepoys from India captured Manila. Spain insisted on ending hostilities lest there be some new disaster. The Spanish alliance had not enhanced France's fortunes either; four more Caribbean islands easily fell into British hands, and, like her Bourbon ally, France too was ready to end the conflict. Strange to relate, Britain also was anxious for peace; domestic intrigues forced Pitt's resignation and the aspiring George III felt that continuing the war would hinder his political ambitions at home and empty the exchequer.

The belligerents met in Paris in the fall of 1762 and after much wrangling signed a peace treaty. Unquestionably it was a victor's peace: France, for all practical purposes, was expelled from North America, and Spain paid dearly for her brief participation in the war. She abandoned all pretensions whatsoever to the Newfoundland fishery; she made concessions in regard to logwood cutting; and, in return for Havana, she ceded Florida.[30] Supposedly to make the loss of Florida more palatable, France in turn ceded Louisiana to her unfortunate ally.

For Florida it was ironic that the capitulation of Fort Morro in Havana rather than the Castillo at St. Augustine should have been the province's downfall. But Spain had no choice. Florida, though a drain on the Treasury, was strategically located: Havana, however, with a superior harbor, was just as strategically located, and was not a financial burden. Even though Spain was abandoning the old convoy system whereby the returning fleets assembled at Havana, this port still was one of the most important in the West Indies. Nevertheless, Spain was humiliated and chagrined at Florida's loss and with reluctance prepared to relinquish it. The treaty provided that Spanish subjects in Florida could remain without molestation and could practice their Catholic religion; but if they chose to leave they could take their private property with them or sell it to the incoming British.[31] Few Spaniards elected to remain. Cuban officials urged all the inhabitants of eastern Florida to migrate to Cuba where they would be furnished land and financial assistance and could worship without question of persecution.[32] Normally the crown furnished transportation, but the Bishop of Cuba, who recently had fled to St. Augustine, personally financed the removal of some of the women and children to Cuba.[33]

The unenthusiastic mass exodus began in the spring of 1763 and was completed early the following year. Transports and cargo ships were loaded almost to overflowing with Spanish troops, their equipment and stores, and with the remainder of Florida's heterogeneous population—unlucky Canary Islanders, Negroes, Mulattoes, Indians, many of whom had good reason to fear for their safety or freedom, and even a handful of Germans who doubtless originally came from Georgia.[34] Soldiers dismantled the Castillo's cannon which had belched defiance at Moore and Oglethorpe and loaded them also aboard ship. To the west similar scenes were enacted. The San Marcos garrison and nearby inhabitants in Apalachee packed up their belongings and sailed for Cuba; even farther west at Pensacola the city's entire population departed for Veracruz. All in all about three thousand Spanish subjects in Florida began life anew in Cuba, as did almost seven hundred more in Mexico. Only a few transferred their allegiance to the British flag.[35]

Britons greeted Florida's acquisition with mixed reactions. In the southern colonies there was nothing but exultation and relief over removal of the hostile Spanish neighbors. Georgia militia and rangers mustered in Savannah's market place and, amid frequent salvos, celebrated the triumphant peace.[36] In Britain, however, the treaty did not receive such unanimous approbation. Pitt and his followers, denouncing the conciliatory policy of the Earl of Bute, were discontented over what they considered unnecessary concessions to

France and Spain, and one of the most irritating was the restitution of Havana for "low, flat, and marshy" Florida, a region "scorched with burning sands" where "the waters stagnate and corrupt." [37] Yet by demanding Florida rather than Havana Bute knew he was more likely to get a quick settlement. And there were arguments justifying the acquisition of Spanish Florida similar to those justifying the taking over of French Canada[38]—neither in itself was considered a particularly profitable colony, but in foreign hands both were a menace to British mainland colonies. In addition to being a thorn in Georgia's side, Florida, commanding the Bahama Channel, was no less important now than in Menéndez's day. Though the peninsula's chief asset was strategic, contemporary publicists exaggerated Florida's infertility. On the peninsula and particularly westward in Apalachee there was excellent farm land.

British troops in 1763 sailed from Havana to take possession of Florida. For the first time in two centuries the Spanish royal banner was lowered at St. Augustine and the Union Jack was raised in its place. Then with little ceremony the last of the Spanish transports departed for Cuba. Spain's tenuous control of *la Florida* which had existed continuously since Menéndez expelled Ribault and his French compatriots from Fort Caroline, at last was destroyed. Actually Spain would still control part of what formerly had been considered *la Florida*—the region now known as Louisiana—and in the future the Spanish flag again would fly over St. Augustine. But when British soldiers mustered in the Castillo's courtyard for the first time, a new day in Florida's history dawned.

Rule,
Britannia!

Chapter 10

The British Empire after the Seven Years War was the most extensive in the world, including almost all of North America east of the Mississippi River, the most valuable sugar islands in the West Indies, some of the more important slaving stations in Africa, and a commanding position in India. From outward appearances the approximately three million white inhabitants in this empire were energetic, prosperous, and bound by law, tradition, and affection to the crown. They were governed in ways varying from considerable self-government in American colonies such as Massachusetts and Virginia to little voice in government in the scattered trading settlements on the coasts of Africa and India. Not only affection and economic advantage within the empire, but also the wooden walls of the British navy strengthened imperial bonds. Britain's successes in the recent war, the extent of her empire, and her haughtiness in the postwar period excited jealousy and left her with few friends on the continent.

France lost many of her colonies to Britain, and, under the leadership of the influential minister, the Duc de Choiseul, was augmenting her war-making potential and marking time for a war of revenge. Spain's policy was similar to France's. Spain also had been humiliated in the recent war, and the pro-French faction, ardent defenders of the family compact, were just as anxious for an opportunity to humble Britain. This, however, was not the unanimous opinion. A small but articulate anti-French group at the Spanish court resented France's influence and desired to sever the Bourbon alliance which relegated Spain to an unequal partner. This was not easy to do and the way was fraught with perils. Spain's empire was second only to Britain's, and there were or soon would be disputes in various quarters of the globe ranging from the upper Mississippi Valley in North America, to the Falkland Islands in the South Atlantic, to the Philippines in the Orient. And Britain for a half century had occupied Gibraltar off the Spanish coast. Britain made little effort to placate Spain, and even though Spain under the enlightened despotism of Charles III and his able ministers was taking great strides towards making her empire more productive, stimulating her industry and agriculture, and strengthening her army and navy, it was obvious that she alone, with a fleet not quite half the size of her rival, was no match for Britain. This unpalatable reality buttressed the hand of the pro-French faction and was all-important in keeping the family compact in force.[1]

France ceded Louisiana west of the Mississippi River and the island of Orleans to Spain to compensate her for Florida's loss, ridding herself of the last fragment of the once-extensive New France by unloading the unprofitable colony on her Bourbon ally. Spain needed no more unprofitable colonies and was unenthusiastic in accepting this gratuitous donation. But if she did not take Louisiana then Britain was willing to oblige, thereby placing aggressive neighbors on New Spain's threshold. Giving New Orleans to Britain would tend to make the Gulf of Mexico a British lake and would point a dagger at New Spain. This Spain had to avoid at all costs. With some misgivings she accepted Louisiana—formerly part of *la Florida*—and in so doing drastically altered the scope of Anglo-Spanish rivalry in North America.

The first Spanish governor, the prominent scientist, Antonio de Ulloa, belatedly took possession of Louisiana in 1766. His immediate problems were manifold: he had to establish Spanish rule over a predominantly French population, to devise means to render Louisiana profitable, and to provide for the colony's defense. Spain took over Louisiana to keep it out of British hands and to create a buffer for New Spain. The first line of defense was the Mississippi River, and from Spain's viewpoint this was a desirable border. In contrast to northern Florida, it was fixed. The broad Mississippi made it easier to defend Louisiana, assuming anything made it easier to defend the almost two thousand mile boundary with only a handful of soldiers and with the closest assistance in Mexico or Cuba. The most important centers were New Orleans near the river's mouth and newer and smaller St. Louis near the junction of the Missouri and Mississippi rivers. In addition, Ulloa and his successors built new forts or improved old French ones at key locations along the extended river boundary: Balize at the river's mouth, two others opposite the British West Florida posts at Manchac and Natchez, one at the mouth of the Arkansas River, another at Sainte Genevieve, and a blockhouse on each side of the Missouri River's mouth. The largest garrison was at New Orleans, and there were only a handful of troops elsewhere; in fact, Spain abandoned some of the above-mentioned posts shortly after she occupied them. Her hold on the Mississippi, the heart of Louisiana and the backbone of a continent, was a shaky one. Spain, no less than Britain, recognized that Louisiana was vulnerable.[2]

It was surprising that the first real danger to Louisiana originated not from without by her British neighbor but from within. Most of the Louisiana settlers were French, and in spite of bonds of a common religion, of similar backgrounds, and of close ties between the mother countries, many had little desire to be ruled by Spain. Her procrastination in occupying Louisiana, the scant number of troops which finally did arrive, the political ineptness of Ulloa, his acute lack of funds—all contributed to the general dissatisfaction and misunderstanding and to the hope cherished by some Frenchmen that France either would not relinquish or would quickly regain this province. Initially the revolt was successful. Armed Acadian and German settlers, fearing they would not be paid for provisions sold to the government and following the leadership of French merchants, forced Ulloa to desert New Orleans and retire first to the mouth of the Mississippi and then to Havana. Soon most of the Spanish troops evacuated Louisiana and the rebels were in complete control.

Spain could not afford to ignore this insult to her authority: not only would she lose Louisiana but the spirit of revolt might prove contagious. She appointed a new governor, General Alexandro O'Reilly, one of Spain's ablest soldiers, who immediately sailed to assume his duties, assisted by two thousand troops. This overwhelming force, the largest Spain would ever put in Louisiana, was more than enough to stamp out the rebellion. O'Reilly entered New Orleans unopposed, arrested many of the leaders, and contrary to expectations, hanged the principals, winning the epithet "bloody O'Reilly." Though O'Reilly and most of the troops soon departed, Spain had forcefully reasserted her authority, and Louisiana was more apprehensive of inroads by her neighbors than of internal unrest.[3]

Louisiana's immediate neighbor was Britain, and judging from past experience there would be squabbles and reason for concern. Disputes there were aplenty from one end of the extensive boundary to the other. Britain was overjoyed to see Spain take over Louisiana, even though enough Frenchmen remained behind "to poison the minds of the Indians, either for their own private interest or as agents for the Spaniards." [4] During the recent rebellion some Britons advocated annexing New Orleans or perhaps foregoing the Manila ransom in exchange for New Orleans, but the ultimate official policy was to give no aid to the rebels.[5] When O'Reilly and his large force came to Louisiana, Britain as a precaution rushed a regiment to West Florida. The garrisons at Fort Bute and Natchez, both on the east bank of the Mississippi, along with the one in Pensacola, had been withdrawn, largely as an economy measure.

One of the most vexing problems centered about the navigation of the Mississippi. There was no question that Britain had the right to navigate this river from its mouth to its source and for its entire breadth. These provisions were in the recent Treaty of Paris and apparently were all that Britain could desire[6]—except that in practice she was able to maintain little commerce on the river. It was laborious for vessels to enter the river's mouth and sail up to New Orleans or beyond. The river meandered, the winds were uncertain, and frequently the only practical way to get upriver in spots was by warping: tying a rope to an object on the bank and winching the vessel upstream, repeating the process as many times as necessary. This was a tedious operation but allowed ocean-going vessels at any time to sail upriver to harbors where they could discharge their cargos. Spain commanded the west bank of the Mississippi and Britain the east bank except near the mouth where Spain controlled the island of Orleans which included both banks. Spain permitted British ships to sail upstream but would not allow seamen ashore on either bank. This deterred warping and, along with not having warehouse facilities at New Orleans, stymied British commerce on the river. Although Britain asserted that the Treaty of Paris granted her free navigation and that warping was essential to free navigation, these arguments made little headway with Spain.[7] Britain pressed her case and doubtless would have pressed it more had O'Reilly and others not stopped much of the contraband trade at New Orleans, had she as an economy measure not withdrawn most of her troops from the Mississippi, and had not Pontiac's Rebellion partially forced her out of the Illinois region.

Britain wanted to navigate the Mississippi to communicate and trade with her own subjects and, equally important, to traffic with the Spaniards. British merchants had outlets in New Orleans; their ships at first regularly visited that city; and they dominated much of Louisiana's commerce until O'Reilly's arrival. He ordered all British merchants to close shop and all British citizens whatever their vocation to leave Spanish soil; he would not permit British ships to tie up at New Orleans or their seamen to set foot on Spanish territory.[8] Even though this stayed much of the commerce which sprang up at the war's end, it did not abolish it. The river boundary was extensive, and it was not in O'Reilly's or anyone else's power to patrol it twenty-four hours a day. At once, and as long as Britain was a neighbor, there was clandestine trade in lower Louisiana, either by Floridians slipping across the river at isolated spots or by their supplying unlicensed French traders already in Louisiana. Another way to win the Indian trade was to entice whole tribes to cross over to the east bank.[9]

The problems of prohibiting contraband in lower Louisiana were magnified many times in upper Louisiana which had St. Louis as its center but which had only a handful of soldiers. British and French-Canadian fur traders as individuals, as employees of the Hudson Bay Company, or later as representatives of the newly-formed Northwest Company ranged far westward from their bases at Montreal and Michilimackinac. Even if anyone had the slightest idea where Louisiana's northern boundary was, these traders would not have respected it. From time to time they crossed the Mississippi and penetrated upper Louisiana via the Missouri, Des Moines, and other rivers. These traders bartered trinkets, guns, and whiskey to the Indians for pelts, and as a result many of the furs which should have gone to Europe via New Orleans pased through Quebec instead. In addition to this widespread illegal Indian trade there was constant intercourse between the Spaniards at St. Louis and the British at nearby Kaskaskia and Fort de Chartres or at more distant Detroit and Michilimackinac. The troops of the St. Louis garrison had a two-year tour and were not paid until the end of that time lest Spanish silver wind up on the east side of the river. With British wares less expensive and in greater supply than those freighted up the Mississippi, the precaution was well founded.[10]

There was maneuvering on both sides to win or maintain Indian friendship after the Treaty of Paris, for without Indian support there could be little trade and neither nation could maintain its authority within its own territory. This the Spaniards well knew in the rebellious Osage country west of the Mississippi as did the British in the Ohio country during Pontiac's uprising. Neither nation respected the Mississippi boundary when dealing with the Indians. Those on the east bank, dissatisfied with British rule, crossed over to St. Louis to be entertained and to receive presents from the Spaniards,[11] while farther west British traders intrigued among the Indians, fostered resentment against the Spaniards, and bartered for their furs. When the Spaniards tried to bring the Osages to terms by cutting off trade, British merchants were only too willing to ascend the Missouri and supply firearms and ammunition in spite of harassment or capture by Spanish patrols.[12] A battle for Louisiana's fur trade was emerging, and Spain was able to do little to alter the tide in her favor.

The petty squabbles between British and Spanish traders in upper and lower Louisiana and the disputes over navigation of the Mississippi River were manifestations of a larger issue. There were three main water entrances to the interior of North America—Hudson Bay, the St. Lawrence River, and the Mississippi River. Firm control of all three, as La Salle and other Frenchmen realized, assured dominion over most of North America. Britain had been master of Hudson Bay for almost a century; she gained the St. Lawrence in 1763; only the Mississippi remained. With all three of these waterways in her possession, France expelled from North America, and Spanish industry in poor position to compete, Britain could expect almost to monopolize American trade north of Mexico. This she was determined to do and for this reason she encouraged contraband with Louisiana, had insisted on free navigation of the Mississippi in the 1763 peace treaty, and demanded the privilege of warping, which would help assure this free navigation.

Spain experienced difficulty in taking over and administering French Louisiana after the war, while Britain, in turn, had a less trying time in administering and peopling Spanish Florida. There was little discontent among the Spaniards here because almost all had departed for Cuba or Mexico. Britain divided the colony into two provinces, East and West Florida, with St. Augustine the capital of one and Pensacola the other. Britain succeeded in attracting settlers to both colonies, most of whom were farmers, while a few were merchants who traded with Louisiana. But Pensacola, with its square stockaded fort and "rabble of dirty fellows," never met expectations nor became a rival to Jamaica as a base for Spanish trade.[13]

Though the Spaniards abandoned East Florida, they did not completely sever their ties with this province or with what Britain maintained was part of this province. British and Spanish fishermen from the Bahamas and Cuba came to the Florida Keys to fish and to take turtles, and each asserted that the other had no right there. Britain declared that the Keys were ceded to her as part of Florida; this Spain denied and said they were and always had been part of Cuba.[14] The Spanish fishermen were more numerous and persistently fished off the Keys and off Florida's deserted west coast, maintaining sporadic contact with the Creeks, occasionally taking them back to Cuba and furnishing them with "rich loud cloaths," [15] but never attempting a formal settlement. Britain was not alarmed so long as the Spaniards made no settlement and did little more than fish; besides, if these fishermen stopped coming it would be more difficult to trade illicitly with Havana.[16]

A characteristic of the period after the Seven Years War was the intensified effort of British merchants to smuggle goods into Spanish colonies and in turn the mounting Spanish opposition through increased vigilance and internal reform to curb this contraband. One such reform was to reduce duties on goods bound from Spain to America which had the practical effect of making French goods dispatched to America via Spain—along with Spanish ones—more competitive with British wares smuggled directly into America. Yet before this and other reforms could take effect, there was the reality of a pent-up demand for European wares—a demand British traders were eager to satisfy. Havana's capture and brief occupation gave them a marvelous opportunity to trade with the city's merchants and provided an excuse to send vessels to other Spanish ports with prisoners above deck and merchandise below. At the same time Jamaica vessels rushed news of peace to the Spanish American mainland. Why it was necessary for these vessels to linger for days or weeks in Spanish ports was never satisfactorily explained. A primary reason for acquiring Pensacola was that it had an excellent harbor convenient to Spanish colonies which in time might rival Jamaica as a center of contraband. After the war Pensacola vessels appeared at New Orleans, Veracruz, Yucatán, and Central American ports while Spanish ships regularly called at this West Florida harbor. Nevertheless, trade based in this city never lived up to expectations.[17]

British traders expanded into the Spanish province of Texas whose trade before had been dominated by the French in neighboring Louisiana. Texas, between the Sabine and Rio Grande rivers, had an extensive, unpopulated coastline with many inlets and coastal islands—an ideal situation for British smugglers. In the decade after the Seven Years War there was considerable commerce between them and Indians who lived along the coast or who gladly came there to trade. At times these adventurers built crude warehouses or forts to facilitate this trade, though this was an exception. Spain periodically sent troops from her nearby presidios at San Antonio and San Agustín or from smaller missions to expel these smugglers from their haunts, but usually they were too wary and nimble to be caught. Spain tried but could not stamp out this new channel of contraband.[18]

A serious controversy arose in 1770 which could have led to war. This new dispute centered around the Falkland Islands in the South Atlantic strategically located off the Argentina coast. Both nations claimed these islands. Britain made good her claim by occupying them in 1766. Spain at once protested and four years later sent an overwhelming force which expelled the intruders, after which Britain demanded an immediate apology and restitution. Spain expected France to back her and girded for war. Britain did likewise. Should there be a rupture her most likely target in North America was New Orleans. Here the French citizens had dour memories of "bloody O'Reilly" and were still restive. Britain could easily approach the city from either West Florida or down the Mississippi, and O'Reilly and his regulars had recently withdrawn. Britain reinforced Pensacola with a thousand men and reoccupied recently abandoned Fort Bute and Natchez on the Mississippi, and she made available a Jamaica squadron to blockade the river's mouth.[19] Her main blow would come down the Mississippi. General Gage began assembling a force in New York which would descend the Ohio and Mississippi rivers, and aided by a secondary attack from Pensacola, would seize New Orleans.[20] Its capture, coming on the heels of

France's loss of Canada, would assure Britain mastery of the Mississippi and almost all of North America above Mexico.

In this crisis, Spain rushed reinforcements to Veracruz, Panama, Havana, and other threatened ports in the Indies but was under no illusions about her ability to defend Louisiana. As O'Reilly, now in Madrid, reiterated, this province was no more than a buffer and to hold it at all costs was a dangerous policy.[21] Spain ordered the Louisiana governor to make whatever defense he could and then to retreat westward. The New Orleans garrison spent almost as much time improving the westward road of retreat as in strengthening the city's fortifications.[22] Gage forwarded supplies and artillery to the Mississippi in preparation for his assault. Before he had a chance to execute it, Spain became conciliatory and agreed to restore the Falkland Islands, thereby averting war. She backed down because France, as in the recent Honduras dispute, furnished no support, and the family compact was further weakened. France, like Spain, recently humiliated by Britain, was not opposed to war in principle but felt this was neither the proper time nor issue.

Spain, had war broken out, entertained several projects: recapturing part or all of Florida, expelling Britain from the Mosquito Shore and Bay of Honduras, and, above all, retaking Jamaica, center of British might in the Caribbean.[23] To attain any of these objectives, except occupying the Mosquito Shore, Spain relied on French naval aid which was not forthcoming. The rebuff in the Falkland Island controversy made Spain more resentful than ever of British arrogance and more desirous than ever for revenge.

The Falkland Islands were thousands of miles from North America, and, assuming they did not become a pretext for an Anglo-Spanish war, should have little effect on the northern continent. Geography was deceiving. The main importance of these islands was as a stopping point for vessels before sailing through the Strait of Magellan or around Cape Horn. For Britons and Spaniards alike there was a logical connection between the Falkland Islands and *Nova Albion*. Britain was intensifying her efforts to trade and acquire colonies in the Pacific and to take up where Drake left off. That *Nova Albion* or California were little mentioned does not alter the fact that they were in the minds of both British and Spanish diplomats during the Falkland Islands dispute.

For several years after this controversy colonial rivalries in America remained dormant. In Louisiana, Texas, and Florida there was the usual contraband trade, but there was no longer any imminent threat to New Orleans. Spain withheld news of a discovery of a silver mine in upper Louisiana which she felt could do little more than lure British adventurers across the Mississippi.[24] In the Caribbean Britain successfully made good her title to a minor island off Puerto Rico.[25] Yet all in all Britons and Spaniards got along well enough in the New World, and Spain was one of Britain's best customers in the Old.

Suddenly in the space of a few years all this changed. War engulfed Britain and most of Europe and was waged in all quarters. Britain erred after the Seven Years War when she assumed she had not "the cause of alarm the Spaniards may find in the disorders of their colonies." [26] Discontent in Britain's North American colonies was the spark touching off a new conflict which gave France and Spain their chance for revenge.

Adelante
España

Chapter 11

Colonial grievances were more deep-rooted and wide-spread than British officials suspected. Many of them were surprised at the uproar over the Stamp Act and Townshend Duty Act but reasoned that the colonists could have little grounds for complaint after the repeal of the latter in 1770. And this might have occurred had not Parliament passed the Tea Act several years later which provoked Boston "Indians" to jettison East India Company tea into Boston harbor. There was no turning back, and events moved rapidly toward Lexington and Concord. Yet even after fighting commenced it appeared that Britain, with the largest empire and most powerful navy in the world, would have little difficulty chastising her rebellious colonists who possessed few of the sinews of war and who were not united in this struggle against the mother country.

Spain and France closely followed events leading to the final break and at once prepared to aid the rebels, not so much because of sympathy with colonial grievances or with incipient republicanism but because of a desire to weaken Britain by any means possible. Each advanced a million livres to further the colonial cause, and they took steps, such as setting up a bogus trading company, to secretly forward military stores. From the beginning Britain was undeceived and lodged protests, but she was careful not to word them so forcefully as to produce an open break should Spain and France not give satisfaction. The British army found it difficult to crush the rebellion, and Britain, fully occupied in New England, New York, and Canada, was not anxious to take on France and Spain as well, in spite of their undercover aid to the rebels.[1]

From the Spanish viewpoint the revolution gave rise to many delicate issues, one of which was whether to support the Americans, and, if so, to what degree. Her answer was to follow France's lead and to ship munitions clandestinely to the rebels. Spanish powder, muskets, bayonets, cloth, and medicine reached the New World through the efforts of the trading firm of Gardoqui and Sons, which from its headquarters in Bilbao transported these supplies to Havana and New Orleans,[2] or else France arranged for their delivery. At Havana American vessels picked up these stores and tried to evade the British blockade and reach the mainland; at New Orleans Americans secretly transferred the munitions to flatboats and tried to slip by enemy West Florida posts upriver. Britain intercepted some of these vessels, but Spanish supplies continued to reach the rebels and were a factor in their successfully continuing the struggle. Those which came upriver from New Orleans were of vital importance in the war in the West. Though Spain supported the rebels during most of the conflict, her aid in subsidies and loans, which ultimately amounted to 645,000 dollars,[3] was never as important as France's. From Britain's standpoint, however, any succor for the Americans was undesirable, and she attempted to intercept these supplies. Britain began doing this before the war during the period when the Americans were feverishly arming themselves, because even then Spain was shipping them munitions.[4] Britain contended that this commerce with the Americans violated her Navigation Acts and avowed Spain "could not but allow the propriety of it." [5] In view of the enormous British smuggling in Spanish America, officials at the Casa de Contratación were hard put to suppress a smile.

Another delicate question with which Spain wrestled was whether to admit American merchantmen and privateers to her harbors. Despite denials to the contrary, Spain soon opened her ports to both merchantmen and privateers, and this policy, particularly the harboring of privateers, was denounced by Britain.[6] Using Spanish and French harbors in both the Old World and the New, these raiders played havoc with British commerce.

Still another Spanish consideration was whether to recognize the rebels. To do so meant war with Britain and was good reason for hesitation. Another aspect was concern over the precedent set by a successful New World revolution. If the British colonies threw off their mother country's shackles, might not the Spanish colonists follow suit? The recent intrigues of Creoles, exiled Jesuits, and Indians gave weight to this consideration. Indeed, Britain bluntly avowed that if Spain aided the North American rebels then Britain would foment unrest in Spanish possessions;[7] and Spain, whose American Indians and Creoles had genuine grievances, realized that Britain might do exactly what she said.

To keep abreast of the rapidly changing situation so that she could better make decisions in regard to recognition, forwarding military stores, and the like, Spain, following the French example, sent agents to the North American colonies. After the outbreak of hostilities the efficient minister of the Indies, José de Gálvez, ordered the Havana governor to send observers to Florida, Jamaica, and other British colonies.[8] There was already a representative at St. Augustine, Luciano de Herrera, one of the few Spaniards who remained there after 1763, who now regularly corresponded with Cuba.[9] Other Spaniards on one pretext or another appeared at Pensacola and Mobile in West Florida. Spanish ships because of "inclement weather" put in at mainland ports, ostensibly to refit or engage in official business, but in reality to gain information. A British vessel blockading the Delaware River intercepted one Spanish official dispatched as an observer at the Continental Congress in Philadelphia. Throwing his commission overboard, he escaped detection but never reached his destination.[10] Later another Spanish vessel brought Juan de Miralles to Charleston, and from here he made his way overland to Philadelphia. Though he was never an accredited minister to the United States, he was treated as such, and both before and after Spain entered the war he coordinated actions of the United States and Spain against their common foe.[11] From her agents in America, her French ally, and English gazettes Spain kept up with the revolution and with satisfaction realized how heavily committed Britain was in this conflict. But lurking in the background was the nagging fear that in some fashion the mother country would patch up her quarrel with the colonists; and united again they would reimburse their mutual losses by appropriating Spanish New World territory.[12]

The Americans, however, apparently were determined to keep up the struggle, and in spite of heavy odds Washington succeeded in keeping General Howe at bay. This made it more likely that Spain, France, and other European nations might not pass up such an opportunity to settle old scores and restore the balance of power. Preparing for a rupture, Spain stepped up her intrigues among the American Indians. In the Illinois country they had bitter memories of Pontiac's Rebellion, and Spain tried to win over many of the tribes. This was no new policy, but after 1775 Spain intensified her efforts, at the same time urging Acadians and other Catholics to settle on the west bank.[13] It was the same story farther south. The New Orleans governor increased presents to Indians on the east bank, while Havana authorities entertained more and more Florida Indians who fondly reminisced about the days of Spanish dominion.[14] At the same time Spain cracked down on contraband trade on the Mississippi and seized almost a dozen British vessels. This almost completely cut off illicit trade that in varying degrees had flourished since the last war.[15]

Spain had a particular interest in regaining Florida. In spite of the fact that it had been a financial drain, this province guarding the Bahama Channel had been in Spanish hands for two centuries, and Spain had reluctantly parted with it. Prospects of recovering Florida and more nearly making the Gulf of Mexico a Spanish lake seemed good. There were three possibilities. Perhaps the rebels might drive Britain out and hand over this province to Spain in return for continued aid or as an inducement to make her openly enter the war.[16] Or, after France entered the war, Spain might demand Florida's restitution from Britain as a price for neutrality. The best prospect, however, was for Spain to seize it herself.

Emboldened by Britain's dilemma in North America, Spain became more aggressive throughout the New World. In turn, Britain, embarrassed by the deteriorating military and diplomatic situation, went out of her way to keep incidents at a minimum so as not to give Spain pretext for entering the war. British men-of-war generally respected the Spanish flag on the high seas, at least at the outset of the revolution; British officials on the east side of the Mississippi scrupulously observed the river boundary; and the superintendent of the Mosquito Shore normally restrained Indian forays. To a limited degree—enough to make Spain aware of the risk involved in a European nation's abetting American rebels—Britain flirted with the venerable idea of supporting a Spanish-American revolution or of seizing the Isthmus of Panama, and kept in contact with exiled Jesuits and others interested in such schemes.[17] British traders, with or without official approval, supplied arms to rebellious Indians in Mexico.[18] But as long as Spain remained technically at peace Britain did not press these schemes for the same reason she did not hold Spain strictly accountable for her clandestine assistance to the rebels; the obvious reason was that Britain was heavily committed in America and needed no additional foes, whether they be Spain, France, or the Netherlands, all of whom were eminent prospects.

A British undertaking initiated before the war, the voyage of discovery of the prominent scientist and explorer, James Cook, was causing Spain anxiety. He was to chart the Pacific, give a detailed account of the regions visited, claim lands not occupied by a European power, and search for the Northwest Passage. These latter provisions alarmed Spain. California bordered the Pacific and on British maps had another name—"Nova Albion." Was Cook's voyage not a natural outgrowth of British occupation of the Falkland Islands, and would he not take up where Drake left off two centuries ago and reinforce Britain's claim to the western part of North America? Spain had recently occupied California and had budding missions and presidios stretching northward from San Diego. She was on the verge of making still another settlement at San Francisco and had no desire to share California with any other power. Besides, in theory the Pacific was a Spanish lake and foreign vessels had no right there. Many countries supported Cook's scientific voyage, and at first Spain reluctantly agreed to let him take on wood and water at the California presidios.[19] But the energetic José de Gálvez, realizing that "Nova Albion" was writ large on British maps and that Spain and Portugal were on the verge of war which assuredly would bring Britain to Portgual's aid, revoked this privilege. He maintained that California's northern boundary extended to the vicinity of present-day Juneau, Alaska, that Spain had a perfect knowledge of these coasts, and that the California governor, normally a pacific person, would use force to maintain the integrity of his province.[20] Gálvez was aware that the new California presidios were in little position to oppose Cook; even so, he ordered them to furnish him no supplies and to seize him should he land. At the same time the Spanish minister urged publication of former Spanish voyages to California to forestall any claim Cook might make by right of prior discovery.[21] Actually his voyage caused little immediate controversy. He reached the Pacific Coast early in 1778, far north of San Francisco according to instructions, and he never made contact with the Spaniards, even though they sent a ship in search of him. He examined the coast from Oregon to Alaska, paying particular attention to the harbor, Indians, and furbearing animals at Nootka Sound on Vancouver Island. Convinced there was no Northwest Passage, Cook returned to the Hawaiian Islands where the natives murdered him, and the expedition soon sailed home.[22]

In Europe events were taking a serious turn. France, heartened by the Americans' defeat of "Gentleman Johnny" Burgoyne's entire army at Saratoga, decided to openly enter the war in 1778 and assumed that her Bourbon ally would follow suit. This assumption was hasty. When France made war on Britain and allied herself with the United States, a secret article provided that Spain would be encouraged to enter the alliance. But Spain, not fully informed of France's decision to enter the war, having settled her boundary dispute in the Plata River region with Portugal, and remembering that France had not rushed to her aid in recent disputes with Britain, was in no hurry to join. Besides she might get Florida, evacuation of the Mosquito Shore, or even Gibraltar as a price for her neutrality. But Spain could not ignore the fact, and France relentlessly hammered it home, that never again would there be such an opportunity to strike at their ancient foe. It was this argument and the fact that Britain would not relinquish Gibraltar that, after a year's delay, induced Spain to enter the war in 1779. This was not the official reason adduced, however; Spain cited British tampering with the Indians from Louisiana to Central America, contraband trade, logwood cutter encroachments, and insults to the Spanish flag on the high seas as grounds for hostilities.[23]

Curious as it at first seems and despite prior aid to the rebels, Spain neither made an alliance with the United States nor officially recognized their independence. Although Spain was willing to go to extremes to humble Britain, including sending munitions to the rebels, she was not inclined to officially recognize United States independence and to support a movement whereby Americans overthrew their mother country's traces. There was too much latent unrest in Spanish colonies to run such a risk. And Spain and the United States had entirely different notions about the fate of the two Floridas, which had become Loyalist asylums, and about navigation of the Mississippi River. Therefore, even though Spain and the United States had a common foe, they made no formal alliance. The two nations did work together in certain areas, and Spain continued furnishing money and munitions to the United States, though parsimoniously from the American standpoint.

In a convention in April 1779 France made widespread concessions to bring Spain into the war: assistance in recapturing both Floridas, Minorca, the Bay of Honduras, and above all Gibraltar; and diplomatic backing at the peace conference to secure the revocation of the British logwood cutting privilege; while Spain on her own, with or without French assistance, envisioned the reconquest of Jamaica, New Providence Island, and the reopening of the Newfoundland fishery.[24]

Britain was not caught off guard when Spain declared war. Her exorbitant demands as a price for mediation and her widespread rearming left little grounds for doubt. Britain hoped for a repeat performance of the Seven Years War in which Spain, after delaying, finally entered, and lost Havana and Manila for her efforts. Manila, which had been restored, again was a likely target as was New Orleans or the Central American isthmus. But the outcome this time was far different. Spain and France had enlarged and improved their land forces and particularly their navies, while Britain's had deteriorated; thousands of redcoats were tied up in America and were unable to cope with Washington's army; at any moment other European nations might openly align themselves against Britain.

On the sea there was a marked contrast with the Seven Years War, because for the first time in many years Britain did not have a larger navy than her combined enemies. The Spanish navy, with around seventy-six ships-of-the-line, was three times larger than at the beginning of the century. The Spanish and French navies combined outnumbered Britain's in addition to the fact that British vessels had been allowed to deteriorate since 1763. The American rebels, who had almost no navy but scores of privateers, and Holland, which had a small navy and soon entered the conflict, placed additional strains on the over-extended British navy. With a good possibility of the Bourbon navies' gaining control of the English Channel and mounting a successful invasion, Britain's maritime strategy by necessity was defensive, and her navy could not meet all the demands placed on it. For British colonies scattered throughout North America, the West Indies, along the African coast, and at Gibraltar and dependent on naval protection for their security, this was of utmost consequence.

Britain's projected attack against New Orleans never got beyond the planning stage. During the Falkland Island controversy Britain, determined to make herself master of the Mississippi, had hoped to seize Louisiana's capital using this river as a main avenue of attack, simultaneously launching a secondary blow from West Florida. After Spain came into the war in 1779, British aims and strategy were essentially the same except that her main thrust would come from West Florida, supported by an attack in upper Louisiana. Former Governor George Johnstone of West Florida urged the ministry to make preparations.[25] Because of the supplies to the rebels funneled through New Orleans, the favorable treatment given James Willing and his followers in New Orleans after their raid on Loyalists along the lower Mississippi River, and American privateers using Spanish harbors, Louisiana's Governor Bernardo de Gálvez knew that Britain, even before Spain entered the war, might attack. Now with Spain definitely in the conflict and Britain gaining control of Georgia and South Carolina and dominating the Southeast, there was a far greater possibility. British designs on Louisiana which had been in the making for a decade might have succeeded except for one thing—Gálvez attacked first.

Even before 1779 Spain had manuevered to recover the Floridas. Perhaps Britain would purchase Spanish neutrality by restoring part or all of Florida or perhaps the Americans would take it and turn it over for a consideration. Whether the Americans were inclined to hand it over was largely influenced by whether Spain was inclined to support an American attack on Florida, which, of course, would have brought Spain into the war. Neither Britain nor the United States delivered Florida, and Spain realized that the only effective course was to take it herself. Laying the groundwork for such an attack, Spain reasserted her title to the Keys and demanded that all British fishermen leave, hoping to remove them and make good her title by diplomacy.[26] At the same time Governor Gálvez tried to win over the Florida Indians and sent an officer to Mobile and Pensacola ostensibly to regulate commercial affairs and relations with the Indians but in reality to examine West Florida's fortifications. As a result, Gálvez at the outset had an accurate picture of the British position in West Florida.[27] In many respects this position was unfavorable. Britain had dispersed her forces at Pensacola and Mobile, and had strung them out along the Mississippi River. They were so far apart that it was difficult for one to relieve another—assuming sea communication was cut off. With the Bourbon fleets menacing the British Isles and Gibraltar and a strong French squadron usually at some American station, Britain was able to provide little naval protection for West Florida. Here the Spanish army and particularly the Spanish navy had a free hand. Britain's dilemma was soon apparent.

Gálvez's first move was to take the Mississippi River outposts at Manchac, Baton Rouge, and Natchez. He hastily raised over a thousand militiamen and Indians, requisitioned small craft of every description, and then set out upstream for Manchac. This was a trading post defended by a wooden fort and stockade and had only a tiny garrison. An assault easily brought victory. Baton Rouge, a few miles farther upriver, garrisoned by four hundred men, was the strongest post on the Mississippi. Here a siege rather than an assault was the answer. The Governor placed his artillery in a commanding position and after a one-sided artillery duel breached the fort's walls and forced the garrison to surrender. The terms included not only this garrison but the smaller one at Natchez as well. Overnight Britain lost her grasp on the lower Mississippi and realized she had better defend Florida rather than aspire to capture New Orleans.[28]

Mobile with its excellent harbor and French-built fort was Gálvez's next target. He sailed into Mobile Bay and, in spite of extensive storm damage and loss of supplies when ships ran aground, successfully debarked his troops and restored order. Reinforced by troops from Havana, he laid siege to the fort; and once again his superior artillery was decisive. The three-hundred-man garrison surrendered, and the relief column from Pensacola, hearing this news before reaching Mobile, retraced its steps over the swamps and bayous. By the end of 1780 Gálvez had made much headway in achieving Spanish objectives in this region.[29]

Pensacola and St. Augustine were the only important remaining British posts, and, if the Governor had his way, Mobile's fate soon would be in store for them. He expected to recover the Floridas and assumed the Americans would help, since it was in their interest to remove this Loyalist stronghold on their southern flank. Congress agreed, though with misgivings over the prospect of Spain's controlling both Floridas and the Mississippi, and authorized almost five thousand men to assemble at Charleston for a descent on East Florida. At the same time the Havana governor prepared to aid the Americans with warships and possibly troops, while Miralles in Philadelphia coordinated plans among Havana, Charleston, Mobile, and Philadelphia.[30] East Florida might have fallen at the same time as

West Florida had not Britain seized Charleston in 1780 and captured most of the American army there.

Though East Florida was spared, this was not the fate of the remainder of West Florida. Pensacola, the provincial capital, had a well-built fort manned by over a thousand regulars and Loyalists. Gálvez, in spite of a hurricane, an unsuccessful attack on Mobile from Pensacola, and procrastination by Spanish officials in the New World, concentrated seven thousand men—from Mobile, New Orleans, Havana, and a French contingent—before the Florida capital. He occupied narrow Santa Rosa Island flanking the harbor's entrance, ran his Spanish and French vessels through the inlet, and then invested the fort. The besieging lines drew tighter, a shell exploded a British powder magazine killing almost a hundred men, and it was soon over. Between Pensacola and Yorktown, each of which had been lost because of naval weakness, Britain had little to boast of in North America in 1781.[31]

When Spain entered the war, Britain planned to capture Louisiana, gain control of the Mississippi, and attack the rebels from the west. Gálvez's prompt action in taking the British posts on the lower Mississippi forestalled any attack from West Florida, but British strategy in upper Louisiana made more headway. Spain's most important post in the north was St. Louis. Once it fell the other small Spanish forts north of New Orleans should quickly capitulate, thereby opening the way to the capital. The British commander at Michilimackinac, lavishly distributing presents, raised a thousand Indians and, accompanied by several hundred Canadians, set out for St. Louis. Fernando de Leyba, the Spanish governor, even with ample warning, was panic-stricken. This city, less than two decades old, was poorly fortified and weakly manned. The prospect of hundreds of savages swarming inside was not a pleasant one. Leyba consolidated the garrison at Ste. Genevieve to the south with his own, rallied the militia, and exhorted everyone to work on the city's incomplete fortifications; even so, he had scarcely three hundred men of all classes to defend the city. After repeated notices, the enemy appeared and stormed the city, but in a sharp engagement were driven off. The Spaniards had reason to be thankful for their successful defense as they helplessly watched Indians torture careless farmers caught outside the city's walls. The attackers retreated some miles and contemplated a second attack, but, disturbed by George Rogers Clark's activities at nearby Cahokia, decided to retreat. Thus, in the long run,

Britain's attempt to wrest upper Louisiana from Spain failed as dismally as did the project against New Orleans.[32]

In upper Louisiana things were going badly for Britain on both sides of the Mississippi. Leyba successfully defended St. Louis; Clark in a surprise move captured Vincennes and Kaskaskia; and these commanders, jointly or on their own, assumed the offensive. The first attack was a combined one against the Indians and British traders on Rock River in the Illinois country, and, if things went well, Detroit might follow. The American Captain John Montgomery, assisted by Spanish troops, surprised British traders and their stores at Rock River, and similar future expeditions kept Britain and her friendly Indians off guard.[33]

But neither Spain nor the United States seriously menaced Detroit as much as each desired to seize this enemy stronghold in the west. In 1781, however, Spain came uncomfortably close. Fort St. Joseph was a small fort built by the French near the southern tip of Lake Michigan, primarily a trading post, one of several which helped Britain maintain her many Indian allies, and at this time was brimming with merchandise. A successful attack here would help forestall Indian raids on St. Louis, would give Spain's Indian allies booty and keep them content, and would give Spain a better title to the Mississippi's east bank in the forthcoming peace negotiations. Sixty Spaniards and Frenchmen, with as many Indian allies, set out from St. Louis in the dead of winter. They ascended the Mississippi and the Illinois rivers until they met ice. Hiding their canoes and loading food and ammunition in their packs, they marched for twenty grueling days over the frozen wilderness before reaching their objective. Secretly winning over the Indians within the fort by promising them a share of the booty, the attackers with little opposition surprised the fort at daybreak. After distributing or destroying everything of value and raising the Spanish flag and taking possession of this post and the entire Illinois-St. Joseph river valleys in the name of Charles III, the raiders abandoned the fort, and with their prisoners swiftly retraced their steps to St. Louis.[34] Subsequent fighting in the Mississippi Valley was indecisive. Periodically St. Louis and Detroit braced themselves for attacks, but fears proved groundless. Except for the usual Indian forays, intrigues by both sides to win Indian favor, and the annoying tactics of Loyalists above Natchez, there was relative quiet in this extensive region.

The leader of these bothersome Loyalists was James Colbert, who held a captain's commission in the British army. He had lived among the Indians from his childhood, had a native wife or two and several children, and a valuable estate worked by one hundred and fifty slaves in the Chickasaw country. After Spain crushed the abortive Natchez rebellion in 1781, many of the Loyalists fled to the interior where they could be safe from Spanish vengeance and where they rallied around their friend and compatriot, Colbert. From the fastness of their forest sanctuary, Colbert and his white and Indian allies periodically lashed out at the Spaniards and harassed communications between New Orleans and St. Louis. In addition to the salt, munitions, or medals for the Indians which failed to reach St. Louis, the Spanish governor bemoaned the loss of his wife whom these raiders also captured. They did not molest her, however, and she was soon released.[35] Colbert's most audacious move came early in 1783 when before daybreak he unsuccessfully stormed the small fort guarding the mouth of the Arkansas River. The signing of a definitive peace treaty later this year put an end to these forays and forced his followers to disperse, though many of them still remained in the Indian country.[36]

Looking at the New World as a whole, Spain had done rather well during the American Revolution—certainly in comparison with the Seven Years War. She repelled all attacks on Louisiana and Nicaragua, captured and retained West Florida, for the most part kept Britain on the defensive in the Bay of Honduras, and at the end of the war captured New Providence Island in the Bahamas and threatened both Jamaica and East Florida. Except for allowing the logwood cutters to regain certain territory in the Bay of Honduras, losing New Providence shortly after its capture, and not overrunning East Florida, the Mosquito Shore, or, with French aid, Jamaica, Spain had little to complain of in America. But in Europe the reverse was true. Here the paramount Spanish objective was the towering rocky fortress of Gibraltar, and in spite of every endeavor of the combined Spanish-French forces by siege, blockade, fireships, and floating batteries, the Bourbon besiegers made little headway against this Pillar of Hercules in almost four years.

After 1781 British resistance stiffened. She held on to Gibralter, defeated a powerful French fleet in the West Indies, thereby rendering a Jamaican invasion less likely, regained New Providence Island, successfully detached the United States from the enemy coalition, and considered using forces no longer needed against the rebels to regain West Florida. But by 1783 all belligerents were weary and ready for peace. Spain at last realized she could not take Gibraltar (France had reached this conclusion months before), and the Yorktown debacle jolted Britain enough to recognize that the United States was destined to win her independence. Peace negotiations got underway in Paris, and compared with twenty years before, conditions had radically changed. No longer was Britain the unquestioned victor; the surprising thing is that she came out as well as she did.

In the definitive peace treaty several nations made important gains. The Americans did quite well for themselves. They got their independence and their western boundary at the Mississippi River. Spain did not fare as handsomely, though she won important concessions. She gained Minorca in Europe and the two Floridas in America, but she did not reopen the Newfoundland fishery or have the Falkland Islands restored. Though Spain had a weak claim by right of conquest to the Mississippi's east bank, she was unable to establish the United States' boundary at the Appalachian Mountains rather than the Mississippi; and though Spain wanted to bar all logwood cutters from the Bay of Honduras, she was merely able to confine them to a restricted area.

Spain regained West Florida, but exactly what was West Florida? As far as Britain and the United States were concerned the northern boundary was the thirty-first parallel. As far as Spain was concerned, whatever parallel it was, it lay considerably northward. She had conquered and occupied Natchez above the thirty-first parallel, and naturally felt Britain was unduly generous in her treaty with the United States with territory not under British control.[37] This boundary dispute at once embittered relations between the United States and Spain; and Britain, by saying that West Florida's boundary was the thirty-first parallel which was not the usual boundary while it was a British province, played a role in laying the groundwork for controversy. For a suitable equivalent, Spain would have let Britain keep West Florida and all the potential quarrels with the United States which possession entailed. If Spain could have exchanged West Florida for Gibraltar, this would not only have secured that important fortress but would also have made Britain and the United States share an uneasy border in the south as was already the case with Canada to the north.[38] Fortune dictated, however, that it would be Spain and the United States who were to be such uncomfortable neighbors in Florida.

Spain had come a long way, especially under the guidance of Charles III and his ministers, in overcoming her decadence of the past century. They and their predecessors were successful in making the governmental administration more efficient at home and in the colonies; they modernized and enlarged the army and navy; and they fostered agriculture, manufacturing, and commerce. The Spanish resurgence was evident in the war. With the reforms of Charles III and his recent gains in the war, he had reason to face the future with optimism. To a considerable degree he had revenged the British navy's earlier insult when as king of the Two Sicilies during the early phase of the War of Austrian Succession, he was given a scant hour to decide whether to remain neutral or to see his beloved Naples demolished.

Commercial Contention and Frontier Intrigue

Chapter 12

The American Revolution was a shock to most Englishmen. Even so, the provisions of the Treaty of Versailles were not so catastrophic as they might have been. In retrospect it can be seen that 1783 was a highly significant date in the development of the British Empire. It marked the demise of the Old Empire, of which the most important part was in America, and the beginning of another empire, the heart of which would be in the East. In Britain, with the fate of the American colonies fresh in mind, there was, or soon would be, disenchantment with the idea of acquiring additional colonies, especially if they had to be peopled by Englishmen.

In spite of a lack of enthusiasm for winning more colonies, Britain after 1783—and the groundwork had already been laid before this date—proceeded to gain another empire, the New Empire, which in time became even larger and more valuable than the former. In many respects Britain did not plan, or even want, this New Empire but, nevertheless, after the Revolution there were basic forces at work which in the long run had their effect. One was the Industrial Revolution which was gaining momentum and caused manufacturers, if not the government, to search for new sources of raw materials and markets. Another was the fact that Britons themselves, with or without official encouragement, were going to virgin lands and forming the nuclei of new colonies. In the vanguard after 1783 were exiled

Loyalists from the American colonies and convicts from Britain who no longer could be transported to the thirteen colonies. After Napoleon's downfall, a mounting stream of immigrants leaving the increasingly crowded British Isles would follow these Loyalists and convicts. Another factor contributing to the development of a new colonial empire was that after 1783 there were Britons who, in spite of the American Revolution, still continued to press for the acquisition and settlement of new colonies in the traditional fashion.

It was not immediately apparent that the American Revolution was such a watershed and the center of the new empire would be in the East already thickly populated by non-Europeans rather than in the Western Hemisphere. Britain still retained Canada and valuable West Indian islands, and for some time it was an open question as to who would permanently dominate the extensive Mississippi Valley. The Spanish empire, most of which was in the Western Hemisphere, was both wealthy and, without French support, vulnerable. The ultimate disposition of uninhabited or sparsely settled fringe areas of this empire—Florida, Louisiana, the northwest Pacific Coast, and similar areas in Central and South America—if not the entire vice-royalties of New Spain, Peru, New Granada, and la Plata, was unsettled. Contributing to this uncertainty were the appealing doctrines of republicanism, liberty, and equality unleashed by the American and French revolutions. For several decades after 1783 the Western Hemisphere was in a state of upheaval and flux. It was not impossible that in the end Britain, who had replaced France in Canada and had designs on the Mississippi Valley, might end up with a greatly expanded empire at the expense of Spain and the United States. Should this occur—and only time would tell—then the center of gravity of Britain's New Empire would still remain in the West or be finely balanced between the West and East.[1]

With the advantages of hindsight it is easy to examine the post–1783 period and speculate and draw general conclusions. At the time, however, most Britons were not concerned with the philosophical implications of the Treaty of Versailles, but instead with specific provisions. Unquestionably this applied to East Florida. This province had become a Loyalist haven, and by the war's end almost seventeen thousand refugees, white and black, swelled the colony's population. They had lost heavily in the war: some barely escaped with their lives; others brought out much of their property and slaves and began life anew farming or lumbering. Details of the peace treaty dashed their hopes: "Where are we to go? What are we to do?" They had eighteen months to find a new refuge, and in this interval they pressed for a revision of the treaty whereby Britain would retain Florida and give Spain an equivalent: Gibraltar, the Mosquito Shore, money—anything.[2] Although the refugees had slight grounds for hope, in the end they were disappointed.

They reconciled themselves to their fate and prepared to move once again; that is, with the exception of John Cruden and his followers. Cruden, a Carolina Loyalist, had come to Charleston after the British captured it in 1780 and had been in charge of confiscated rebel property which included thousands of slaves. After Yorktown he and his associates, including men of rank in the colonies and in the mother country, wanted Britain to seize West Florida and retain East Florida as asylums for Loyalists and their Negroes. When it appeared in 1783 that Britain would not retain either Florida, Cruden simultaneously attempted to get Spain to cede autonomy to his numerous followers in East Florida and promoted an armed uprising that would give him part of Florida in spite of Spain. Lack of sufficient political support in Britain and determined Spanish opposition proved the downfall of this "mad scheme," which in fact was not as reckless as his critics charged.[3] Beginning in the summer of 1783, despite Cruden, the evacuation went on without incident and was essentially completed within two years. The Loyalists dispersed to the Bahamas, the West Indies, Nova Scotia, England, Louisiana, and the Mosquito Shore.

Fifteen transports convoyed the new Spanish governor, Vicente Manuel de Zéspedes, and five hundred soldiers to St. Augustine. After delays and re-routing because the main channel was closed, they belatedly reached their destination. The Castillo de San Marcos's low silhouette was a familar and welcome sight. Amid salutes of twenty-four-pounders and volleys of musketry the Union Jack was lowered and the Spanish ensign raised in its stead.[4] Some five hundred Italians, Greeks, and Minorcans, most of whom were Catholics brought in by the British, elected to stay and to take the oath of allegiance to the new flag. A large majority of the British were Protestants; this was one reason why they did not or could not remain. Whereas in 1763 few Spaniards elected to stay in Florida, after 1783 only a few hundred British remained in East Florida.

Reoccupying both Floridas involved more than merely reopening St. Augustine's channel. There was the question of scattered Loyalists in the hinterland far from Spanish control; there was the usual problem of contraband trade; there was the dispute with the United States over West Florida's boundary; and above all there was the Indian question. How was Spain to win them over and keep them under control? During the American Revolution the Loyalist merchants, William Panton and Robert Leslie, were forced to move their base of operations from South Carolina and Georgia to St. Augustine. By the war's end they dominated the Indian trade in the Southeast, supplying the natives with munitions, clothes, and hardware in return for deerskins. The Indians depended on European goods for their existence; if Spain did not supply them through gifts or trade then someone else would, and there was no doubt that Americans or adventurous contrabandists would like to fill this void. To control the Floridas effectively Spain had to win over the Indians, and to win them over she had to furnish the accustomed manufactured goods.

The problem was obvious; its solution was more difficult. From where would these goods come? Since Spain was unable to supply most of them and since France was already furnishing a large percentage of Spain's manufactures, it was natural for Spain to turn to her Bourbon ally. Even before the war was over Spain made an arrangement with a French firm to take over the southern Indian trade, but because the firm suffered heavy losses at the hands of the British navy, it soon went bankrupt.[5] With misgivings, but with no immediate alternative, Spain accepted Panton, Leslie, and Company's proposals that they remain in Florida and be given in effect a monopoly of the Indian trade. As these British merchants repeatedly hammered home, any interruption of this trade would drive the Indians into the American camp. And should this happen, Panton and Leslie hinted that they would have no choice but reluctantly to follow the Indians' example. By allowing their company to continue trading with Spanish approval, the Indians would be kept well disposed and out of American arms, and it was in the common interest of Spain, the Indians, and Panton to stem the westward American surge. Even more than Panton's agents, Florida authorities urged Spain to accept these proposals. In the long run perhaps the Spanish textile and other industries would be strong enough to supply the Florida market, but for now the Indian trade had to be maintained, and there was no other solution.[6] Spanish officials in Europe were less enthusiastic about the concession to Panton, Leslie, and Company and were more concerned about the long range disadvantages. Should Britain and Spain go to war, how would the company wield its influence over the Indians? Or if the company withdrew in wartime as was perfectly legal, would this not alienate the Indians at an inopportune juncture? In spite of suspending Florida's future on a "thread so easily broken and corrupted as the capriciousness and good will of a half dozen English agents," [7] Spain at first tolerated this firm and in several years gave it the desired monopoly. For years this company dominated trade in the Southeast. Spanish industry was never able to satisfy Florida's needs, and Panton's monopoly, continuing during peace and war, gave ample proof of the Spanish dilemma.

There was a similar pattern in upper Louisiana. Since 1763 the Canadian Hudson Bay or Northwest companies had commanded trade in this region whether it was in the northwestern part of the United States, or throughout upper Spanish Louisiana. In violation of the 1783 peace treaty with the United States, Britain retained Detroit, Niagara, and other American forts, though Britain alleged the United States first violated other provisions of the treaty. From these posts and similar ones in Canada large quantities of British wares made their way southward to both sides of the Mississippi. There was a steady stream from Detroit and Fort Michilimackinac to Kaskaskia and Cahokia where they were illegally picked up by Spanish traders from St. Louis. The Spanish governor here, fortunately for the traders and probably for his personal benefit, was a good friend of the Canadians.[8] Goods not distributed by Spanish merchants were dispensed by the British themselves. The Revolution temporarily diminished British commerce on the upper Missouri River, but it was resumed with vigor after 1783, and Canadian traders or their Indian representatives became a common sight among the Mandan, Omaha, Pawnee, Oto, and Osage villages. In short, by one fashion or another Britain almost exclusively reaped the advantages of trade in upper Louisiana, and Spain's ineffectual efforts to build forts on the Des Moines, Minnesota, and Iowa rivers to stop this commerce made scant headway.[9]

The question of British contraband in upper Louisiana and legitimate or contraband trade in Florida was one aspect of a broader issue—ultimate control of the entire Mississippi Valley. Spain's hold on both Florida and Louisiana was feeble, as was the United States' dominion over the vast area between the Appalachian Mountains and the Mississippi River. It was true that Americans were pouring into the West, but they frequently were dissatisfied with the East, dependent on the free navigation of the Mississippi River, and some were inclined toward establishing an independent western state and allying with the British or the Spaniards. The Canadian governor sent an agent, Dr. John Connolly, into the Ohio country in 1788 to determine if the frontiersmen really were going to separate from the East and if, at an appropriate time, they might cooperate in an attack on New Orleans. It was not surprising that some immediately requested British arms, though both Dorchester and Whitehall said that Britain could not definitely commit herself now.[10] But, if the decision had been up to Phineas Bond, a prominent Loyalist now British consul at Philadelphia, there would have been no reason whatsoever for delay.[11]

There was no hiding the fact that most of the Mississippi Valley was actually controlled by the Indians who looked to the British in the north and to the Spaniards, through Panton, Leslie, and Company, in the south. There was a widespread belief by foreigners after 1783 that the infant United States would break up, and it was obvious that Spain had a weak grasp on Louisiana and Florida. These considerations made the activities of British traders in the upper Mississippi Valley on both sides of the river, the actions of Panton, Leslie, and Company or other British merchants who attempted to supplant them in the south, and the apparently petty intrigues of Loyalists and others in the West and their contacts with Canada and the West Indies of far more consequence than was warranted by just the peltry trade or land speculation.

After the war Britain's foreign trade expanded, and there was a relentless search for new markets. Florida and Louisiana absorbed their share of Manchester and Liverpool wares, and the rest of Spanish America provided a far larger market. Spanish industry had declined and had been in an unsatisfactory state since the latter part of the sixteenth century. Charles III and his immediate predecessors had enacted many reforms, and the textile and other industries were reviving and expanding. But even a revitalized Spanish industry was pressed to meet the demands of a growing population at home and frequently was unable to satisfy the needs of the millions of Spanish-American subjects. Despite this Spanish industrial revival, most manufactured goods destined for Spanish America did not originate in Spain but in France, Italy, Britain, or another European country.

In sharp contrast to Spain's industry, Britain's had grown steadily since the sixteenth century and now, with the application of power to her machinery, was on the threshold of vastly increasing her output. Britain was determined that she, rather than Spain or France, should profit from Spanish-American wealth.

This is why she was so interested in the trade of Florida and Louisiana and is why at the same time she was flirting with larger stakes —a virtual New World trade monopoly. The best prospect after 1783 centered around a successful Spanish-American revolt. Discontented Creoles, Indians, and banished Jesuits, citing Spain's conduct during the American Revolution, insisted Britain had every excuse to back such a revolt. And there was unrest in Peru, New Granada, and Mexico. In Peru Spain had suppressed the Indian followers of executed Tupac Amarú, but there were still periodic outbreaks and widespread resentment. In New Granada the Creoles and Indians had recently revolted against excessively high taxes, and, though Spain had put down the insurrection, there was still agitation and discontent. In Mexico there was always the possibility that the Indians might follow the Peruvian example and attempt to reestablish Montezuma's empire. Mysterious personages appeared in London—personages like Luis Vidal requesting aid to continue the revolt in New Granada,[12] or Francisco de Miranda, a visionary Creole working for a rebellion in his native Venezuela in particular and all Spanish America in general,[13] or Francisco Mendiola who insisted that Mexico was ripe for revolt.[14] All of them were courteously received by the new prime minister, the younger William Pitt, or other officials, but none wrangled a positive commitment from the government. These revolutionaries had the impression that, although Britain could not underwrite their schemes now, the uncertain international scene might bring a policy change in the future. For the time being Britain officially steered clear of involvement, but this did not apply to all her subjects. Merchants in Britain and Loyalists in America had now or soon developed a lively interest in revolutionary plots and pressed Whitehall for support.

One of the more colorful, and from Spain's viewpoint one of the more tempestuous, of the intriguers was William Augustus Bowles, who was soon to plunge the Southeast into turmoil. Born in Maryland, he remained loyal to the crown after the outbreak of the Revolution and made his way to Philadelphia when General Howe occupied it in 1777. Commissioned ensign in a provincial regiment, he participated in the General's overland retreat to New York. Then Bowles, only fifteen years old, and his regiment were ordered to Pensacola. Shortly after arriving he was charged with desertion and stricken from the rolls. Throwing his regimental coat into the sea, this youth was taken in by a Lower Creek chieftain, became a member of his family, married his daughter, and ultimately became a chief himself. Later reinstated in his regiment because of bravery in leading Indian war parties, Bowles was at Pensacola when Gálvez attacked in 1781 and was almost blown up when the fort's magazine exploded. He was captured for his efforts and, along with the other prisoners, was paroled and shipped to New York which was still under British control. Shortly after the war he returned to the Indian country where the Creeks elected him war chief, and he became a figure of some stature among the natives.[15]

In the postwar period there were a number of whites or half-breeds among the Indians, many former Loyalists still not reconciled to the peace. The most influential of these at first was Alexander McGillivray, the son of a Scottish merchant and a French-Indian half-breed squaw. Although receiving his education in Charleston and Savannah McGillivray during the Revolution, like his Loyalist father, developed a bitter hatred toward the Americans and after the war treated Bowles as a rival and interloper rather than as a fellow chief. His education and ability and the fact he was one-quarter Indian himself allowed McGillivray to become spokesman for most of the Creeks. Their prime objective was to keep their lands in the face of mounting western American expansion. To achieve this intricate feat McGillivray had to weigh and play off rival aspirations of the Americans, Spaniards, unruly Creek warriors, and even the British: he was a close friend and employee of Panton and Leslie and was their most important representative in the Indian country.[16]

Panton's relationship with the Spaniards and his monopoly were proving satisfactory and profitable. Other British merchants, however, eyed the Florida trade and in devious ways sought to make inroads on his monopoly. Indeed, they eyed the entire Mississippi Valley from the Gulf of Mexico all the way to Hudson Bay where they envisioned continuing the British-dominated wartime alliance between the northern and southern Indians which would present a common front to the Americans and might allow Britain to colonize part of this wilderness. And regardless of British policy, there was a mounting feeling among influential Indians of different tribes all along the frontier that they must unite to contain the Americans. Britain's desire to control the Indians west of the mountains was another manifestation of her taking over where France left off in North America, and by now the transformation was complete. Whereas in the past France tried to control Hudson Bay and the St. Lawrence and Mississippi rivers to contain or squeeze Britain off the Atlantic Seaboard, now Britain, who already had Hudson Bay and the St. Lawrence, was trying to become master of the Mississippi Valley and to restrain the westward expansion of her former subjects. British interest in and designs on the Mississippi Valley at this time, however, were generally pushed by individuals without specific official backing and were an indication in the post-1783 period that, in spite of the collapse of the Old Empire during the American Revolution, forces were at work which in time would make Britain a greater colonial power than ever.

A number of prominent figures in one fashion or another were implicated in this grandiose design for control of most of North America: Governor Dunmore in the Bahamas, Revolutionary hero Elijah Clarke in Georgia, Senator William Blount in Tennessee, Governor Guy Carleton, Lord Dorchester, and Lieutenant Governor John Graves Simcoe in Canada, important statesmen in Britain, and merchants who were already established in Canada and the Bahamas and who wanted to extend their operations. Indication that the British government in part was in sympathy with this project was the repeated assertion that it still retained the right to navigate the Mississippi, although it had lost all territory bordering that river; and in negotiations with the United States or with individual Americans Britain discussed annexing the Old Northwest and Vermont to Canada or making them British spheres of influence.[17] Panton and Leslie did not support Britain's design on the West because of their connection with and dependence on the Spaniards, and because there was no reason for them to be dissatisfied with their present monopoly.

Then Bowles stepped in. His experiences in the army and among the Indians threw him into contact with merchants, frontiersmen, and Indians who wanted a separate state in the heart of North America. Some of these merchants were agents of Miller, Bonnamy, and Company on New Providence Island who were interested in the scheme of a western Indian buffer state in general and were concerned with gaining a share of the Florida trade and breaking Panton's monopoly in particular. In the Southeast the Creeks were waging a fierce struggle against the Georgians and Tennesseans who were encroaching on Indian lands. Spain's support to the Creeks varied in proportion to the resoluteness of her policy toward the advancing Americans. The Indians were not overly concerned with subtleties of Spanish-American relations but demanded a constant source of arms and munitions to ward off the Georgians and Tennesseans. Usually it was in Spain's interest to see that Panton kept the Indians well supplied with firearms. In the late 1780s, however, most of the Creeks, including McGillivray when the Spaniards cut off his subsidy in 1788, felt Spain was far too niggardly in furnishing weapons. Spain was playing a double game—urging the Indians to protect their lands from the encroaching whites and also encouraging the frontiersmen to break away from the United States. Because of Indian hostility on the frontier it was impossible to pursue both policies simultaneously, and in 1788 Spain wooed the settlers on the Tennessee and Cumberland by curbing Indian attacks. In this crisis Bowles offered to go to New Providence and immediately open trade with his friends at Miller, Bonnamy, and Company. This new commerce would be reliable, would give Panton competition thereby raising the price of skins and reducing the price of manufactures, and would not be subject to the caprice of Spanish authorities.

Bowles and several Indians sailed to Nassau in 1788 to make final arrangements with the West Florida Loyalist, John Miller. And Miller was not the only backer. The island's governor, John Murray, Earl of Dunmore, who was a close friend of Miller and stood to gain personally should Panton's monopoly be broken, gave his unstinted support. Dunmore, as the ousted royal governor of Virginia, had no love for the Americans and was in sympathy with his counterparts in Canada toward creating a western buffer state. He had been in Charleston just before the end of the Revolution and had become involved in Cruden's "mad scheme" to make the Floridas a haven for Loyalists both white and black, and he could never get out of his mind the advantages of a Gulf Coast Loyalist refuge.[18] Both he and Miller had been in London and had used their influence in favor of having the government establish Nassau as a free port to facilitate illegal commerce with Spanish Florida.[19] With Miller's backing and Dunmore's blessing Bowles returned to Florida aboard a fourteen-gun vessel laden with merchandise and carrying thirty-six whites. Many of them were Loyalists with Florida ties, a few had commissions—though they were not authorized by Whitehall—and all in their various capacities would assist Bowles in his commercial and political ventures.[20]

Bowles's first attempt to break Panton's monopoly failed. His party landed in East Florida at Indian River but was never able to win over permanently a majority of the Creeks who remained loyal to McGillivray and Panton. McGillivray temporarily considered abandoning Panton and the Spaniards but, after Spain quickly increased her subsidy of arms and munitions, reasoned it was better to maintain the existing Spanish relationship, which, in spite of its faults, was working reasonably well, rather than embark on a new venture fraught with unknown perils. Because McGillivray and most of the Creeks, although they wavered, did not rally behind Bowles and because additional food and trading goods never arrived from New Providence, Bowles and his compatriots wandered about Florida until finally food became so short and their condition so desperate that twenty-eight saw no alternative but to throw themselves on the mercy of the Spaniards, who sent them to Spain. Thus came to an inglorious conclusion the first phase of the Bowles-Miller-Dunmore conspiracy.[21]

These promoters realized that there might be setbacks along the way but that in the end they would succeed, and ultimate victory would bestow ample rewards. Bowles's next move was to return to Nassau with five Indians, all of them Creek or Cherokee chiefs. Here Dunmore and Miller, hoping that Spain and Britain would soon drift into war, agreed that Bowles and his fellow chiefs should go to London and present their plea directly to the government—a plea that the populous Creek-Cherokee nation be considered independent and be taken under British protection similar to the arrangement with the Indians in the Old Northwest. Foul weather forced Bowles to return briefly to Florida before continuing to Canada in the early summer of 1790. Sailing upriver to Quebec, he conferred with Governor Dorchester and outlined the general scope of his mission to him as well as to chiefs of the Iroquois Confederacy who were also in Canada. The Creeks and Cherokees and Dunmore in the south and the Six Nations of the Iroquois Confederacy and the Algonquin tribes in the north—most of whom sided with Britain during the Revolution and who now were insisting on the Ohio River as their boundary—all stood to profit should Bowles's mission be approved and successfully executed.[22]

Bowles and his companions, their fare paid by Dorchester, sailed from Halifax and arrived in London in the fall of 1790. They could not have picked a more appropriate time to plead for official backing, because the Nootka Sound crisis was at its peak. Spain had seized British vessels at Nootka Sound on Vancouver Island and had called into question ownership of the whole Pacific Northwest. If neither modified its extensive claims, war was likely, and both had been feverishly arming just as the Creek and Cherokee chiefs docked in England. Though Spain backed down just before Bowles was to be presented to the king, Pitt listened attentively to his proposals—as he had to those of Miranda and other Spanish-American revolutionaries—which Britain could put to good use in any difficulty with Spain. Bowles, magnifying the number of his followers, maintained that only a little outside help would permit the twenty-thousand-strong Creek-Cherokee nation to throw off Spanish control, that their Chickasaw and Choctaw allies, also twenty thousand strong, doubtless would join him, that six thousand volunteers from Tennessee and Kentucky after capturing New Orleans would willingly march overland to Mexico, and that the thousand Loyalists in the Indian country would aid in any of these attempts. But Spain finally backed down, and for the time being Pitt shelved all the projects directed against Spanish America in a convenient niche at Downing Street. Bowles's only tangible commitment was permission to send vessels duty free to the Bahamas—indirect recognition of his Indian nation's sovereignty. While in London Bowles also held a series of conferences with the Spanish ambassador, but the ambassador would not readily agree to let the Indians develop two new Florida ports or to the contention that they were masters of all Florida with the minor exceptions of St. Augustine, San Marcos, and Pensacola. After a six-months' visit in which Pitt granted only a small part of their demands, Bowles and his fellow chiefs returned to Nassau.[23]

Though Pitt did not countenance Bowles's plan and did not extend courtesies due to this Loyalist and his fellow chiefs as representatives of a sovereign nation, the prime minister listened sympathetically and did not denounce their ideas. If Bowles, Miller, Dunmore and the others concerned went ahead and established an independent nation with two new ports of its own and broke Panton's monopoly, then official backing might be forthcoming. But if Britain offered official support now it could lead to war with both Spain and the United States which Pitt did not want to risk. Bowles and his companions sailed to an isolated area between San Marcos and Pensacola in West Florida, resolved to carry out their plan. Determined opposition from McGillivray, Panton, and Spanish authorities prevented this "daring rogue" from winning wholesale converts among the Indians, even though many were dissatisfied with concessions made by McGillivray in his recent treaty with the United States.[24] Because of Spanish countermeasures supplies did not regularly reach Bowles, and he needed presents and trade goods to show the Indians the advantages of siding with him. Therefore he appropriated Panton's warehouse at San Marcos. But even this did not win sufficient converts, and he took the desperate gamble of negotiating directly with the Spanish governor at New Orleans, stressing the advantages of an independent Creek-Cherokee nation as a buffer to the Americans, and insisting it would achieve a cardinal Spanish objective by protecting Mexico, costing the Spanish treasury nothing.

With gusto Leslie relayed the news to his partner that the Spaniards had induced "squire Bowles" to visit New Orleans.[25] Regardless of a safe conduct pass and Indian threats of retaliation should their leader not return, Leslie expected that this would prove to be Bowles's downfall. In the long run this British merchant was not deceived, though the outcome at first was in doubt. Some months after Bowles's capture, McGillivray died, opening the question as to who would succeed him, and Bowles with his following among the Lower Creeks, even in Spanish eyes, was a candidate. But the two parties reached no satisfactory agreement, and Governor François Hector Carondelet first confined this "Irish adventurer," and ignoring Indian threats, protestations, and testimonials, later shipped him off to Havana.[26] From there he was sent to Spain where authorities requestioned him and for awhile considered installing him as McGillivray's successor, though ultimately they sentenced him to prison. No place seemed more appropriate to serve out this term or more removed from the Indian country than half way around the world in the Philippines.[27]

Even with Bowles out of the way his chief lieutenant, William Wellbank, also a former British Loyalist officer, remained among the Creeks and Cherokees, and kept up the correspondence with the northern Indians and Canadian authorities, but he had even less success than Bowles. The Creeks murdered him in 1794.[28] And a subsequent Loyalist sent over by Miller to replace Bowles and Wellbank fared no better.[29] Undaunted by these setbacks Miller and Dunmore kept trying to establish two ports in the Indian country, one on the peninsula and the other to the west of San Marcos, and continued to entertain influential Indians in Nassau and to grant them British commissions and medals.[30] But the Spaniards seized Miller's and Dunmore's vessels bound for Florida and thwarted their every move. With Bowles safely bound for the Orient, Spanish authorities closed the book on the turbulent episode of this audacious adventurer—at least so they thought.

Had Spain not backed down at the time of the Nootka crisis and averted war, Bowles might have succeeded and never faced Spanish imprisonment. Seizure of British merchant vessels at Nootka Sound was the culmination of a dispute that had been in the making over many years. The question was whether much of the Pacific coast should be called "Alta California" or "Nova Albion." In recent decades there had been renewed interest in this region sparked by Russian advances and by Cook's voyages. Cook explored much of the coastline in 1778, including Nootka, and, largely because of prospects for a lucrative fur trade, considered this a region "certainly . . . of some consequence." [31] Both before and after Cook's voyage Spaniards explored the Pacific Northwest to offset any claim that Cook or the Russians might make and to promote the settlement of "Alta California" which now stretched northward to San Francisco. In the 1780s, spurred on by Cook's account of otters and other fur-bearing animals, British merchant ships made intermittent appearances in the vicinity of Nootka. These vessels came from the Far East, perhaps openly flying the Union Jack or perhaps surreptitiously the Portuguese ensign.[32]

The Mexican viceroy in 1789 ordered Captain Estevan José Martínez to sail to Nootka, to make a permanent settlement, and to prevent foreigners from trading there whether they be British, Russian, Portuguese, or American. He reached Nootka in the spring of that year and aggressively following his instructions first seized a vessel flying the Portuguese flag, then three flying the Union Jack.[33] It was these latter seizures at remote Nootka Sound that almost led to a general European war. At first both nations tried to keep in the background the question of title to the Pacific Northwest and concentrated instead on what damages, if any, were due as a result of the seizures. But as the crisis deepened each nation asserted its exclusive title to this region. Britain cited the voyages of Drake and Cook, the merchants who traded here before 1789, and the fact that Spain had no settlement north of San Francisco as ample proof. In turn, Spain maintained her mariners had reached Nootka long before Cook and that all of "Alta California" belonged to Spain by right of discovery, occupation, and the papal donation.

It took some months for news of happenings at Nootka to reach Europe and for each side to assert its exclusive title. At first William Eden, the special ambassador extraordinary at Madrid, thought mounting foreign concern in the Northwest Coast was "more interesting in the Lore of geographical Science than in any other point of View." [34] He was wrong. Neither Britain nor Spain made any concessions, and both appealed for outside support: Spain to France, and Britain to the United States and to anyone fostering a Spanish-American revolution. As has been seen Bowles and Dunmore pushed their project of an independent Creek-Cherokee Indian state, which might be only part of a larger nation carved out of the Mississippi Valley at the expense of Spain and the United States. Only recently the Canadian governor had sent Dunmore's Loyalist friend and fellow speculator in western land, Dr. John Connolly, down from Detroit to the Ohio to talk to dissatisfied frontiersmen.[35] Britain sounded out the official opinion of the new United States government, but the Americans were never enthusiastic about any expedition that would merely replace Spain with Britain in New Orleans.[36] American frontiersmen, argued the British consul at Philadelphia, even without their government's approval, could not only take New Orleans but also could further Miranda's dream of wresting Mexico from Spain.[37] Miranda, however, did not restrict his view to Mexico, for he envisioned ousting Spain from all of the New World and setting up one or more independent states. An essential ingredient in this ambitious undertaking was British support; in return Britain would critically weaken Spain and in the future would dominate New World trade.[38] The prospect was as appealing to Pitt as it was to London merchants.

Both sides girded for war and sought outside backing. Pitt placed the navy on a war footing, intrigued with Miranda and Bowles, weighed proposals for attacks on Louisiana, Florida, Mexico or South America, prepared an expedition in the Far East destined for the Philippines or the American Pacific Coast, and sent troops to Belize as a first step in recapturing the Mosquito Shore. For her part Spain strengthened her army and navy, reinforced her key ports in America, but was under no illusion over the difficulty of defending Nootka against a Far Eastern expedition or Louisiana and Florida against a joint British-American attack. To Spain it made little difference whether the United States officially supported the attack or whether westerners, who were determined to gain New Orleans with or without official sanction, executed it.

From the outset of the crisis Spain had appealed to France to honor the family compact and not to allow Britain to gain territory and prestige to offset that lost in the recent war. But for France in 1789–1790 the most exciting events were not in distant Nootka but at home with the storming of the Bastille, the Great Fear that terrorized both peasants and nobles in the countryside, the meeting of the Estates General, and the resulting confusion in drawing up a constitution and limiting the monarch's power. In short, France was in turmoil and would not or could not lend her customary support to Spain. In view of this, in view of Britain's extensive military preparations and her intrigues with American Indians, Loyalists, Creoles, and Kentucky and Tennessee frontiersmen, and in view of the vulnerability of Nootka, Louisiana, and Florida, Spain had little choice but to back down. Her plight was obvious to Britain.

The Spanish capitulation was evident in the convention signed in the fall of 1790. Spain admitted what to others was obvious: that the Pacific was not a Spanish lake and that effective occupation was the only sure title to American territory. She agreed that north of that portion of California already occupied, both countries had the right to trade and make settlements, though it was ambiguous whether they could be permanent.[39] The net effect was to support Britain's contention that her merchants had every right to trade at Nootka, that the seizures were illegal, and that compensation was due the injured parties. Without question the convention applied to the entire Pacific Coast and granted Britain the right to trade and make at least temporary settlements above Spanish ones in North America and below those in South America. Spain maintained that it definitely did not apply to the Atlantic Coast and it did not give Britain title to Honduras any more than it gave Bowles or his followers title to any of Florida's deserted coastline.[40] It was not relinquishing her exclusive claim to Nootka that bothered Spain so much—Nootka itself was relatively unimportant—rather it was the interpretation of this convention by Britain and others regarding portions of any Spanish colony not actually settled.

This convention did prevent war, though it did not completely wind up the controversy. There was disagreement over the exact amount of damages due, whether British whaling vessels were to be admitted to South American ports, and particularly exactly what rights each nation had at Nootka. Spain assumed that she was obliged to return only the huts and other property actually seized ashore at Nootka and after doing so had a right to remain. Britain said no, and it was over this issue that George Vancouver and Juan Francisco de la Bodega y Quadra disagreed when they met at Nootka in 1792. It was not until two years later with the signing of a subsequent convention that the two countries put the dispute to rest. Spain agreed to lower her flag at Nootka and to have the British one raised in its stead. Then both parties retired, neither would make a permanent settlement here, though both could return to traffic with the natives.[41] Although Spain retained vague rights at Nootka, she realized that because of aggressive British and Russian advances in this region, because of the distance of Nootka from any Spanish settlement, and because of the difficulty of getting Spanish colonists to settle on either the Atlantic or Pacific North American coasts, she would do well to make good her claim up to the Strait of Juan de Fuca or even Bodega Head considerably southward.[42]

After the Nootka scare the two nations drew closer together. The radical Jacobins now were directing the French Revolution; they proclaimed a republic, guillotined their king and hundreds of others, and began to spread their deadly doctrines throughout Europe. Neither the Spanish nor British governments readily embraced republicanism and regicide, and they along with other nations joined a coalition to stamp out this dangerous movement. Thus 1793 witnessed the eighteenth century rarity of Britain and Spain as allies. The radical European change was reflected in America. Even when Vancouver and Bodega y Quadra differed in interpreting the 1790 convention, their relations were most cordial, and Vancouver and his men were shown every courtesy when they later stopped at the infant Spanish cities in California.[43] In fact Spain, with her close French commercial ties at home disrupted, threw open all New World ports to British warships and merchantmen alike.[44] The two new allies even contemplated joint action against the French colony of Saint Domingue, but the fluid situation caused by the slave uprising on this island and the conflicting objectives of the British in Jamaica and the Spaniards in Santo Domingo undermined possible collaboration there.[45]

In the Mississippi Valley there was much talk of cooperation.

Britain was on the verge of war with the United States and was disturbed by General Anthony Wayne's army's marching into the Northwest Territory supposedly only to chastise the Indians; yet Britain occupied forts on American soil and traded with and encouraged Wayne's adversaries. Spain on the other hand was apprehensive over the designs of the new French minister to the United States, Edmond Genêt, when he tried to recruit an American force serving under the French banner to attack Florida and Louisiana. Because Britain's main concern was in the north and Spain's in the south and because Wayne restricted hostilities to the Indians and Genêt's project collapsed, there never was any active military cooperation between the two allies. But in the correspondence between Canada and Louisiana much store was placed on a western Indian confederation under British or British-Spanish protection to restrain the American Jacobins.[46] In a letter to Spanish authorities Dorchester avowed that Bowles could be most influential in bringing about such a general confederation and was mystified why Spain had arrested and continued to hold him.[47] And Simcoe's lieutenant had gone from upper Canada to London and was pressing the government to negotiate the retrocession of West Florida, which would allow Britain to shield Spanish Louisiana from the Americans and increase British control over the Mississippi Valley.[48] In the United States President Washington feared the hostile British-Spanish alliance had gone much further than was actually the case.[49]

Another example of Anglo-Spanish harmony was in regard to commerce. Spain, theoretically possessing a monopoly of trading with her colonies, fell far short of meeting their wants, and in one fashion or another France or Britain usually made up the difference. Now at war with France, Spain was more sympathetic to proposals by British merchants, and she sanctioned trade which they probably had been illegally carrrying on in the past. One case was Louisiana where Spain, though she continued to arrest Canadian interlopers, authorized Andrew Todd to underwrite the Missouri Company for trade in upper Louisiana.[50] British merchants now could legally engage in this trade, but the pelts would reach Europe via New Orleans rather than Quebec which was both economically and politically advantageous to Spain. Even though Spain made many concessions she did not agree to every British commercial proposal, such as that of Captain Charles Stevenson, one of Simcoe's influential Canadian subordinates, to open the Mississippi to British ships.[51]

After the Revolution Britain, like the United States, had been trying to secure free navigation of the Mississippi, and Spain was no more anxious to grant this concession to Britain than to the United States.[52]

For two reasons the brief interval of Anglo-Spanish cooperation vanished: one was that on short notice it was hard to reconcile centuries-old colonial differences; the other was the rapidly changing European situation which saw the Jacobin Reign of Terror come to an end, and Spain first make peace with her ancient ally and then in 1796 openly enter the war against Britain. Both the Old World and the New witnessed indications of the Spanish shift. Whereas at first Spaniards courteously entertained Vancouver or his associates at San Francisco, Monterey and the other California ports, now they were coldly received, given only minimum supplies, and hardly allowed to set foot ashore. Spain was well on the way to closing all her ports to British ships which was feasible now that French goods were more readily available. In Louisiana Spain strengthened St. Louis and through force and use of the Missouri Company planned to disrupt the extensive contraband trade on the upper Missouri; while at the same time she intrigued with Frenchmen on both banks of the Mississippi who might want to strike at Canada in the forthcoming war.[53] During this same period Britain revived contacts with Kentucky and Tennessee frontiersmen, dangling New Orleans before their eyes, and she now considered acquiring West Florida by force rather than negotiation.[54]

In all quarters it was obvious that the fleeting period of Anglo-Spanish cooperation, loosely held together by a common dread of Jacobinism, was rapidly coming to a close. For the balance of the century Spain resumed her alliance with France, even a Republican France, and the Anglo-Spanish conflict in American resumed unabated.

Spain's Disquieting Ally

Chapter 13

Spain had anticipated an open break with Britain for months. New World controversies such as the increase of illegal British trade on the Missouri River, Britain's treaty with the United States in 1794 which hinted that Britain might join the Americans and use force to obtain free navigation of the Mississippi River, and Spain's cession of Santo Domingo to France were all factors. More significant, however, were the aggressive actions of the British navy in the Mediterranean and the new Franco-Spanish alliance—an alliance imposed by French arms in which Spain was a subordinate partner.[1] As war appeared imminent, Spain rushed reinforcements to the Indies and alerted her American officials.

Hostilities renewed old fears at St. Louis that Britain would strike directly down the Mississippi River or would step up her commerce and intrigues with the Indians and undermine Spanish influence. The New Orleans governor considered that one method of protecting Louisiana was for Spain to strike at Canada from the west while French troops, cooperating with disaffected French Canadians, delivered the major blow on the St. Lawrence.[2] In reality it was improbable that Canada would succumb to such a Franco-Spanish onslaught—though Canadians never got it out of their minds that Jacobinism was not going to ascend the Mississippi River[3]— and the St. Louis commandant instead made plans to build a chain of forts stretching from St. Louis up the Missouri River, across the mountains to the ocean, terminating at Nootka or another port to the south. The location of Louisiana's northern boundary was uncertain, and this was the best way to map it out to Spanish advantage. These forts would destroy British commerce in upper Louisiana and deny Canadians intercourse with New Mexico to the south.[4]

Such a chain of forts, stretching over fifteen hundred miles, was expensive. The newly-founded Missouri Company had a monopoly of upper Louisiana's trade, and in turn assumed responsibility for building these forts which not only would be focal points for the fur trade but also would protect the northern frontier. This company, however, was Spanish in name only; the Irishman Andrew Todd was a partner who provided most of the capital. Todd was no stranger to Louisiana and the Missouri River. In the past his Canadian firm had argued that, in spite of the 1783 peace treaty, Britain should retain posts in the United States Northwest and that the Indians should make the Ohio River their boundary so that Canadians rather than former rebels could control the fur trade. But Britain's agreement to relinquish these posts in the 1794 Jay Treaty was the *coup de grâce* for the profitable operations of Todd's firm. Even so, this treaty might be a blessing in disguise. Upper Louisiana was a vaster and potentially more lucrative area, and Todd had valuable contacts there. After Jay's Treaty he offered, using New Orleans and St. Louis as bases, to exploit these contacts, to provide goods for the Indian trade, and to assist in building the Missouri River forts. In short, he offered—and Spain accepted the offer—to underwrite the Missouri Company. His firm would keep the Indians as well disposed toward Spain in Louisiana as the firm of Panton and Leslie was in Florida. Had Todd not died in New Orleans and the Missouri Company failed for lack of financial backing, Spain might have secured a measure of control over the Missouri River.[5]

Canadian merchants still dominated commerce on the upper Mississippi, Minnesota, and Missouri rivers. They erected a small fort at the Mandan villages on the Missouri; a Spanish expedition sent out by the Missouri Company captured it and "instantly hoisted the Spanish flag"; and a subsequent Canadian party soon recaptured it and ran up their own ensign.[6] This alternate raising and lowering of rival flags was duplicated elsewhere, though Spain made no headway on her string of forts. Before retreating in the 1794 Jay Treaty, Britain had hoped to make the Ohio the American boundary; after

1794 the main boundary controversy shifted westward where Britain was trying harder than ever to make the Missouri Canada's southern boundary.

At the outset of the war in 1796, British officials and individual citizens renewed interest in Louisiana and the Floridas which Bowles, Dunmore, Dorchester, Simcoe, and others had manifested before. While Canadian merchants unofficially but successfully competed for the trade in upper Louisiana, Britain, just before the final rupture, forcefully reasserted that previous treaties guaranteed her free navigation of the Mississippi River.[7] At the same time scores of Providence Islanders were on the Florida Keys and in the Creek Nation and posed the threat that the Bowles project might be revived at a moment's notice. Britain's dream of carving out a client state in the heart of North America and of linking it with Canada, though never publicly proclaimed or officially sanctioned, was not far from the surface. Former Loyalists, wealthy merchants and lowly Indian traders, ambitious colonial officials, and disgruntled American frontiersmen, all had a stake—not always the same—in wresting Louisiana and the Floridas from Spain.

The first attempt on this Spanish territory was a failure: this was the so-called Blount Conspiracy in which bankrupt Senator William Blount of Tennessee was to have played a major role. Since Congress exposed this scheme and it was never put into operation, it is difficult to ascertain details. In its broad outline it was a project whereby British land forces in Canada and naval forces in the Gulf of Mexico would cooperate with Tennessee, Kentucky, and Georgia frontiersmen and with former Loyalists in the Indian country to seize Louisiana and the Floridas. British subjects and Loyalists assumed that both Floridas and Louisiana would go to Britain who in turn would allow the Americans free use of New Orleans and Florida ports.[8]

There were several prominent figures in this undertaking: the impoverished Senator Blount from Tennessee; John Chisholm, ex-Loyalist and Indian trader, who wielded influence over both whites and Indians in the Creek-Cherokee country; Dr. Nicholas Romayne, now more a land speculator than a physician, who would be Blount's chief London agent; the British minister in Philadelphia, Robert Liston, who sympathetically conferred with the conspirators and forwarded their plans to Whitehall; the new Canadian governor-general, Robert Prescott, who at the outbreak of hostilities assembled troops and Indians at the Great Lakes and prepared to strike at Louisiana with or without the frontiersmen's assistance; and the Florida governor, Enrique White, who apparently was dissatisfied with Spain and willing to cooperate.[9] All of these individuals, and others besides, sometimes working closely with one another, sometimes pursuing different ends and ignorant of what the others were doing, busied themselves during 1796 and 1797. Chisholm and Blount, directly or indirectly, approached Liston in Philadelphia and were favorably received. The British minister paid Chisholm's passage to London and also investigated the possibility of Canadians' furnishing munitions.[10] At the same time Blount dispatched his good friend Dr. Romayne to England. Both of these emissaries primarily wanted to secure the cooperation of the British fleet in blockading New Orleans and Pensacola while land forces assaulted these ports. For almost two months they dickered with Secretary of State William Grenville and other officials but were put off on one pretext or another, until finally Grenville positively refused them any assistance.[11]

The question raised is, why? This project, if successfully executed, would seize the Floridas and Louisiana at very little cost from Spain and would weaken her in the present conflict. One reason cited—the most sensational one—was that Blount's incriminating correspondence inopportunely came to light and prematurely exposed the whole scheme. Undoubtedly this disclosure angered the United States Senate. Here was a senator on his own initiative organizing an expedition in the United States against a power with which she was at peace. Blount's unauthorized conduct resulted in his expulsion from the Senate and in the collapse of the whole undertaking. This, however, is not a definitive explanation for the project's downfall. If Britain helped raise an expedition on United States soil, then unquestionably this was a violation of neutral rights which might have serious repercussions. But where her own interests were involved, Britain usually did not worry about American neutral rights, and there is little reason to believe that had there been no other motives she would have abandoned this ethic. Only four years before, the French minister to the United States, Edmond Genêt, openly tried to recruit an American expeditionary force to seize the Floridas and Louisiana from Spain with whom France at this time was at war. Britain had no more scruples about this sort of thing than France. Even after the unfavorable publicity given Blount and Chisholm in the impeachment proceedings, Liston still was intriguing to replace the latter with a Canadian trader, who, according to the provisions of the Jay Treaty, could circulate unnoticed in the Indian country.[12]

Unquestionably the prospect of an open break with the United States concerned Britain. But she was also influenced by the fact that she might obtain her objectives and a great deal more without incurring American enmity. Why not officially cooperate with the United States, who, in spite of her recent treaty with Spain, still had serious misunderstandings with that nation? In this fashion Spain might lose not only the Floridas and Louisiana but Mexico and even all of Spanish America. This would weaken Spain, while Britain could acquire commercial ascendancy or sovereignty over some of these newly-acquired territories. In the United States there were influential persons, notably Alexander Hamilton, supposedly in official retirement but actually dominating many policy decisions, or Rufus King, the ambassador in London, or General James Wilkinson, military commander in the West, who were only too anxious to participate in such a joint undertaking.[13] Because Jay's Treaty had smoothed over some of the glaring differences between Britain and the United States and because France was beginning to seize large numbers of American merchantmen on the high seas, it appeared logical that the United States and Britain should draw closer together against their common foe, France, and France's Spanish ally. This influenced Britain in not committing herself to the Blount Conspiracy and instead to intriguing with United States congressmen and cabinet members to secure a formal understanding.[14] It was ironic that both in the United States and in Britain those who most detested revolutionary Jacobinism were the ones most zealous in promoting revolution in Spanish America. In this instance, however, the dread that France herself might take over Spanish America outweighed the danger of flirting with revolution.[15]

Spain knew she might lose Louisiana and the Floridas as a result of the Blount Conspiracy, of an official Anglo-American combination, or even of French pressure to cede New Orleans to Britain in a general peace settlement,[16] and she hoped to forestall such a disaster. She stocked St. Louis with food and munitions; she sent spies to the Lakes region to determine how advanced Canadian preparations were;[17] she raised a Negro regiment at St. Augustine to protect the East Florida frontier;[18] she tempted impoverished General Elijah Clarke with lands and money if he would enlist Georgia frontiersmen to help defend Florida rather than cooperating with Britain and using these troops to attack the province;[19] and all the while her minister in Philadelphia exposed Blount's and Chisholm's machinations and demanded that the United States strictly enforce her neutrality. Spanish vigilance, the collapse of the Blount Conspiracy, the downfall of negotiations in 1797 that could have led to a general peace, and the fact that the United States patched up her differences with France and did not enter into a close British alliance removed the imminent peril that Britons and Americans would jointly move against Louisiana and Florida, or that Britain would acquire New Orleans by diplomacy.

Though the danger to these colonies abated, it did not disappear. It was one thing for Britain to involve herself in raising a military force on United States territory directed against Spanish colonies; it was quite a different matter launching a direct attack from British soil. In this fashion Louisiana and the Floridas were fair game, and the United States could have little diplomatic grounds for protest. Still eyeing much of the Mississippi Valley, Britain listened favorably to projects of her own subjects, which in themselves could deprive Spain of these colonies. And at this moment there reappeared in the West Indies a tumultuous figure—none other than the recent fugitive from Manila exile, William Augustus Bowles. Apparently his star had permanently waned when Spain captured him and imprisoned him in the Philippines. But in 1797 the Manila governor sent him back to Spain, possibly because Spain was considering turning Louisiana over to France, and in these changed circumstances Bowles might be willing and able to advance Bourbon interests; or, more likely, because he was inciting anti-Spanish feeling among the native Filipinos. He never reached Spain, however, because he jumped ship off the African Coast, made his way to Sierra Leone, and ultimately set foot at Dover.[20] At this time Britain was fully committed to the war against France and Spain, and the Blount Conspiracy recently had been exposed. Grenville, the Duke of Portland, William Windham—the most extreme anti-French cabinet members who championed an aggressive campaign against the enemy—and Pitt himself all reconsidered Bowles's plea for setting up a nominally independent Indian state in the Creek-Cherokee country, while at the same time they pondered the recommendations of General Simcoe and Canadians who for years had felt geography dictated that Canada should have access to the Mississippi and control of at least one bank.

Aboard a British vessel, Bowles made his way to the West Indies, first to Barbados and Jamaica and then to New Providence. In this same period Simcoe was also in the West Indies, commanding forces which unsuccessfully attempted to capture Saint Domingue. It is unlikely that Bowles had a meeting with this former Canadian governor, but the Spaniards feared the outcome of any joint scheme fostered by these two, one who wielded great influence over Indians in the north and the other over them in the south.[21] Both directly from the government and from private merchants—and primarily from the latter—Bowles collected munitions and trading goods and enlisted a few followers, some of whom were French royalist exiles of "sound principles" from Saint Domingue. To all appearances his plan now was essentially the same as in the past: he would set up an Indian state which would have close ties with Britain and New Providence Island merchants and possibly could be associated with similar semi-independent states in northern and southern Louisiana. This time the governmental organization of the State of Muskogee was more complex; there were judges, a collector of customs, and other civil officials, an army and navy, and a national flag. Bowles, still retaining the title Director General, set about drawing up a constitution.

Although on the surface his plans were identical to those at the time of the Nootka crisis, actually by the end of the 1790s circumstances were quite different. In 1790 Europe was at peace, and his hopes of carving out a semi-independent state were based on the fact that the area between the Appalachian Mountains and the Mississippi River was largely under Indian control. These Indians looked to and traded with the Canadians in the north and the Spaniards, through Panton, Leslie, and Company, in the south, and it was the latter arrangement that Bowles had intended to alter. Many Americans in the West were dissatisfied with seaboard rule and might cooperate, and, of course, Spanish dominion over Louisiana and Florida was weak.

By the end of the decade, however, almost all of Europe was at war; the United States in 1794 had defeated the Indians north of the Ohio River and in a short time Britain evacuated all forts on American soil. There was less likelihood of a general Indian confederation in the Mississippi Valley dominated by Britain. And Spain in the late 1790s was France's ally, openly at war with Britain. There were rumors that Spain already had ceded Florida and Louisiana to

France. This could be only the beginning, and the tricolor soon might wave over all Spanish America. To gain official backing Bowles in 1798 primarily relied on the argument that he could be an instrument of preventing France from acquiring Florida, Louisiana, and eventually far more in America.[22]

Aboard a light-draft warship of the Royal Navy he sailed for Apalachee, though unfortunately the vessel ran aground near the mouth of the Apalachicola River, and he lost much of his ammunition and supplies. Spaniards speculated about the designs of Bowles and Britain at this time. They feared a Canadian attack on St. Louis in conjunction with an assault on New Orleans delivered by several thousand troops sailing directly from Britain.[23] There was talk of reviving the Blount Conspiracy even though Blount himself was on his death bed. The United States had patched up her differences with France, the pro-French Republican Party was in power, and prospects for an Anglo-American alliance were fading. As Dr. Romayne on the verge of his trip to London was quick to point out, Britain was not likely to reach an official arrangement with the United States government and had better make an unofficial one with the frontiersmen.[24]

Bowles doubtless knew of many of these projects and realized that his undertaking could be integrated with them. Back in Apalachee he renewed old friendships while denouncing Panton and Leslie's monopoly and stressing the advantages of a direct trade with his merchant friends in New Providence independent of the capriciousness of Spanish authorities. Fortunately Bowles did not have to contend with McGillivray, who now was dead. His base of operations was north of San Marcos where he tried to enlist the Indians and to induce them to bring him their skins for trade.

As soon as Bowles landed the Spaniards knew exactly where he was and what he was up to. The Louisiana governor sent out soldiers with orders to bring Bowles back dead or alive—and they nearly succeeded. They surprised his camp at the junction of the Chattahooche and Flint rivers, captured some of his white and Indian followers, and just missed their leader. Minus his gold-braided coat and most of his other raiment, the Director General barely made his way to safety in the forest.[25] But Bowles was yet to have his day. He reassembled his followers and once again overpowered Panton's store at San Marcos. But this time he went further by capturing the nearby Spanish fort and its one-hundred-man garrison. Bowles and his several hundred Indian allies invested the fort and began a regular siege. After a short time, for reasons which are difficult to fathom, the Spanish commander surrendered. The Director General's prestige now was at an all time high. Not only had his Indian nation captured a fortified post from the enemy, but also they had helped themselves to the rich booty at Panton's store. Fort San Marcos on the St. Marks River gave Bowles command of a much-needed port and facilitated his communications with Nassau.[26] Rumors that Spain had ceded Louisiana to France were more prevalent than ever, making Bowles confident of official backing. His hopes were more than wishful thinking because the cabinet was considering acquiring key Spanish-American ports to keep them out of French hands, and New Orleans had a high priority.[27] But Bowles's success and enthusiasm proved to be short-lived. The Spaniards, chagrined at losing a well-provisioned fort to Florida savages, determined to avenge the insult. The Pensacola governor, with every man and shallow draft warship at his command, sailed upriver to San Marcos, bombarded the fort, and after several hours forced the defenders to take to the woods.[28]

The remainder of Bowles's Florida career was anticlimactic. Patrolling Spanish vessels made it increasingly difficult to maintain correspondence with New Providence. At times he wandered into Georgia, and immediately authorities there set upon him. Both state officials and those in Washington had other plans for the Floridas and did not want them to fall into the hands of either Bowles, Britain, or France. Other than carrying on sporadic warfare with the Spaniards, fruitlessly trying to engineer a land-sea attack on San Marcos or Pensacola, and maintaining an intermittent trade with the Bahamas, Bowles's most aggravating pursuit was commissioning privateers to prey on the Spaniards. Shortly after he arrived in Florida, privateers flying the Muskogee ensign appeared in the Gulf of Mexico. Most of them were New Providence ship captains who had a personal interest in Muskogee's sovereignty.

The Treaty of Amiens in 1802 bringing peace to Europe marked the downfall of the State of Muskogee. Making extensive concessions to France and hoping that this peace would be permanent, Britain withdrew all backing whatsoever from Bowles, and the New Providence governor announced that in the future sailors in Muskogee's navy would be considered pirates—in some cases an apt description.[29] The Spaniards read with astonishment reports of the death sentences handed out to some of these mariners, and recognized that this new governor was no Dunmore.[30] Bowles, himself, after wandering in the wilderness for several years, was seized by the Indians and turned over to the Spaniards. In a last-ditch gamble to head an independent Indian state, he had attended a native council in 1803 at the Hickory Ground on the Coosa River to win election as King of the Four Nations. He had staked his career on the not unfounded hope that Britain would intervene in Florida and Louisiana to keep them out of French hands. But no British expedition appeared, and after several days' deliberation the Indians turned against him and accepted the proposals of Spanish and United States agents for cancelling Indian debts, ceding additional land, and receiving an annual subsidy. An integral part of the agreement was that the Indians had to hand over Bowles. First Benjamin Hawkins, the United States representative, took him into custody and in turn delivered him to the Spaniards who for a second time sent this adventurer first to New Orleans and then to Havana. The Havana imprisonment brought Bowles's career to a close, for within two years he died. Perhaps he was destined to perish at Spanish hands, but with his versatility and his propensity for the melodramatic, the fates were unkind in allowing him to waste away in a dank Morro cell.[31]

With one or two notable exceptions, the intense international rivalry in Florida and the Mississippi Valley between Britain, Spain, France, and the United States was coming to a close, and the United States was winning the prize. When Bowles returned to Florida this rivalry was reaching a climax, though the crucial struggle was not being waged in Florida, the Louisiana delta, or on the Missouri, but instead in the council chambers of the Tuileries and the Escorial. By the Treaty of San Ildefonso of 1800, Spain, as a result of French prodding for a decade, secretly ceded Louisiana to France in return for Tuscany. Napoleon had visions of resurrecting France's New World empire with Louisiana and Saint Domingue as a nucleus. But he was unable to overcome the rebellious blacks and tropical disease in Saint Domingue. Once again European war clouds were becoming ominous, and he decided to abandon his colonial ambition and to sell Louisiana to the United States. Jefferson accepted the offer and added New Orleans and the rest of the Mississippi Valley to the United States, thereby doubling its size. Soon a stream of immigrants pressed into Louisiana, and as time passed it became more difficult through force or intrigue to deprive the United States of her new acquisition. By obtaining Louisiana, the United States, like France earlier, severed Spanish Florida from the northern provinces of New Spain.

When Britain and Spain drifted into war in 1796 Britain again entertained hopes, with or without United States approval, of becoming master of Louisiana and the Floridas, if for no other reason than to keep them out of French hands. This was at the heart of the Blount and Bowles affairs, and at a moment's notice Spain faced the prospect of losing these colonies. At the same time Spain also had her hands full along the Pacific Coast. In the past the Nootka conventions had prevented war, but both before and after the outbreak of hostilities, British ships had the annoying habit of hovering off Monterey, San Diego, Acapulco, and other Pacific ports. Some of these vessels clandestinely traded with the Indians and Spaniards, others began to nab Spanish prizes, and all doubtless were on the lookout for the Manila galleon.[32] In addition to the aggravating presence of foreign merchantmen and warships off the Pacific Coast, Spain believed that Britain might make a full-fledged settlement at or near Nootka. Why else were so many of her vessels seen near upper California or why was Alexander Mackenzie making his way across the frozen Canadian wastes to the ocean? Certainly a permanent settlement in Nootka's vicinity must be tied in with these enterprises.[33] Or even if Britain did not establish a major foothold in California, overtures to her Russian ally to strike at Spain via California were hardly less encouraging.[34] Spain strengthened her Pacific squadron and seized a handful of careless British seamen, but could not stop the mounting foreign contraband and fur trading.

Spain, Britain, France, and the other belligerents in 1802 secured a respite from the warfare which had raged for over a decade. In the Treaty of Amiens Britain made her peace with France and Spain, and agreed, to the disgust of Grenville and Windham, to restore most of her overseas conquests, though Trinidad was a notable New World exception.[35] Some considered this an all inclusive and permanent peace, but hopes were soon shattered. Napoleon by diplomacy and the threat of force continued to extend his control over Italy and Switzerland, while Britain did not evacuate Malta. The peace proved to be only a short-lived truce, and in 1804 Pitt took the initiative in forming still another coalition against France and her allies.

Spain procrastinated openly entering the war. At once, however,

Napoleon pressured her to furnish him a subsidy and men-of-war, and in reality Spain, somewhat against her will, sided with France from the start. Pitt recognized this and, though technically at peace, ordered the seizure of Spanish treasure ships to keep this money from reaching Bonaparte. In a sharp encounter British frigates captured the treasure ships, and it was only a question of months before Spain too was officially at war.

Breaking out of hostilities raised all the old American problems and dangers and new ones as well. The venerable project of winning part or all of Louisiana and eventually a great deal more once again came to the forefront. This time the design was known as the Burr Conspiracy. As in similar attempts to set up a separate state in the heart of North America, the details are hazy. Apparently the former vice president of the United States, Aaron Burr, wanted to detach the western part of his country, to join it with part of the Floridas on the east and New Spain on the west, and then to establish himself as a western potentate.[36] Like the Blount and Bowles intrigues in the past, British naval cooperation in the Gulf was a requisite, and as a reward Britain probably would receive preferential commercial privileges in this extensive domain rather than actual sovereignty. Burr approached the British minister in Washington, Anthony Merry, who approved of the project; Burr then sent agents to London and Jamaica to obtain naval support and in both places they mingled with Spanish-American revolutionaries who were advocating their own particular schemes;[37] but in spite of Merry's endorsement in Washington and that of first lord of the admiralty, Viscount Melville, in London, Burr wrangled no positive commitment. His feeble attempt to take New Orleans was a fiasco. He was captured and lucky to save his neck in the subsequent trial.[38]

Burr felt that his promise of commercial privileges in the heart of North America would be a powerful bait for naval cooperation. The economic warfare waged through Napoleon's Continental System and Britain's Orders in Council disrupted usual patterns of trade in both Europe and America. It adversely affected British outlets on the continent, and it inhibited Spanish and French commerce in the New World. Up to now a large percentage of the manufactured goods that had come to Spanish America were of British or French origin. After the outbreak of hostilities in the 1790s and particularly after the Franco-Spanish naval disaster at Trafalgar in 1805, it became increasingly difficult for Spanish or French goods to reach the New World or for Spanish Americans to dispose of their raw materials and bullion legally. This situation was made to order for British merchants and was the major reason why Spain permitted Panton, Leslie, and Company to remain in Florida during both peace and war, why Andrew Todd was allowed to underwrite the Missouri Company, and why Spain made similar concessions elsewhere in Spanish America.[39]

Spain was aware of this unsatisfactory state, but the alternatives were worse; to deny British goods to the Spanish Americans—assuming this were possible—would impose hardships and might touch off a rebellion. At the same time Spain was cognizant of another fact: after many prior false alarms Britain definitely was outfitting a major expedition against Spanish America. Britain could not dispute the fact that Napoleon was military master on the continent, but the vulnerable overseas colonies of France and her allies were another matter. An influential figure in the operation against Spanish America was Miranda, who after almost two decades and countless setbacks, now was on the brink of success. The overall military commander was Arthur Wellesley, soon to become Duke of Wellington. He considered several plans of attack, and one of the most promising was to strike at Veracruz and from this base either conquer or promote insurrection throughout New Spain, most of which would become a subject province or independent with close British ties.[40] If Mexico were the primary objective, then Britain probably would seize Pensacola and Mobile to expel Spain from the Gulf of Mexico, and to penalize the pro-French Republicans in the United States whose main support was in the South.[41] Depriving Spain of Mexico would divert the output of the silver mines in San Luis Potosí and Zacatecas from the mother country—and ultimately from France— and instead would channel this bullion directly to Britain, who would be in a stronger position to be paymaster of the coalition against Napoleon.

Warships, transports, and thousands of troops began assembling in England's southern ports, while the "traitor Miranda" stepped up his intrigues in both hemispheres. Spain received reports of these hostile movements, rushed warnings to Pensacola, Mobile, and other likely targets, and undertook all possible New World defensive measures. Units of the British expedition late in 1806 assembled at Falmouth on England's southwestern tip and prepared to unleash an attack which in time could sever Florida and all Spanish-American colonies from the mother country.[42] With some ten thousand regulars poised at Falmouth, with British agents in Mexico stirring up the already discontented Creoles and Indians,[43] and with mounting dissatisfaction on the peninsula over Napoleon's having forced his brother onto the Spanish throne, there was little to reassure Spaniards about the future of their empire.

Strange
Bedfellows

Chapter 14

The British expedition destined for the Indies in 1807 never sailed—at least not to the New World. Instead the government ordered it to the Iberian Peninsula, to fight with rather than against the Spaniards. Europe in the years after the outbreak of the French Revolution witnessed many changes, and one of the most memorable was the sudden Spanish nationalistic uprising against the French. To enforce the Continental System and to bring Britain to her knees, Napoleon had to control all European ports. He made an agreement with Spain whereby French troops could cross Spanish soil to invade Portugal, and he pressed both Charles IV and his son, Ferdinand, to abandon their claim to the Spanish throne in favor of his own brother, Joseph. At the same time French troops passing through Spain to Portugal occupied key strong points and paved the way for Joseph's assumption of power. The Spanish people, incensed at the overthrow of their hereditary monarchy and at the high-handed, anti-clerical tactics of the French troops, spontaneously rose against these soldiers as they streamed into the peninsula. And this unexpected rebellion is why the British expedition sailed to the Iberian peninsula to fight on the side of the Spaniards rather than to the New World.[1]

In one respect Britain's policy toward Latin America underwent a fundamental change, yet from another standpoint it remained essentially the same. Britain ceased inciting a Spanish-American revolution in order to maintain the good will of the Supreme Spanish Junta and to keep it wholeheartedly committed to the struggle against Napoleon. Britain's long range objective had been to channel Spanish colonial bullion and raw materials into British rather than Spanish coffers; if this could now be achieved peaceably through Spanish cooperation rather than war, so much the better. Britain, as she saw it, had a strong case for legally assuming much of Spain's colonial commerce. Spain herself was weakened and at any moment might succumb to Napoleon's legions; should this happen the Spanish cause would be doomed. British troops and subsidies were a major factor in keeping Napoleon from becoming master of the Iberian Peninsula. In gratitude for this considerable aid and to allow her the means to continue it, Britain argued that she must freely traffic with Spanish America.[2]

Even with the peninsula engulfed in turmoil and having only a makeshift provisional government Spain could not overlook her longstanding New World differences with Britain, nor would she abandon her traditional mercantilistic policy. In spite of mounting pressure, she refused—with a brief exception in 1810 when French armies overran Andalusia and most of Spain—to open her colonial ports indiscriminately to British merchantmen. Spanish officials were ordered to continue enforcing the laws of the Indies by not admitting any foreign trading vessels to Spanish ports—even if these vessels belonged to an ally. British ship captains, as in the past, were informed that they were not allowed to trade in Spanish ports, though because of the new alliance the notification now was more tactfully worded.[3]

Circumstances, however, forced Spain to deviate from her general policy of barring foreign commerce. The obvious reasons were that French manufactures were scarce in Andalusia and, especially, that Britain controlled the sea. Though she never got all the concessions she wanted, Britain became more of a factor in the legitimate commerce of the Spanish colonies than ever. And behind the scenes contraband trade flourished unabated. Legally or not, Britain was enjoying the fruits of an even larger percentage of Spanish-American commerce, and this helped to take the sting out of the Continental System. Britain, after Trafalgar and the outbreak of anti-French hostilities on the peninsula, replaced France as the dominant power trading with Spanish America, regardless of whether this commerce was carried on directly in the New World or indirectly through Spain.

There never was any doubt that Panton, Leslie, and Company (reorganized as John Forbes and Company after Panton's death) would remain in Florida.

Commercial relations with Spain and her colonies were of paramount importance at Whitehall and Cádiz. Another issue pondered at Whitehall, though rarely mentioned at Cádiz, was what would happen to the Spanish colonies if Joseph Bonaparte entrenched himself on the peninsula. After the outbreak of the Spanish war, Britain shied at promoting revolution in the New World, once again shelved Miranda's project to separate part or all of Spanish America from the mother country,[4] and at Spanish insistence did not allow the disgraced Burr to remain in London where he had been promoting a British attack on the Floridas.[5] At the same time Britain made it perfectly clear that under no circumstances would she permit Napoleon to take over the Spanish colonies. Wellington was ordered to take his command to New Spain should he and the Spanish insurgents make no headway in Old Spain, and Britain was willing to advance funds to aid Spanish colonial governors to keep out French troops. She still maintained her contacts with Spanish Americans who would be willing, should Bonaparte consolidate his power in Spain, to proclaim their independence and to form close British commercial ties; and she considered various ways to acquire the Floridas in order to keep them out of French and American hands.[6] As the war dragged on relatively few Spaniards rallied around Joseph Bonaparte. Wellington and the Spaniards, after heartbreaking setbacks, began to make steady progress against the French; and for the duration of the war Britain and Spain, fighting side by side, on the surface were the best of allies. For the time being their mutual detestation of the French and their common desire to bring about the Corsican's downfall relegated colonial disputes to the background.

One novel situation produced by the Spanish war was the situation in the Floridas. Britain had always had designs on these provinces. She won them in 1763 and reluctantly gave them up twenty years later; and subsequently she, or at least a number of her subjects, tried to regain them and much more as evidenced by the Bowles and Blount affairs. The United States also wanted both Floridas. She claimed West Florida by virtue of the Louisiana Purchase and was threatening to make good this claim which in some fashion might include East Florida as well. The Supreme Junta, beset by revolutions on both sides of the Atlantic, entreated her new British ally to come to her rescue in Florida. Britain did, and she now was in the unique position of trying to maintain rather than undermine the territorial integrity of Spanish Florida. In the past scores of Americans had drifted into West Florida, and many assumed that it was a question of time before this province became part of the United States. News of events on the Spanish peninsula in 1808 gave them their chance. In the confused interval when Florida authorities were wondering just which was the proper Spanish government, the inhabitants around Baton Rouge pledged their allegiance to Ferdinand VII and on their own set up an emergency administration. It was obvious at the time that this emergency government provided for an almost independent state and was merely the first step toward American annexation. In the immediate aftermath of the 1810 Baton Rouge rebellion the United States positively asserted that West Florida was part of Louisiana and, with the enthusiastic cooperation of a majority of the inhabitants, occupied all of this province eastward to the Pearl River. In 1813, because of her claim under the Louisiana Purchase and fear that Spain might prevail on her British ally to defend or take over Florida, the United States occupied Mobile and the remainder of the province up to the Perdido River. And her repeated offers to buy Pensacola and East Florida and the encroachments of neighboring Georgians did not augur well for the future.[7]

In the critical five-year period between the Spanish upheaval on the peninsula and the final American occupation of almost all of West Florida in 1813, Spain relied heavily on her new ally to keep this province out of United States hands. The British charge d'affaires in Washington put forth the novel contention that his country guaranteed Florida to Spain by virtue of the 1783 peace treaty and made remonstrances when the United States began massing troops in neighboring Louisiana, when she seized half of West Florida in 1810, and then when she threatened to take over the remainder.[8] He insisted that the United States should not take advantage of Spain while she was engaged in a heroic life or death struggle with Napoleon and offered to mediate.[9] The United States fully intended to profit from Spain's misfortunes and stood to gain little from mediation. She did not respond to the British overtures, and soon was at war with Britain, making any mediation out of the question.

A number of Spanish and British inhabitants of East Florida were concerned that through purchase, internal revolution, or direct assault the United States might acquire this province. It was for this reason that members of Forbes and Company, British diplomats in the United States, and leading Spaniards in Florida, implored Britain to take over this province, to make it another Canada, and to keep it out of American hands.[10] Since the Supreme Junta in the name of the imprisoned Ferdinand vii, with massive British aid, was engaged in a bitter but successful struggle for its very existence, it was no more expedient for Britain to acquire East Florida than it was for her to back a separatist movement in New Spain. Instead when Britain went to war with the United States in 1812 and Spain nearly followed suit, the British navy was an important factor in upholding Spain's unsteady control over East Florida and the small remaining portion of West Florida.

The War of 1812 further complicated the New World picture. The British practice of impressment, her maritime restrictions on neutral commerce, and the desire of the United States to use war as an opportunity to conquer Canada and Florida induced President Madison to deliver his war message in June 1812. The United States believed Britain was urging her Spanish ally, who apparently needed no prodding, to join in the war and used this as one reason for threatening to occupy the remainder of West Florida.[11] Nothing could be further from the truth. Spain, engrossed with tumults in the New World and Napoleon in Europe, needed no more enemies. She promised Britain to render all possible aid against the United States—as long as it did not commit Spain to hostilities.[12] Though she had ample grounds for war in view of the seizure of part of West Florida and the United States's aid to the Spanish-American revolutionaries, she could not afford a break at this time. At first Spain encouraged British warships and troops to visit East Florida to deter further American aggression.[13] For Britain the war with the United States was of secondary importance; her primary concern was Europe and Napoleon and in keeping Spain in the struggle against the Corsican. Therefore Viscount Castlereagh, the foreign secretary, never insisted that Spain break with the United States and recognized that, for the time being, neutrality was the most realistic policy for his hard-pressed ally.[14]

At the beginning of hostilities in 1812, Britain was not able to send significant reinforcements to the New World, and her strategy was defensive. But after the first year, after Napoleon's disastrous retreat from Moscow and his defeat the following year at Leipzig, and after Wellington was on the verge of sending Marshal Soult reeling north of the Pyrenees, then both Britain and Spain could afford the luxury of paying more attention to America. Now Britain contemplated two powerful attacks against the United States: one launched from Canada aimed at New York; the other, with the active or passive cooperation of the Spaniards in Florida, and possibly the French Creoles in Louisiana, directed against Louisiana. Indeed the decades-old dream of a Mississippi Valley state to contain the rapidly expanding United States, and which in some fashion would be linked with British Canada as a buffer between the United States and New Spain once again was in the air.[15]

There were three parties—Britain, Spain, and the Indians—who had designs on Florida, Louisiana, and New Orleans. These parties at times had conflicting interests, and their cooperation frequently was confused and illogical—certainly this applied to the Indians. Even before the war Britain had supported the dream of the Shawnee Indian Tecumseh and his brother, the Prophet, in organizing all the western Indians into a general confederation to restrain the Americans. In the Battle of Tippecanoe in 1811 William Henry Harrison partly destroyed the confederation as it was taking shape in the Northwest.[16] The Creeks and other southern Indians for the time being remained aloof, but two years later went on the warpath with a vengeance. With the advantage of hindsight, it is obvious that their timing could hardly have been more inopportune. By immediately joining the confederation they would have presented a common front to the Americans; or if delay were unavoidable, then it would have been more effective to wait and join the thousands of British regulars who soon streamed into Florida and Louisiana. As it turned out the Creeks began hostilities in 1813, were crushed by Andrew Jackson in the Battle of Horseshoe Bend the following year, and as the British began launching their massive attack against Louisiana and West Florida, these Indians had already lost over half of their land and some two thousand warriors.[17] Had the Indians waited and combined at full force with the British, the New Orleans encounter with Jackson might have taken a different turn. Ironically the Canadian governor, urging the southern Indians to begin hostilities immediately, contributed to this mishap, though at the time he probably had no knowledge of the expedition against Louisiana.[18]

Spain's role was no less baffling and inconsistent. Clearly Spain hoped to recover West Florida and to expel the Americans from

Louisiana, and she was generally well-disposed toward cooperating with Britain in achieving this end. Clearly Spain wanted British warships to protect Florida, and if an American attack seemed imminent, would welcome redcoats as enthusiastically here as on the peninsula. However, there was another factor: allowing Britain to use Florida as a springboard for a Louisiana attack might involve Spain in war with the United States, and a break at this time was the one thing Spain was trying to avoid. Confused and uncertain, Spain simultaneously encouraged and discouraged British troops to come to Florida.

Britain counted on Spanish cooperation in Florida and believed her ally would profit as a result. Admiral Alexander Cochrane, commanding the British fleet in America, was aware of the Creek disaster at Horseshoe Bend, but he also knew that many of the surviving Red Stick warriors had sought refuge in Florida. He urged them to join him and promised that great fleets and thousands of soldiers would soon appear off the coast for support. These veterans, who had just sent Napoleon to a little island, could not fail to defeat the Americans and help recover Indian prestige and lands. Many of the Indians, who had just fled into Florida and were bitter toward the Americans, were eager to join the British banner. Colonel Edward Nicholls in the first part of 1814 arrived at the Apalachicola River with several thousand stands of arms, a thousand swords, and two field pieces and began distributing them, organizing the Indians into companies, and building a fort at Prospect Bluff fifteen miles upstream.[19] The colonel hurriedly returned to London where he integrated his Indian plans into the grand design and then hastened back to Florida. He took his command westward to Pensacola where his Indians were joined by several hundred British regulars and units of the Royal Navy—the advance party of the British expeditionary force expected shortly.[20]

The relations between Nicholls and the Pensacola governor were perplexing and at times strained. In the past the Spanish government had indicated it would welcome British troops into any of the colonies, including Florida, and according to Nicholls, Governor Mateo González Manrique of Pensacola issued him a written invitation.[21] The Havana governor, however, was concerned that these troops might provoke an American attack, or if they entrenched themselves at Pensacola and on the Apalachicola River, there was good reason to fear that British statesmen might find a way to keep them there. Therefore he ordered Manrique not to let them land.[22] But land they did, and at first, to outward appearances, the British and Spaniards got on well enough. Nicholls continued to enlist Red Sticks who refused to accept the verdict of Horseshoe Bend and Jackson's harsh treaty. He drilled them and several hundred Negroes in Pensacola's streets, dressed them in the brightest scarlet, and promised them that any day sails of the British expedition would dot the harbor.

Spain was reluctant to let Nicholls use the Apalachicola River and Pensacola because it might commit her to a war with the United States. It almost did. The overall British plan was to use Pensacola and Mobile as bases and from there for the regulars and Indians to move either directly against New Orleans or more likely to some point upriver from which they could isolate the capital, cooperate with the dissatisfied Louisiana Creoles, and force the Americans to submit.[23] Jackson assumed this was the British strategy and realized he had to move against Pensacola immediately; that the United States was not at war with Spain was a minor consideration. With three thousand frontier militia he marched against the city and demanded that Spain make good her neutrality by allowing him to take over Pensacola's fortifications.[24] Fort San Miguel in the city was the bastion of Spanish authority in the western part of Florida as the Castillo de San Marcos was in St. Augustine, and Manrique would no more allow Jackson to garrison San Miguel than he would extend this privilege to Nicholls. Jackson attacked the outer defenses, forced the combined British and Spanish troops to fall back, and because the Spaniards would not permit Nicholls to enter San Miguel and continue the fight, the British commander withdrew to his ships while Manrique surrendered. Before Nicholls finally departed he loaded Captain George Woodbine and his Indian followers aboard and then blew up Fort San Carlos de Barrancas some miles away which guarded the harbor mouth.[25] With the British abandoning Pensacola as a base to strike at Louisiana, Jackson pulled out of the city and avoided a break with Spain. Neither side, in spite of the Pensacola affair, was anxious for a rupture. The United States had its hands full dealing with the Canadian invasions, the threatened secession of the New England Federalists, and the impending attack on Louisiana; Spain was busy restoring order on the peninsula and quelling the Spanish-American revolts. At this time neither wanted a full-scale war, and neither made an issue of the Pensacola incident.

The setback at Pensacola and an earlier repulse at Mobile denied Britain ports from which to launch her attack against Louisiana. These two reverses, the earlier one at Horseshoe Bend, and the delay of the British expedition in reaching the Gulf were all nearly fatal as far as Indian cooperation in the Louisiana campaign was concerned. Had the over four thousand Creek warriors effectively cooperated with Britain's six thousand regulars it is likely that Louisiana would have flown the same ensign as Canada, or possibly it might have been returned to Spain in the diplomatic maneuvering at the war's end. Denied Pensacola and Mobile as bases for an indirect attack on New Orleans, the British decided they had no alternative but a direct assault. The rout of General Pakenham's six thousand peninsula veterans and the loss of a third of his command, including a majority of the officers, was a signal victory for Jackson, particularly since his composite force was inferior in numbers. His crushing victory at New Orleans, coupled with other American victories on the Canadian border the preceding year, marked the final downfall of British dreams to dominate at least part of the Mississippi Valley which statesmen, merchants, and adventurers had entertained for over two decades. In the long run Britain was no more successful than the Comte de Frontenac, LaSalle, or the Ibervilles in trying to dominate the heart of North America by firmly controlling the Mississippi, the St. Lawrence, and Hudson Bay. The civil officials for the proposed British crown colony of Louisiana who accompanied the expedition had no alternative but to reembark with the survivors, and aboard one of the ships was Pakenham's body in a barrel of rum, bound for burial at St. Paul's Cathedral.[26]

Memorable events had been taking place in Europe preceding the Battle of New Orleans. Napoleon was defeated in the Battle of the Nations at Leipzig in 1813 and the following year fled to Elba. Shortly after his downfall representatives of the victorious powers began gathering at Vienna to redraw the map of Europe, while at the same time United States commissioners were unsuccessfully haggling over peace terms with their British counterparts at the Flemish city of Ghent. The Vienna delegates were startled when Napoleon suddenly returned to France for a whirlwind hundred days which culminated in Waterloo and his exile to Santa Helena. With the Corsican menace definitely removed, the Vienna statesmen returned to their labors. Their primary concern naturally was Europe, and colonial issues were of minor importance. When raised the issues usually pertained to which overseas conquests Britain would keep or which ones she would agree to return to the Netherlands or to France.

Surprisingly enough, amid constant fêtes, masked balls, excursions, and reconstructing the European map, delegates at the Austrian capital took under consideration the question of Louisiana and West Florida. During the nine months that they were in session they were cognizant of the formidable expeditions Britain had dispatched to Canada and the Gulf of Mexico and they knew about the New England dissatisfaction which led to the Hartford Convention. Most assumed that the United States would be defeated and that she would lose territory in both the north and the south. The checks the American army gave the Canadian invaders on Lake Champlain and the Niagara River in 1814 made it unlikely that the United States would lose any territory in this quarter. But the New Orleans attack did not come until early in 1815, several months before the statesmen had tidied up the loose ends at Vienna, and throughout most of the Congress it was generally presumed that the United States would lose Louisiana to a British or British-Spanish assault. And in the aftermath disgruntled New England Federalists might well secede.

The problem perplexing Britain's Viscount Castlereagh, Spain's Pedro Gomez Labrador, and other interested delegates was not whether the United States would retain Louisiana, but instead what should be its final disposition? Those powers that had an historic interest in this province—Britain, Spain, and France (not Napoleonic France but France of the restored Bourbon Louis XVIII)—all had their own solutions and invariably each differed. British statesmen feared that in some devious fashion France would reassert her claim to Louisiana and then would try to acquire it through diplomatic swapping.[27] For a combination of reasons, however, France's representative, Charles Maurice de Talleyrand-Perigord, had little to say about Louisiana. Britain, of course, expected to conquer West Florida and Louisiana with or without Spanish cooperation. Though she hastily signed the Treaty of Ghent with the United States in December, 1814, partly because of the threat of Napoleon's return from Elba, there was no reason to assume that Britain would automatically restore these provinces to the United States if Jackson were defeated (the Battle of New Orleans was in January, 1815). Quite the contrary, there is reason to expect that she would keep them, or at least demand an equivalent, and that she would insist that these additional provisions be added to the peace treaty. Wellington's victory at Waterloo would have strengthened Britain's bargaining position.[28] The dream of controlling two of the most important North American rivers, the St. Lawrence and Mississippi, along with Hudson Bay, was a long-standing one and not to be abandoned lightly once success was so close at hand. Though Britain never had to finally make up her mind about what to do with New Orleans, she might have taken the advice of her subjects who were arguing that now was her last chance to link Louisiana and the Floridas to Canada and to bar the inexorable American expansion.[29]

Spain was just as confident as Britain that the United States was on the verge of losing West Florida and Louisiana and took all measures short of military intervention to regain one or both of these provinces. Labrador at Vienna tried to strengthen Spain's claim to Louisiana and insisted that Napoleon had illegally sold this colony and that after his downfall it should be returned to Spain.[30] In correspondence with Britain, Spain dwelt on the dangers of the expanding United States whose population was doubling almost every twenty years and who in the future would be an important trade rival, and suggested that if Louisiana were returned to Spain—to whom it rightfully belonged—then it would stunt the growth of a potential leviathan. Naturally Britain would have to guarantee Spanish Louisiana's territorial integrity after handing it over, though Spain might be willing to part with one or both of the Floridas in return.[31] Castlereagh was not inclined to relinquish New Orleans or all of Louisiana should they be captured and certainly not to prop up either as a Spanish colony.

The Vienna diplomats, with more immediate issues at hand, fortunately did not have to redraw the map in the heart of North America; General Jackson spared them that ordeal. As a result of the settlements in 1814–1815 the United States kept Louisiana, including almost all of West Florida; Spain retained East Florida and a tiny bit of West Florida; and Britain's New World territorial gains were limited to Spanish and French West Indian islands and an unofficial enhancing of her position in the Bay of Honduras and on the Mosquito Coast. Peace returned to the Old World but not to the

New. The cataclysmic forces unleashed by the French Revolution and by Napoleon's venture into the Spanish peninsula were not resolved at Vienna. From Florida to La Plata Spain's colonies continued in real or threatened turmoil. Britain and Spain, the European nations with the largest colonies and economic stakes in the Western Hemisphere, soon discovered that, as in the past, their interests conflicted.

Finale

Chapter 15

The French Revolution, the rise and collapse of Napoleon's empire, and the decade immediately following the Congress of Vienna marked one of the most eventful periods of Spanish history. Particularly under the enlightened despotism of Charles III Spain made a remarkable recovery from the decadence of a hundred years earlier. But Charles III died in 1788 and neither of his successors, the vacillating Charles IV, or his son, the unscrupulous Ferdinand VII, was as capable. The court intrigues of Charles IV, of his Queen, María Luisa, and of her lover, the youthful, ambitious minister, Manuel Godoy, were in themselves enough to undermine some of the recent advances. Far worse than court cabals were the impact of the French Revolution on Spain, Napoleon's invasion of the peninsula, and the arbitrary thrusting of Joseph on the Spanish throne. As a result it was many years before life returned to normal in either the mother country or her American colonies.

Most Spanish-American officials and a majority of the New World inhabitants had not recognized Joseph Bonaparte and in varying degrees supported the Supreme Junta or the subsequent Council of Regency which governed in the name of the imprisoned Ferdinand VII; and Florida authorities like those elsewhere accepted the liberal 1812 constitution framed by the Cortes at Cádiz. After Napoleon's downfall and the restoration of Ferdinand to the throne, and after he then summarily overthrew the 1812 constitution, Spanish liberals on both sides of the Atlantic were suppressed and dismayed. Those in America who formerly supported this overrated monarch now began to swell the ranks of extremists who all along had been pressing for independence. After the expulsion of French troops from the peninsula, Spain dispatched sizable reinforcements to the New World and apparently snuffed out most of the separatist movements. Nevertheless, the determination of the American Creoles and Mestizos, the difficulty of suppressing revolution in colonies thousands of miles from Europe, and continuing unrest in the mother country demonstrated that the rebel cause was not hopeless, and by 1830 Spain was expelled from almost all of the New World.

One of the first provinces to fall was Florida—East Florida and the tiny remaining portion of West Florida—and the handwriting here had long been on the wall. This territory, like other Spanish colonies, underwent rapid changes of authority, but the colonists of this frontier outpost did not take advantage of the confusion to launch a concerted independence movement. Instead the most dangerous threat came from the expanding United States which desired to round out her borders in the Southeast—that she had no valid claim did not alter the peril.

Britain was also involved in the Florida tangle and conceivably could have taken this colony off Spanish hands. In the recent war Britain had been heavily committed in this quarter and had organized the Indians in the Southeast and built forts on the Apalachicola River. During the Congress of Vienna and the immediate aftermath there was no assurance she would pull out, though after the New Orleans disaster it was not likely that she would remain unless Spain voluntarily ceded or sold the colony. But Spain at this time was not inclined to hand over Florida—unless Louisiana could be an equivalent—and Britain prepared to withdraw Nicholls and his command from their bases on the Apalachicola River.

In the Louisiana-Florida campaign the British and Spaniards had suffered setbacks, but they were not as calamitous as those of their Creek allies. These Indians, routed by Jackson at Horseshoe Bend and expelled from almost half their lands, with British assistance had hoped to recover both their lands and their prestige. But when British forces withdrew from New Orleans and Nicholls and his detachment, much against the commander's will, later evacuated the Apalachicola River, the Creeks were left to their own resources—

a cheerless prospect. In the recent past Britain considered the Creeks an independent nation and maintained that their rights would not be forgotten and that their lands would be restored if only they joined the war against the United States.[1] They did, though with little effect, and in the future neither Britain, the United States, Spain, nor anyone else paid much attention to their rights. At first, in the negotiations at Ghent Britain insisted that the Indian tribes were independent nations whether they were within the boundaries of the United States or not, but after the reverses along the Canadian border in 1814 and after the victorious powers at Vienna began to quarrel, Britain dropped this extreme demand and settled for the *status quo ante bellum*.[2] To British statesmen in London this meant that Britain was abandoning her dream of creating an Indian buffer state along the Canadian boundary. But to British officials on the scene in Florida the *status quo ante bellum* and the specific provisions stating that Indians with whom the United States was at war would have returned to them territories which they possessed in 1811 meant that the Creeks would regain their lands and implied British intervention if necessary. It was with this understanding that the Red Sticks who had supported Nicholls were prevailed upon to endorse the treaty.[3] The United States insisted, however, that in 1815 she was at peace with the Creeks, that the 1814 Treaty of Fort Jackson, though signed by few Red Sticks, was valid, and that half of the lands possessed by all the Creeks before the war now rightfully belonged to the United States.[4] Hundreds of Americans enthusiastically seconded their government's position and in an amazingly short time poured into the fertile black belt of the Old Southwest and effectively occupied it. These developments came as no surprise, and, though Admiral Cochrane, and briefly even Lord Bathurst, secretary for war and colonies, made a strong legal case that Britain had shamefully deserted the southern Indians, Britain made no forceful protests.[5]

She had abandoned the Creeks with only minor exceptions. One was the leaving of munitions and cannon at the Prospect Bluff Fort where she contended the Indians could prosper and defend themselves against any enemy.[6] This might have happened if British merchants had continued a thriving trade with the Indians and if Britain had assumed an unofficial protectorate over the natives. This is precisely what Nicholls, who argued with logic that the Treaty of Ghent sanctioned British intervention, hoped would happen and is why he lingered at the fort some months after the proclamation of peace. But pressure from both Washington and Madrid brought about his recall, and he dejectedly made his way to England. It was becoming obvious to him and to the Creeks that the United States was going to make good its interpretation of the treaty, that the Americans were going to occupy the Creek lands, and that the Indians need not look to Britain for support.

Nicholls, accompanied by several Creek chiefs, reached London in the fall of 1815 and, along with Cochrane, continued to uphold the cause of these "Creeks who have sacrificed everything for us" and now are being abandoned.[7] Under his guidance, Hillis Hadjo, one of the most outspoken Red Sticks whom Nicholls had taken into his own lodgings, wrote a petition to the Prince Regent requesting an audience where the chief could personally present the calumet and inform the ruler of the Creeks' pitiable condition. As a result of the recent reverses they had lost hundreds of their most able warriors; the Americans had taken over their hunting grounds; while many of their squaws and children were naked and on the verge of starvation. The only remedy was for the Prince Regent to take the Muskogee nation under his wing, to maintain the fort at Prospect Bluff, and to insure a regular trade with the Indians.[8]

But the Prince Regent would not grant Hillis Hadjo's demands. Instead he suggested that the Creeks repair their domestic difficulties and have friendly intercourse with the United States, and both the Prince Regent and the Indians realized what that meant.[9] The government ordered Nicholls not to bring over any more chiefs whose mission would be doomed to failure and who could only be a drain on the exchequer. The Vienna settlement had ended a quarter century of fighting, and Britain was tired of war. In the full flush of victory against Napoleon in 1814–1815 she failed dismally in Florida and Louisiana and could only write off the New Orleans campaign as a costly blunder. The Creeks, as well as Britain, must pay for this failure. The Creek alternative was for Britain to assume a protectorate over the Indians and to continue an active trade via the Apalachicola River. To do so could reopen the conflict with the United States and would strike a sensitive chord in relations with Spain.

Arriving in London after 1815 without official encouragement, other Creek chiefs told of the grievous condition of the Indians, demanded a fixed trade with Nassau or Jamaica, or, if there were no other solution, requested that the Creeks be transported to another

British colony. The response was the same given to Hillis Hadjo; like this chief they were rejected and given transportation back to Florida, but whereas Hillis Hadjo received a hundred pounds to ease his misery, the subsequent chiefs were lucky to get a farthing.[10] Around 1810 the Creeks could muster over seven thousand braves and controlled some thirty-six thousand square miles; five years later they were pressed to muster half that many men, they had lost the better portion of their domain, and many were on the verge of starvation. They had been pawns in a determined three-way struggle in the Southeast, and even McGillivray or Bowles must have realized that pawns usually do not checkmate kings. There was no clouding the fact that the Battle of Horseshoe Bend and the failure of the Anglo-Spanish-Indian campaign eliminated the Creeks as a significant factor in this part of the continent. Soon talk of an Oklahoma reservation would be more than wild rumor.

Britain after 1815 had no strong desire to assume a protectorate over the Creek nation or to acquire Florida. But judging from accounts circulating in the United States, it was hard to fathom the British policy. The Prospect Bluff fort disturbed the Americans; it was some months before Nicholls left, and his interpreter, Lieutenant William Hambly, an old Indian trader, remained on the scene and for a brief period acted as his deputy.[11] Both the United States and Spain feared that Britain might try to maintain her influence among the Creeks, and both protested. But Nicholls retired, and in 1816 in an encounter with United States forces the fort was blown up and the stores destroyed or given to the Indians who participated in the attack.[12] Though in the future New Providence Island merchants appeared in the Creek nation and had a voice in its councils and British military adventurers revived Bowles's dreams, it was becoming obvious, particularly after the destruction of the fort, that Britain was going to let the Creeks fend for themselves.

Even if Britain did not remain a serious contender in the Southeast in a clandestine fashion, there was another possibility—she might buy Florida. The tempo of Spanish-American revolutionary movements increased just before 1820, and Spain was committed elsewhere. Since the design of making the Gulf of Mexico a Spanish lake was shattered and Spain had given up neighboring Louisiana and most of West Florida, the remainder of Florida had lost much of its value. Because this province was relatively worthless, because retaining it might lead to hostilities with the United States, and because it had always been a drain on the exchequer, there were ample grounds for selling it to Britain—at least so speculated United States authorities.[13] At first after Napoleon's downfall Spain believed that she could put her American house in order and retain Florida. But the specter of a war with the United States and the successes of the Spanish-American rebels made the possibility of a British sale more attractive. Britain's dream of dominating much of the Mississippi Valley, however, had received a fatal check at New Orleans, and with no prospect of controlling North America's heartland, Britain had little use for Florida. She never offered to buy this province and rejected all future Spanish overtures for a purchase.

It was obvious to both Spain and Britain that whoever had Florida had a colony of little value but one that provided a hornet's nest of problems with the United States. At no time was this truer than in 1817. Many of the Red Sticks who had survived Horseshoe Bend, who were bitter over the Treaty of Fort Jackson which they had not signed, who had later served under Nicholls, and who were chagrined when their lands were not restored after the Treaty of Ghent, had sought refuge in Florida. They and runaway Negro slaves frequently sallied across the border and raided the settlers who were streaming into the Creek lands. Spain could not control these Indians and Negroes, and this was the most vexing problem on the Florida frontier. Had there been good will on both sides, this complaint, and the ones Spain had against the United States for aiding the Spanish-American rebels, could have been adjusted. But expansionists in the United States were eyeing Florida, were unwilling to compromise, and were determined to take over all of this province and to use the Indian-Negro border raids as a pretext. No expansionist was more positive in his views than Jackson, and it was he and his frontier militia who dashed into Florida and captured all the important posts except St. Augustine. It is open to question whether Jackson exceeded his authority in seizing Florida, though the General in his own mind apparently was convinced that he was carrying out the administration's wishes.

One thing, however, is certain: his action could have led to war with two European powers. One was Spain and the grounds for hostilities were obvious; the other was Britain and the reasons were more complex. San Marcos, where many of the Indians and Negroes sought refuge, was the first Spanish fort captured by Old Hickory. These fugitives absconded before Jackson arrived, but this did not deter him from seizing the fort from the Spaniards.[14] Inside was Alexander Arbuthnot, a Scottish trader from the Bahamas, who wanted to take over the remnants of the trade formerly enjoyed by Panton and Leslie and, like Nicholls, insisted that the Treaty of Ghent sanctioned British intervention in behalf of the Creeks. Jackson promptly placed him under arrest, and a youthful officer, Robert Ambrister, who was captured nearby, soon joined this elderly merchant. Accused of inciting the savages to war on peaceful civilians, Jackson hanged one and shot the other. It was these executions which could have caused a rupture with Britain. Castlereagh, the foreign minister, did not make an issue out of this affair, even though the court martial's grounds for execution were flimsy and Arbuthnot and Ambrister had as much legal right in Florida as Jackson. On and off since 1783 Britain had flirted with the idea of regaining Florida or at least a protectorate over the Creeks. But after the New Orleans debacle in 1815 and defeats along the Canadian border the preceding year, the government renounced any design on Florida. Arbuthnot and Ambrister failed to take into account this policy shift and paid for it with their lives. The same applied to the Creek chieftain, Hillis Hadjo, who had been to London after the war in an unsuccessful bid for British support and now was enticed aboard a gunboat flying the Union Jack near San Marcos. But rather than a New Providence ship bringing supplies and munitions, it was one of Jackson's warships. In 1816 Hillis Hadjo was enjoying the pleasures of cosmopolitan London; 1817 found him dangling from the end of a rope at San Marcos.[15]

Britain was deeply involved with several aspects of Jackson's Florida invasion: one was the potentially explosive Arbuthnot-Ambrister affair which might have led to war; another was an attempt to avoid future hostilities by mediating this Spanish-American crisis. Spain turned to her recent ally and asserted that the two nations who had cooperated in crushing the usurper Napoleon should renew their concert against the United States which adhered to the Corsican's demonic principles. Spain demanded that Britain mediate this dispute with the Americans, that before negotiations began the United States evacuate Florida, and that Britain be willing to use force to see that they did.[16] Even though in return Spain held out the lure of Florida commercial concessions, Britain did not jump at the bait. With American immigrants pouring into the Southeast and with the several crushing defeats of the Creeks, the Florida Indian trade, now largely confined to the peninsula, had lost much of its appeal. After 1815 Britain abandoned designs of becoming entangled in Florida and in no fashion would commit herself to using force to prop up the rickety Spanish regime here. Nevertheless, she was opposed to the United States's acquiring more territory, she hoped that Spain could retain Florida, and, with no strings attached, she offered her good offices. The United States, having nothing to gain by arbitration, flatly turned this overture down.[17] She considered Arbuthnot, Ambrister, and similar adventurers a manifestation of sinister British designs on Florida, and she was determined to acquire Florida now or in the immediate future. Events proved that arbitration was not necessary. A strong reaction developed in the United States against Jackson's arbitrary invasion, and President Monroe withdrew the troops. But the American secretary of state, John Quincy Adams, insinuated that Spain must control the Indians —as dissatisfied as ever about the Treaty of Fort Jackson—or there would likely be another invasion, and this time the troops would remain. For Spain, deeply involved elsewhere in America, prospects for the future were not heartening.[18]

Jackson's invasion and the execution of Arbuthnot and Ambrister nearly led to a rupture with Britain. Castlereagh later claimed that if he had but lifted his finger the cabinet would have demanded war.[19] In Britain, and even in the United States, especially among the partisan followers of Henry Clay, there was concern over the harsh verdicts handed down by the court martial. Jackson, however, considered both of these men guilty and was only sorry that he was not able to shoot another. The English adventurer who nimbly eluded Jackson's clutches was Lieutenant George Woodbine, "the notorious Woodbine," one of the scores of British soldiers seeking his fortune in troubled waters of the New World after peace returned to Europe. He had served under Nicholls in 1814–1815 and was directly responsible for drilling the Florida Indians. After Nicholls' departure, Woodbine appeared frequently in Florida and the Americans considered him at the root of Indian-Negro depredations. It was with a heavy heart that Jackson learned that his quarry had escaped.[20]

When not in Florida, Woodbine was usually in Jamaica where he had obtained a commission from General Gregor McGregor. This Scottish soldier was one of many professionals participating in the independence of Spanish America. He had served under Miranda and now was one of Bolívar's most valuable lieutenants. Apparently without Bolívar's official approval, McGregor hoped to free Spanish East and West Florida and in some fashion to link them with Britain or with other Spanish-American colonies which might win their independence. Both Woodbine and Ambrister, and perhaps Arbuthnot, were associated with McGregor. However, opposition from Britain and the United States marked the downfall of McGregor's design, and the Scottish soldier was able only to occupy Amelia Island off the East Florida coast for a brief period in 1817. The munitions which Woodbine was assembling in Jamaica to arm the thousands of Florida Indians and Negroes were of no avail. Florida remained in turmoil, but the curtain lowered on Woodbine's role in this theatre.[21]

Because of Spain's inability to contain the resentful Red Sticks and Negroes, because, as a consequence, the United States probably would take over this colony by force, because Britain or other European countries would not give Spain any effective support, and because the revolutionaries elsewhere in Spanish America were becoming increasingly bold and successful, Spain reluctantly realized that the most expedient course was to hand over Florida to the grasping Americans and to bargain for the best terms possible. This is what she did in the Adams-Onís Treaty of 1819 in which she relinquished her claim to both Floridas and received several benefits, including a definite boundary between the United States and New Spain that recognized Texas as part of New Spain.[22]

Ceding Florida was the last resort for Spain, and both before signing the treaty and in the two years that lapsed before ratifying it she vainly sought some other recourse. She delayed ratification, hopefully trying to exact additional concessions from the United States, or in hopes of obtaining foreign intervention in Spanish behalf. During the period in which the Florida cession hung in the balance, Spain repeatedly turned to her erstwhile ally. She wanted Britain to intervene in a positive fashion which would forestall giving up Florida. Or if Britain would not lend diplomatic support backed by force—and Castlereagh made it clear that there would be none—then from the Spanish point of view it was "less unfortunate" to see Florida wind up in British rather than United States hands.[23] At least Britain and Spain, both with Gulf Coast colonies, might make common cause in containing the Americans. In a roundabout way Spain offered to sell this colony: Britain would advance six million dollars so that Spain could fully satisfy the United States claims, and in turn Britain would get Florida as security.[24] There was little possibility that Spain could repay the six million and an excellent possibility that Britain would acquire Florida. Castlereagh would have nothing to do with this, and, though sympathizing with Spain's dilemma, advised ratifying the treaty.[25] Belatedly Spain did, and when General Jackson for a third time within a decade marched into Pensacola, this time as governor, it marked the final phase of the contest of Florida which had begun in de Soto's time.

After the Florida cession in 1821 and the successful Mexican revolution the same year, Anglo-Spanish rivalry in North America ceased. It had begun unpretentiously in the sixteenth century when English ships from the West Country began fishing off Newfoundland and when John Hawkins began squinting at Florida; and, as one examines Britain's diplomatic maneuvers concerning Florida after 1815, it is apparent that this rivalry could hardly have ended with less fanfare. To be sure if one had accompanied Governor Moore or Oglethorpe against St. Augustine or Montiano against Frederica there would have been sufficient excitement and pageantry. Yet what was truly significant over the years was the fact that thousands of Englishmen, or Europeans under English auspices, had poured into America, and that English merchants and manufacturers, lured by American raw materials and by growing markets among whites and Indians, had stimulated English colonization and expansion. Since Spanish immigrants, with few exceptions, regularly went to Mexico and South America and Spanish merchants and manufacturers hardly ever were in a position to exploit Florida's resources effectively, it is hard not to conceive that, even if Spain had taken Frederica in 1742, this would have merely delayed the inexorable English advance.

After the American Revolution, of course, the main question was whether Britain would attach part or all of the Mississippi, Ohio, and Missouri river valleys—including the Floridas and possibly California—to Canada. This issue was in the balance from 1783 until 1815. The question was resolved in 1815 because Britain, now with a healthier respect for the power of the United States, was exhausted after the quarter-century struggle against France. Coming more under the influence of Adam Smith's *laissez faire* doctrines which placed little emphasis on colonies, she put aside the dream of carving out a colony in the heart of North America at the expense of Spain and the United States. It was not surprising that Britain did not encourage the southern Indians after 1815. Possibly both Hillis Hadjo and Nicholls finally realized that, after almost three centuries, Britain had abandoned her policy of acquiring territory in North America at Spain's expense.

Abbreviations

Add. MSS	British Museum: Additional Manuscripts
AGI	Archivo General de Indias, Seville
AGN	Archivo General de la Nación, Mexico
AGS	Archivo General de Simancas
AHN	Archivo Histórico Nacional, Madrid
AHR	American Historical Review
B. M.	British Museum
Bol. AGN	*Boletín, Archivo General de la Nación*
CO	Colonial Office
Col. S.C. Hist. Soc.	*Collections of the South Carolina Historical Society*
CSP	*Calendar of State Papers*
DOM.	Domestic
EF	East Florida Papers, Library of Congress
EHR	*English Historical Review*
FHQ	*Florida Historical Quarterly*
FO	Foreign Office
For.	Foreign
GHQ	*Georgia Historical Quarterly*
HAHR	*Hispanic American Historical Review*
Hist. MSS Com.	Great Britain, Historical Manuscripts Commission
L.C.	Library of Congress, Washington, D.C.
leg.	legajo
mod.	moderno
núm.	número
PRO	Public Record Office, London
SRNC	Spanish Records of the North Carolina Historical Commission
SP	State Paper Office
WMQ	*William and Mary Quarterly*
WO	War Office

Notes

Chapter 1

1. Capitulaciones de los Reyes Católicos con Don Cristóbal Colón, Santa Fé, Apr. 16, 1492, Joaquín Pacheco, Francisco de Cárdenas, Luis Torres de Mendoza, *et al.*, eds., *Colección de documentos inéditos relativos al descubrimiento, conquista, y colonización de las posesiones españolas en América y Oceanía, sacados en su mayor parte, del real Archivo de Indias* (Madrid, 1864–1884), XIX, 432. From around 1480 Bristol merchants were looking for and apparently found a land or island usually called Brazil. Located in the Atlantic to the west of Europe, and in reality perhaps part of America, this land could be a convenient way station on a westward voyage to Cathay, and knowledge of the existence of this land may have stimulated both Columbus and the Cabots in their voyages. See James A. Williamson, *The Cabot Voyages and Bristol Discovery under Henry VII* . . . (Cambridge, 1962), pp. 3 ff., and David B. Quinn, "The Argument for the English Discovery of America between 1480 and 1494," *The Geographical Journal,* CXXVII (1961), 277–285.

2. One of the most recent scholarly accounts of Columbus is Samuel E. Morison, *Admiral of the Ocean Sea, A Life of Christopher Columbus* (Boston, 1942).

3. Herman van der Linden, "Alexander VI and the Demarkation of the Maritime and Colonial Domains of Spain and Portugal, 1493–1494," *AHR*, XXII (1916), 20.

4. Treaty of Tordesillas, June 7, 1494, Frances G. Davenport and Charles O. Paullin, eds., *European Treaties Bearing on the History of the United States and Its Dependencies* (Washington, 1917–1937), I, 95, 99.

5. Capitulación con Juan Ponce de León, Burgos, Feb. 23, 1512, Pacheco, *et al.*, *Documentos inéditos*, XXII, 27–30.

6. Andrés G. de Barcia Carballido y Zúñiga, *Ensayo cronológico para la historia general de la Florida*, trans. Anthony Kerrigan (Gainesville, 1951), pp. 1–2.

7. Gonzalo Fernández de Oviedo y Valdés, *Historia general y natural de las Indias, islas y tierra-firme del mar océano* (Madrid, 1851–1855), III, 621–623; Fred-

erick T. Davis, "History of Juan Ponce de León's Voyages to Florida, Source Records," *FHQ*, xiv (1935), 26, 64; the most recent, though not definitive, biography of Ponce de León is Vicente Murga Sanz, *Juan Ponce de León: fundador y primer governador del pueblo puertorrigueño, descubridor de la Florida y del Estrecho de las Bahamas* (San Juan, 1959).

8. Peter Martyr, *The Decades of the Newe Worlde or West India* . . . , trans. Richard Eden (London, 1555), p. 319.

9. Oviedo, *Historia general*, iii, 628; Barcia, *Historia general*, pp. 5, 9.

10. A convenient summary of these expeditions, though superceded in spots by more recent scholarship, is Woodbury Lowery, *The Spanish Settlements within the Present Limits of the United States, 1513–1561*, 2d ed. (New York, 1959).

11. *Ibid.*, 376.

12. Charles G. M. B. de la Roncière, *La Floride française, scène de la vie indienne, peintes en 1564 par Jacques LeMoyne de Morgues* (Paris, 1928); Charles A. Julien, *Les voyages de découverte et les premiers établissements (xve–xvie siècles)* (Paris, 1948); along with Francis Parkman, *France and England in North America, Pioneers of France in the New World* (Boston, 1865) are the best accounts of Frenchmen in Florida.

13. Royal Capitulación y Asiento with Pedro Menéndez de Avilés, Madrid, Mar. 20, 1565, Jeannette T. Connor, ed. and trans., *Pedro Menéndez de Avilés; Memorial by Gonzalo Solís de Merás* (Gainesville, 1964), pp. 122, 259–261.

14. Verne E. Chatelain, *The Defenses of Spanish Florida, 1565–1763* (Washington, 1941), p. 44.

15. Royal Capitulación, Connor, *Menéndez de Avilés*, p. 261.

16. Menéndez to Philip ii, St. Augustine, Oct. 15, 1565, Eugenio Ruidíaz y Caravia, *La Florida, su conquista y colonización por Pedro Menéndez de Avilés* (Madrid, 1893), ii, 94–95.

17. The best account of this mission is Clifford M. Lewis and Albert J. Loomie, *The Spanish Jesuit Mission in Virginia, 1570–1572* (Chapel Hill, 1953).

18. Juan López de Velasco, *Geografía y descripción universal de las Indias, recopilada por el cosmógrafo-cronista Juan López de Velasco, desde el año de 1571 al de 1574* (Madrid, 1894), p. 157.

19. Henry P. Bigger, ed., *The Precursors of Jacques Cartier, 1497–1534, a Collection of Documents Relating to the Early History of the Dominion of Canada* (Ottawa, 1911), p. xxii.

20. Daniel W. Prowse, *A History of Newfoundland from the English, Colonial, and Foreign Records* (London, 1895), p. 48; Harold A. Innis, "The Rise and Fall of the Spanish Fishery in Newfoundland," *Transactions of the Royal Society of Canada*, 3d ser., xxv (1931), 51 ff.

21. Anthony Parkhurst to Richard Hakluyt, 1578, Eva G. R. Taylor, ed., *The Original Writings and Correspondence of the Two Richard Hakluyts* (London, 1935), i, 128.

22. There are several valuable works dealing with the economic life and commerce of Seville and the Spanish empire: Huguette et Pierre Chaunu, *Séville et l'Atlantique, 1504–1650* (Paris, 1955–1959); Ramon Carande Thobar, *Carlos V y sus banqueros, la vida económica de España en una fase de su hegemonía* (Madrid, 1943); Albert Girard, *Le commerce français à Sèville et Cadix au temps des Habsbourg; contribution à l'étude du commerce étranger en Espagne aux XVIe et XVIIIe siècles* (Paris, 1932); Clarence H. Haring, *Trade and Navigation between Spain and the Indies in the Time of the Hapsburgs* (Cambridge, 1918); a delight-

ful account of Seville is Ruth Pike, "Seville in the Sixteenth Century," *HAHR*, XLI (1961). In 1717 the Casa de Contratación was moved from Seville to Cádiz, and Cádiz became the monopoly port for the American trade.

23. A satisfactory, though not exhaustive, account dealing with this subject is Lillian E. Fisher, *Viceregal Administration in the Spanish-American Colonies* (Berkeley, 1926); of greater value are Clarence H. Haring, *The Spanish Empire in America* (New York, 1947) and Silvio A. Zavala, *Hispanoamérica septentrional y media, período colonial* (Mexico, 1953).

Chapter 2

1. Williamson, *Cabot Voyages*, pp. 3 ff.; Quinn, "Argument for English Discovery of America," pp. 277 ff.

2. Richard Hakluyt, *The Principal Navigations, Voyages, Traffiques, and Discoveries of the English Nation* (London, 1598–1600), VII (1903 edition), 143.

3. Henry Harrisse, *John Cabot, the Discoverer of North America and Sebastian His Son, a Chapter in the Maritime History of England Under the Tudors, 1496–1557* (London, 1896), pp. 55, 126, 141.

4. Davenport and Paullin, *Treaties*, I, 95.

5. An excellent discussion of the Papal Bulls is in Linden, "Alexander VI and the Demarkation of the Maritime Domains of Spain and Portugal," p. 20. Of value also are Manuel Giménez Fernández, *Nuevas consideraciones sobre la historia, sentido y valor de las bulas alejandrinas de 1493 referentes a las Indias* (Seville, 1944) and Lewis U. Hanke, *The Spanish Struggle for Justice in the Conquest of America*, 2d ed. (Philadelphia, 1959), 25 ff.

6. Ruy Gonzales de Puebla to Ferdinand and Isabella, July 25?, 1498, Harrisse, *Cabot*, p. 396.

7. Reales cédulas en que se contiene el asiento hecho con Alonso de Hojeda, Granada, June 8, 1501, Pacheco, *et al.*, *Documentos inéditos*, XXXVIII, 470.

8. Martín Fernández de Navarrete, *Colección de los viages y descubrimientos que hicieron por mar los españoles desde fines del siglo XV, con varios documentos inéditos concernientes á la historia de la marina castellana y de los establecimientos españoles en Indias* (Madrid, 1825–1837), III, 41.

9. Reales cédulas . . . con Hojeda, June 8, 1501, Pacheco, *et al.*, *Documentos inéditos*, XXXVIII, 470.

10. Información de testigos hecho por orden de la Audiencia de Santo Domingo, Nov. 26, 1527, Pacheco, *et al.*, *Documentos inéditos*, XL, 306; Crown to Judges of the Audiencia of Santo Domingo, Madrid, Mar. 27, 1528, Irene A. Wright, ed., *Spanish Documents Concerning English Voyages to the Caribbean, 1527–1568* (London, 1929), p. 57; Henry P. Biggar, "An English Expedition to America in 1527," *Mélanges d'histoire offerts à M. Charles Bémont par ses amis et ses élèves à l'occasion de la vingtcinquième année de son enseignement à l'École pratique des haute études* (Paris, 1913), pp. 459 ff.

11. Details of French attacks on Spanish America in the first half of the sixteenth century are in Charles G.M.B. de la Roncière, *Histoire de la marine française* (Paris, 1899–1932), III, 129 ff.

12. Thomas Rymer, ed., *Foedera, Conventiones, Literae* . . . 2d ed. (London,

1726–1735), xii, 411–429. Apparently the Treaty of Medina del Campo was never officially ratified. [John D. Mackie, *The Earlier Tudors, 1485–1558* (Oxford, 1952), pp. 96–97.]

13. Carande, *Carlos V y sus banqueros*; Girard, *Le commerce français à Séville et Cadiz*; Haring, *Trade and Navigation*; and Gordon Connell-Smith, *Forerunners of Drake, a Study of English Trade with Spain in the Early Tudor Period* (London, 1932), p. liv; Philip A. Means, *The Spanish Main, Focus of Envy, 1492–1700.*

14. A good account of English participation in the fishery is Prowse, *History of Newfoundland* and Harold A. Innis, *The Cod Fisheries; the History of an International Economy* (New Haven, 1940).

15. Thomas Blake arrived in Mexico City around 1534 and served under Coronado. Conway transcripts, Account 3739, L. C.

16. Roger Barlow, *A Brief Summe of Geographie*, ed. Eva G. R. Taylor (London, 1932), p. liv; Philip A. Means, *The Spanish Main, Focus of Envy, 1492–1700* (London, 1935), p. 41. Cabot for many years was pilot major for the Casa in Seville and served both England and Spain during his eventful career. Considering him as an English national exclusively, of course, is misleading.

17. The 3. unfortunate voyage made with the Jesus . . . 1567 and 1568, Clements R. Markham, ed., *The Hawkins' Voyages during the Reigns of Henry VIII, Queen Elizabeth, and James I* (London, 1878), pp. 70 ff; a good popular account based on secondary sources is Rayner Unwin, *The Defeat of John Hawkins; a Biography of His Third Slaving Voyage* (New York, 1960). See also James A. Williamson, *Sir John Hawkins, the Time and the Man* (Oxford, 1927), pp. 142 ff.

18. There is abundant material on the fate of these prisoners in Mexico in the Conway transcripts; Juan de Castañeda to ?, Convento de Tezcuco, Sept. 1, 1609, *Bol. AGN*, iv (Mar.-Apr. 1933), 244–246.

19. David Ingram, *The Land Travels of Davyd Ingram and Others in the Years 1568–9. From the Rio de Minas in the Gulph of Mexico to Cape Breton in Acadia*, in P. C. J. Weston, ed., *Documents Connected with the History of South Carolina* (London, 1856), pp. 5–24.

20. Guerau de Spes to Crown, London, Aug. 5, 1570, Martín Fernández de Navarrete, Miguel Salvá, Pedro Sainz de Baranda, *et al.*, eds., *Colección de documentos inéditos para la historia de España* (Madrid, 1842–1895), xc, 384.

21. Philip Nichols, *Sir Francis Drake Revived* . . . (London, 1628) gives a detailed, reasonably accurate account of this raid; a more modern account is in James A. Williamson, *The Age of Drake*, 4th ed. (London, 1960), pp. 117 ff.

22. During part of the sixteenth and most of the seventeenth centuries European nations generally agreed that hostilities in the New World would not automatically cause a rupture between the mother countries in the Old World—"no peace beyond the Line." The line was a right angle formed by the prime meridian —passing through either the Canary or Azores islands—and the Tropic of Cancer. (Introduction to Tready of Cateau-Cambrésis, 1559, Davenport and Paullin, *Treaties*, i, 220–221.) There are many examples in medieval times of a ruler of several kingdoms simultaneously being both officially at war and at peace with a given foreign kingdom. The concept of "no peace beyond the line" in many respects was a carryover from the past.

23. Mendoza to Philip ii, London, Feb. 20, 1580, *CSP, Spain, Elizabeth*, iii, 8–9; *ibid.*, Nov. 7, 1581, 208.

24. Los puntos en que habló Henrrique Cobam á su Mag^d . . . 1575, AGS, estado, leg. 829.

25. Mendoza to Philip ii, London, Sept. 25, 1579, *CSP, Spain, Elizabeth*, ii, 698.

26. Guerau de Spes to Crown, Aug. 5, 1570, Navarette, *et al., Documentos inéditos, España*, XC, 384; declarations by Oxenham, etc., Zelia M. M. Nuttall, ed. and trans., *New Light on Drake, a Collection of Documents Relating to His Voyage of Circumnavigation, 1577–1580* (London, 1914), p. 11; Martín Enriquez to the Inquisitor Bonilla, Mexico, Feb. 18, 1580, *ibid.*, p. 376.

27. Norman M. Penzer, ed., *The World Encompassed and Analogous Contemporary Documents Concerning Sir Francis Drake's Circumnavigation of the World* (London, 1926), 59–64; Kenneth R. Andrews, *Drake's Voyages; A Reassessment of Their Place in Elizabethan Maritime Expansion* (New York, 1967), pp. 76–79; details of Spanish countermeasures to Drake in the Pacific are in AGI, patronato, leg. 2–5–2/21.

28. Francis Pretty, Voyage of Thomas Candish, 1586–1588, Hakluyt, *Principal Navigations*, XI, 320–325.

29. Eva G. R. Taylor, "Early Empire Building Projects in the Pacific Ocean," *HAHR*, XIV (1934), 299; Antonio de la Ascensión, Relación breve en que se da noticia de descubrimiento . . . hasta . . . cabo Mendocino, Mexico, Oct. 12, 1620, Pacheco, *et al., Documentos inéditos*, VIII, 554.

30. Many details of Spain's building a fleet of galleys in the South Sea (1579–1590) are in AGI, patronato, leg. 2–5–2/25, núm. 2, ramos 1–10.

Chapter 3

1. The best accounts of Stucley are Richard Simpson, ed., *The School of Shakespeare* (London, 1878), I, 1–156, and John Izon, *Sir Thomas Stucley, c. 1525–1578, Traitor Extraordinary* (London, 1956). See also J. Leitch Wright, Jr., "Sixteenth Century English-Spanish Rivalry in la Florida," *FHQ*, XXXVIII (1960), 267 ff.

2. Ribault had frequently been in England in the past and had worked here with the aged Sebastian Cabot. He had also commanded English Protestants when they aided the French Huguenots in their struggle against the French Catholics. Barlow, *Brief Summe of Geographie*, p. iv; Menéndez de Avilés to Crown, St. Augustine, Oct. 15, 1565, Horace E. Ware, ed. and trans., "Letters of Pedro Menéndez de Avilés," *Proceedings of the Massachusetts Historical Society*, 2d ser. VIII (Boston, 1892–1894), p. 438.

3. Bishop Quadra to Philip II, London, May 1, 1563, Navarrete, *et al., Documentos inéditos, España*, LXXXVII, 512–513.

4. *Ibid.*, June 26, 1563, 531; La Roncière, *La Floride française*, pp. 29–30; Jeanine Jacquemin, "La colonisation protestante en Floride et la politique européenne au XVIe siècle," *Bulletin de la Société de l'Histoire du Protestantisme Francais*, CI (1955), 187.

5. Quadra to Philip II, London, June 19, 1563, Navarrete, *et al., Documentos inéditos, España*, LXXXVII, 524–525. In the future Hawkins would make similar overtures to the Spanish ambassador.

6. Guzman de Silva to Philip II, Oct. 22, 1565, *ibid.*, LXXXIX, 216–217.

7. *Ibid.*, Dec. 4, 1564, 63–64; Challoner to Cecil, Dec. 24, 1564, *CSP, For., Elizabeth*, VII, 272.

8. Guzman to Philip II, London, Aug. 27, 1565, Navarrete, *et al., Documentos inéditos, España*, LXXXIX, 178.

9. "Laudonnière's Historie of Florida," Hakluyt, *Principal Navigations*, IX, 77–81.

10. Hawkins to Elizabeth, Padstow, Sept. 20, 1565, Hist. MSS Com., *Report on the Pepys Manuscripts* . . . (London, 1911), p. 66.

11. John Sparks, *Voyage Made by the Worshipful M. John Hawkins . . . 1564,* Markham, *Hawkins' Voyages*, pp. 56–63.

12. Philip II to Bernardino de Mendoza, Madrid, Oct. 31, 1578, Navarrete, *et al., Documentos inéditos España*, XCI, 297; Guzman to Philip II, London, Oct. 22, 1565, *ibid.,* LXXXIX, 218.

13. Mendoza to Philip II, London, Mar. 31, 1578, *ibid.,* XCI, 205–208.

14. "Instructions . . . given to Frobisher . . . for a voyage to Meta Incognita," Richard Collinson, ed., *The Three Voyages of Martin Frobisher, in Search of a Passage to Cathaia and India by the North-West, A. D. 1576–8 . . .* (London 1867), p. 214.

15. Humphrey Gilbert, "A Discourse How Hir Majestie May Annoy the King of Spayne," Nov. 6, 1577, David B. Quinn, ed., *The Voyages and Colonizing Enterprises of Sir Humphrey Gilbert* (London, 1940), I, 172–174.

16. Mendoza to Gabriel de Zayas, Aug. 14, 1578, Navarrete, *et al., Documentos inéditos, España*, XCI, 271.

17. Mendoza to Philip II, London, July 11, 1582, *ibid.,* XCII, 396–397.

18. *Ibid.,* Apr. 26, 1582, 358.

19. "George Peckham's True Report," Nov. 12, 1583, Quinn, *Gilbert,* II, 445.

20. "Discourse of Western Planting by Richard Hakluyt, 1584," Taylor, *Hakluyt Correspondence,* II, 239–242; David B. Quinn, ed., *The Roanoke Voyages, 1584–1590, Documents to Illustrate the English Voyages to North America under the Patent Granted to Walter Raleigh in 1584* (London, 1955), I, 32.

21. Licentiate Aliagra to Crown, Santo Domingo, Nov. 30, 1585, Irene A. Wright, ed., *Further English Voyages to Spanish America 1583–1594, Documents from the Archives of the Indies at Seville Illustrating English Voyages to the Caribbean, the Spanish Main, Florida, and Virginia* (London, 1951), 16.

22. Richard Grenville to Walsingham, Plymouth, Oct. 29, 1585, Quinn, *Roanoke Voyages,* I, 219–220.

23. Alonzo Santos Saez to Crown, St. Augustine, July 11, 1586, AGI, Santo Domingo, leg. 54–5–14.

24. "Discourse and Description of the Voyage of Sir Francis Drake and Mr. Captain Frobisher, Set Forward the 14th Day of September, 1585," Julian S. Corbett, ed., *Papers Relating to the Navy during the Spanish War, 1585–1587* (London, 1898), p. 25; James Covington, "Drake Destroys St. Augustine: 1586," *FHQ,* XLIV (1965), 81 ff.

25. Gabriel de Luxon and Diego Fernández de Quiñones to Crown, Havana, July 1, 1586, Wright, *English Voyages, 1583–1594,* p. 185.

26. Juan de Posada to Crown, St. Augustine, Sept. 2, 1586, *ibid.,* p. 205; Quiñones to Crown, Havana, Sept., 1586, Irene A. Wright, ed., *Historia documentada de San Cristóbal de la Habana en el siglo XVI, basada en los documentos originales existentes en el Archivo General de Indias en Sevilla* (Havana, 1927), II, 65.

27. "Relation of Pedro Morales and Nicholas Burgoignon," Hakluyt, *Principal Navigations,* IX, 112–115.

28. Edward Stafford to Walsingham, Paris, Aug. 20, 1586, *CSP, For., Elizabeth,* XXI, pt. 1, 73.

29. Quiñones to Crown, Havana, Sept. 1586, AGI, Santo Domingo, leg. 54–2–4.

30. Marqués to President of House of Trade, St. Augustine, June 17, 1586, Wright, *English Voyages, 1583–1594*, p. 164.

31. Marqués to Crown, St. Augustine, Dec. 12, 1586, AGI, Santo Domingo, leg. 54–5–9.

32. The best account of the debates over the future status of Florida is ir Charles W. Arnade, *Florida on Trial, 1593–1602* (Coral Gables, 1959).

33. Luís Jerónimo de Oré, *The Martyrs of Florida (1513–1616)*, trans. Maynard Geiger (New York, 1936), p. 48.

34. Vasques y Obros to Juan de Ybarra, Havana, July 22, 1588, AGI, Santo Domingo, leg. 54–1–34; Consejo del Rey to Ybarra, Mar. 31, 1589, *ibid.*

35. Demands to be made by her M^d Comesioners . . . , Cotton Vespasian, CXIII, B. M.; Charles Cornwallis to Conde de Lemos, Aug. 1607, *ibid.*, CVI. For Vitoria's belief as to what constituted Spain's just title to the Indies and for his influence on contemporaries and posterity see Hanke, *Spanish Struggle for Justice*, pp. 150 ff.

36. The most waighty, secret, and last Instruction given by Philip II to his son, Sept. 13, 1598, PRO, SP, 94/6.

37. Davenport and Paullin, *Treaties*, I, 256.

Chapter 4

1. Charles M. Andrews, *The Colonial Period of American History* (New Haven, 1934–1938), I, 79.

2. William W. Hening, ed., *The Statutes at Large, Being a Collection of All the Laws of Virginia from the First Session of the Legislature in the Year 1619* (Richmond, 1809–1823), I, 58–59.

3. Pedro de Zúñiga to Philip III, London, Dec. 24, 1606, AGS, estado, leg. 1007.

4. Ferdinando Gorges to Robert Cecil, Plymouth, Feb. 4, 1606, James P. Baxter, ed., *Sir Ferdinando Gorges and His Province of Maine. Including the Brief Relation, the Brief Narration, His Defence, the Charter Granted to Him, His Will, and His Letters* (Boston, 1890), III, 126–127. Apparently Challons was to have struck out directly across the Atlantic rather than taking the usual route through the West Indies. This violation of orders contributed to Gorges's ire. Richard A. Preston, *Gorges of Plymouth Fort; a Life of Sir Ferdinando Gorges, Captain of Plymouth Fort, Governor of New England, and Lord of the Province of Maine* (Toronto, 1953), pp. 143–144. Another vessel sent out by the Plymouth Company in 1606 commanded by Martin Pring did make a successful reconnaissance of the Maine coast.

5. "The Voyage of M. Henry Challons," Samuel Purchas, *Hakluytus Posthumus or Purchas His Pilgrimes, Contayning a History of the World in Sea Voyages and Lande Travells by Englishmen and Others* (London, 1625), XIX (1905 edition), 284–293; Memorial . . . of Enrique Chalons, May, 1607, Cotton Vespasian, VI.

6. Charles Cornwallis to Conde de Lemos, Aug. 1607, *ibid.;* memorial of Chalons, May 1607, *ibid.*

7. Cornwallis to Earl of Salisbury, Feb. 6, 1606/7, Harleian MSS, 1875, B. M.

8. Zúñiga to Crown, Highgate, Sept. 10, 1608, AGS, estado, leg. 1008.

9. "Observations by George Percy," Edward Arber and Arthur G. Bradley, eds., *Travels and Works of Captain John Smith, President of Virginia, and Admiral of New England, 1580–1631* (Edinburgh, 1910), I, lxxi.

10. Sarmiento de Acuña to Crown, London, Oct. 5, 1613, AGS, estado, leg. 1009; Matthew P. Andrews, *Virginia, The Old Dominion* (New York, 1937), p. 67.

11. Council in Virginia to Council of Virginia in England, Jamestown, June 22, 1607, Hist. MSS Com., *Third Report* (London, 1872), p. 54.

12. Cornwallis to Privy Council, June 9, 1608, Cotton Vespasian, XI.

13. El consejo de estado, Nov. 10, 1607, AGS, estado, leg. 984; *ibid.*, July 3, 1610, leg. 844; *ibid.*, Feb. 14, 1612; Irene A. Wright, "Spanish Policy Toward Virginia," *AHR*, XXV (1920), 448–479.

14. ? to ?, London, June 29, 1608, AGS, estado, leg. 984.

15. Godfrey Davies, *The Early Stuarts, 1603–1660,* 4th ed. (Oxford, 1949), pp. 51 ff; AGS, estado, leg. 2518 gives details on many aspects of the proposed marriage.

16. Pedro de Ybarra to Crown, St. Augustine, Jan. 4, 1606, AGI, Santo Domingo, leg. 54-5-9; Arnade, *Florida on Trial,* pp. 12 ff.

17. Ybarra to Crown, St. Augustine, Dec. 26, 1605, AGI, Santo Domingo, leg. 54-5-9.

18. Tanto de las diligencias que se hicieron sobre atraer a la obediencia de S. M. las Provencias de horruque y Aiz, 1605, AGI, patronato, leg. 1-1-1/19.

19. Ybarra to Crown, St. Augustine, May 16, 1607, AGI, Santo Domingo, leg. 54-5-9.

20. Arthur Hopton to Viscount Dorchester, Madrid, Aug. 22, 1631, Stowe MSS, CLXXXVI, B. M.; Barcia, *Historia general,* p. 195.

21. Arber, *Smith,* I, 158.

22. *Ibid.,* 13; Philip L. Barbour, "Captain George Kendall, Mutineer or Intelligencer?" *Virginia Magazine of History and Biography,* LXX (1962), 297 ff.

23. Dudley Carleton to John Chamberlain, London, Aug. 18, 1607, *CSP, Colonial,* I, 7. Little is known about Waiman or what prompted him to flee England; possibly Capt. Waiman was Capt. George Weymouth.

24. Ralph Winwood, *Memorials of Affairs of State in the Reigns of Q. Elizabeth and K. James I. Collected (Chiefly) from the Original Papers of the Right Honourable Sir Ralph Winwood, Kt. Sometime One of the Principal Secretaries of State . . .* (London, 1727), II, 439; ? to President of Indies, July 19, 1608, AGI, indiferente general, leg. 147-5-8; David W. Davies, *Elizabethans Errant; The Strange Fortunes of Sir Thomas Sherley and His Three Sons as Well in the Dutch Wars as in Muscovy, Morocco, Persia, Spain, and the Indies* (Ithaca, 1967), pp. 141–142. It is interesting to note, though possibly merely coincidence, that Kendall, Shirley, and Waiman—assuming that the George Kendall in the Netherlands was the same as at Jamestown and that Waiman was Weymouth—all had been followers of or associated with Essex or Southampton and all probably were Catholics.

25. Consulta of the Council for War in the Indies, Mar. 5, 1611, Wright, "Spanish Policy Toward Virginia," p. 463.

26. Mary Ross, "The French on the Savannah, 1605" *GHQ,* VIII (1924), 189; Ybarra to Philip III, St. Augustine, Dec. 26, 1605, AGI, Santo Domingo, leg. 54-5-9.

27. Consulta, Mar. 5, 1611, Wright, "Spanish Policy Toward Virginia," pp. 463–467.

28. Crown to Alonso de Velasco, Madrid, June 17, 1611, Alexander Brown, *The Genesis of the United States* (Boston, 1890), I, 476.

29. Relación del viaje que hizo a las Indias hasta la Virginia . . . Don Diego de Molina, Antonio Pérez, y Francisco Lymbry, in Duke de Lerma to ?, el Pardo, Nov. 13, 1611, AGS, estado, 1008.

30. Depositions of John Clark and Others at Havana, 1611, Wright, "Spanish Policy Toward Virginia," pp. 470–473.

31. Molina to Velasco ?, Virginia, 1613, in Velasco to Crown, Aug. 2, 1613, AGS, estado, leg. 1009.

32. "Notes of Virginia Affairs . . . taken out of Master Ralph Hamor's Booke," Purchas, *Pilgrimes*, XIX, 99.

33. Molina to Acuña, Virginia, June 14, 1614, AGS, estado, leg. 1009.

34. Purchas, *Pilgrimes*, XIX, 117.

35. Molina to Velasco ?, Virginia, 1613, in Velasco to Crown, Aug. 2, 1613, AGS, estado, leg. 1009.

36. Molina to Acuña, Virginia, April 30, 1614, in Acuña to Crown, London, Oct. 17, 1614, AGS, estado, leg. 1009.

37. James P. C. Southall, "Captain John Martin of Brandon on the James," *Virginia Magazine of History and Biography*, LIV (1946), 39.

38. Depositions of Clark at Havana, 1611, and examination of Clark in Madrid, Feb. 18, 1613, Wright, "Spanish Policy Toward Virginia," pp. 470–473, 476–479.

39. Wright, "Spanish Policy Toward Virginia," p. 455.

40. John Digby to Carleton, Madrid, Nov. 3, 1613, *CSP, Colonial*, I, 16.

41. *Ibid.*, Oct. 10, 1612, 14.

42. John Rolfe to Edwin Sandys, Jan. 1619, Susan M. Kingsbury, ed., *The Records of the Virginia Company of London* (Washington, 1906–1935), III, 244.

43. Privy Council to George Yardley, Whitehall, Apr. 19, 1626, William L. Grant, James Munro, and Almeric W. Fitzroy, eds., *Acts of the Privy Council of England, Colonial Series* (London, 1908–   ), I, 99–100.

44. El consejo de estado, Apr. 18, 1614, AGS, estado, leg. 844; Digby to Thomas Edmondes, Madrid, Sept. 14, 1613, Stowe MSS, CLXXIV.

45. AGS, estado, leg. 985.

46. Digby to Carleton, Nov. 3, 1613, CSP, *Colonial*, I, 16.

47. Capt. John Pennington to Duke of Buckingham, Catwater, Apr. 5, 1626, *CSP, Dom., Charles I*, I, 304.

48. Capt. Richard Plumleigh to Lords of the Admiralty, The Downs, Aug. 29, 1630, *ibid.*, IV, 335.

49. Proceedings and debates, June 17, 1607, Leo F. Stock, ed., *Proceedings and Debates of the British Parliaments Respecting North America* (Washington, 1924–1941), I, 17.

50. Wesley F. Craven, "The Earl of Warwick, A Speculator in Piracy," *HAHR*, X (1930), 463.

51. John Winthrop, *Winthrop's Journal, "History of New England," 1630–1649*, ed. James K. Hosmer (New York, 1908), Aug. 27, 1639, I, 310; *ibid.*, June 1646, II, 272.

52. Countless of these petitions between the years 1610–1620 are in the Stetson Col., University of Florida Library, Gainesville.

53. Luis Horruytiner to Philip IV, St. Augustine, Nov. 15, 1633, AGI, Santo Domingo, leg. 54–5–18.

54. Gerónimo de la Torre to Crown, Madrid, Nov. 10, 1655, AGI, Santo Domingo, leg. 58–1–26.

Chapter 5

1. Ayllón's Chicora and the English Carolina had similar bounds. San Jorge was in the vicinity of Charleston and Santa Elena applied to the Port Royal region. Throughout this chapter the author frequently has relied on his "Spanish Reaction to Carolina," *NCHR*, XLI (1964), 464 ff.

2. Charles I's charter to Robert Heath, Oct. 30, 1629, Mattie E. E. Parker, ed., *North Carolina Charters and Constitutions, 1578–1698* (Raleigh, 1963), pp. 62 ff.

3. Proposals by Mons. Belavene, July 24, 1629, *CSP, Colonial*, I, 99; Directors to Mons. Bonnavolia, March ?, 1630, *ibid.*, 109; petition of Edward Kingswell to Privy Council, Sept. 1634, *ibid.*, 190–191.

4. Henry Huncks to Earl of Carlisle, July 11, 1639, *ibid.*, 300.

5. Crown to Viceroy of New Spain, Buen Retiro, Nov. 16, 1655, AGN, reales cédulas, originales, tomo 5, expediente 101.

6. Two examples of this promotional literature are Edward Williams, *Virginia: More Especially the South Part Thereof, Richly and Truly Valued: Viz. the Fertile Carolana, and No Lesse Excellent Isle of Roanoak . . .* (London, 1650); and Edward Bland, *The Discovery of New Brittaine. Began August 27. Anno Dom. 1650* (London, 1651).

7. William Hilton, Samuel Goldsmith, Lucas Greenlese, *et al.*, "William Hilton's Voyage to Carolina in 1662," ed. J. Leitch Wright, Jr., *Essex Institute Historical Collections*, CV (1969), 99–102; Wesley F. Craven, *The Southern Colonies in the Seventeenth Century, 1607–1689* (Baton Rouge, 1949), pp. 317–320.

8. John T. Lanning, *The Spanish Missions of Georgia* (Chapel Hill, 1935), p. 203. Timucua is the coastal area of northern Florida, Guale roughly corresponds to coastal Georgia, and Santa Elena to the Port Royal region of South Carolina.

9. Religious of Santa Elena to Crown, Florida, Sept. 10, 1657, AGI, Santo Domingo, leg. 54–5–20; Juan de Salamanca to Crown, Havana, Nov. 1, 1658, AGI, Santo Domingo, leg. 54–1–18.

10. Council of the Indies, Madrid, May 13, 1653, AGS, estado, leg. 991.

11. The Heath charter and the 1663 and 1665 charters are in Parker, *North Carolina Charters*.

12. William Hilton, Anthony Long, and Peter Fabian, *A True Relation of a Voyage Upon Discovery of Part of the Coast of Florida from the Latitude of 31° to 33°45' North Latitude* (London, 1664), in *Collections of South Carolina Historical Society* (1857–1897), V, 21.

13. Alonso Arguiles to Hilton, Santa Elena, Sept. 23, 1663, *Col. S. C. Hist. Soc.*, V, 28.

14. Hilton to Arguiles, *Adventure*, Sept. 23, 1663, *ibid.*, p. 27.

15. Hilton *et al.*, *True Relation*, p. 21.

16. Ibid., p. 25.

17. Robert Sanford's Relation, 1666, Alexander S. Salley, Jr., ed., *Narratives of Early Carolina, 1650–1708* (New York, 1911), pp. 104–105.

18. Andrews, *Colonial Period of American History*, III, 201.

19. Francisco de la Guerra y de la Vega to Charles II, St. Augustine, Aug. 8, 1668, AGI, Santo Domingo, leg. 54–5–18; Doña Estefania Ponce de Léon to ?, March 4, 1679, AGI, Santo Domingo, leg. 54–5–19. Searles's alias was John Davis.

20. Verner W. Crane, *The Southern Frontier, 1670–1732* (Durham, 1928), pp. 6–7.

21. Details of Peñalosa's proposals and of his conferences with the English king and advisors around 1670 are in AGS, estado, leg. 994 and 995.

22. Treaty of Madrid, 1670, Davenport and Paullin, *Treaties*, II, 193–196. Herbert I. Priestley in *The Mexican Nation, A History* (New York, 1923), p. 3, states that this treaty made the Savannah River the boundary between Georgia and Spanish Florida. Fisher in *Viceregal Administration*, p. 3, makes the same claim. There is no reason at all to say that the Savannah is the boundary, particularly since Georgia was not founded until over a half century later. Chatelain in *Florida Defenses*, p. 65, says the treaty made the boundary between Carolina and Florida a line running due west from Port Royal Sound. If the boundary could be definitely established, it should be around Charleston, not the Savannah or Port Royal. In fact, a boundary was never definitely established based on this treaty in Carolina or anywhere else.

23. Woodward to Sir John Yeamans, Albymarle Pointe in Chyanhaw, Sept. 10, 1670, William L. Saunders, ed., *The Colonial Records of North Carolina* (Goldsboro, 1886–1890), I, 208–209.

24. Informe de la junta de guerra de Indias en que se da cuenta a S. M. de lo que participa el sargento mayor del presidio de la Fla. sobre . . . San Jorge, Madrid, Feb. 12, 1674, AGI, Santo Domingo, leg. 58–2–14.

25. Manuel de Condoya to Charles II, St. Augustine, Mar. 21, 1672, AGI, Santo Domingo, leg. 54–5–11. By not publishing the treaty Condoya was merely following the English example. The Jamaica governor supposedly had not officially notified Henry Morgan of this treaty before he sailed from Jamaica to sack Panama.

26. Crown to Viceroy of New Spain, Madrid, June 20, 1671, AGN, reales cédulas, duplicadas, expediente 263; instrucción . . . a Antonio Sebastian Toledo, Oct. 22, 1673, *Instrucciones que los vireyes de Nueva España dejaron a sus sucesores* . . . (Mexico, 1873), I, 167.

27. Maurice Mathews' relation of St. Katherina (Wallie), 1670, Salley, *Narratives of Carolina*, pp. 114–115.

28. West to Lord Ashley, Kyawaw, June 27, 1670, *Col. S. C. Hist. Soc.*, v, 174.

29. *Ibid.*, Charles Town, Sept. 3, 1671, p. 338; Meeting of Grand Council, Charles Town, Jan. 10, 1672, *ibid.*, pp. 373–374.

30. Chatelain, *Florida Defenses*, pp. 63–67.

31. Mark F. Boyd, "The Fortifications at San Marcos de Apalachee," *FHQ*, xv (1936), 3–8; Mark F. Boyd, Hale G. Smith, John W. Griffin, *Here They Once Stood, the Tragic End of the Apalachee Missions* (Gainesville, 1951), pp. 8–10.

32. Hita Salazar to Crown, St. Augustine, Sept. 6, 1677, AGI, Santo Domingo, leg. 58–1–26.

33. Junta de guerra de Indias, Mar. 6, 1674, AGI, Santo Domingo, leg. 58–2–14.

34. Juan Marqués Cabrera to Charles II, Dec. 8, 1680, AGI, Santo Domingo, leg. 54–5–11.

35. William E. Dunn, *Spanish and French Rivalry in the Gulf Region of the United States, 1678–1702; the Beginnings of Texas and Pensacola* (Austin, 1917), p. 71.

36. Herbert E. Bolton, "Spanish Resistance to the Carolina Traders in Western Georgia (1680–1704)," *GHQ*, IX (1925), 124–125.

37. Razón de lo sucedido en las provincias de la Florida . . . , May 20, 1683, AGI, Santo Domingo, leg. 54–5–11.

38. James Colleton to Gov. of Florida (?), in Diego de Quiroga y Losada to Crown, St. Augustine, Apr. 1, 1688, AGI, Santo Domingo, leg. 58–1–26; instructions to Colleton, Mar. 3, 1687, *CSP, Colonial*, XII, 338.

39. J. Leitch Wright, Jr., "Andrew Ranson: Seventeenth Century Pirate?" *FHQ*, XXXIX (1960), 135–144.

40. Charles II to Sir John Nisbet of Dirleton, July 10, 1671, *CSP, Dom., Charles II*, 378.

41. George P. Insh, *Scottish Colonial Schemes, 1620–1686* (Glasgow, 1922), p. 191.

42. Examination of several Yamasee Indians, May 6, 1685, Alexander S. Salley, Jr., ed., *Records in the British Public Record Office Relating to South Carolina, 1663–1710* (Atlanta, 1928), II, 66.

43. Lords Proprietors to Colleton, Mar. 3, 1687, *CSP, Colonial*, XII, 336; ? to Seth Sothell, 1696?, Saunders, *Records of North Carolina*, II, 846–847; M. Eugene Sirmans, *Colonial South Carolina; A Political History, 1663–1763* (Chapel Hill, 1966), p. 44.

44. ? to Seth Sothell, 1696?, Saunders, *Records of North Carolina*, II, 846–847.

45. Torres to John Archdale, Jan. 24, 1696, Archdale Papers, L. C.; Marqués de Mancera to Alexander Stanhope, Madrid, Sept. 4, 1693, PRO, SP 94/73.

46. The best account of this is in Jonathan Dickinson, *God's Protecting Providence, Man's Surest Help and Defence, in Times of Greatest Difficulty* . . . (Philadelphia, 1699) .

47. Details of Anglo-Spanish designs on Saint Domingue are in AGI, patronato, leg. 2–5–1/26, ramo 5, and in La Roncière, *Marine française*, VI, 253–254.

48. Commons House Journal, Nov. 10, 1697, Alexander S. Salley, Jr., ed., *Journals of the Commons House of Assembly of South Carolina for the Two Sessions of 1697* (Columbia, 1913), p. 19.

49. Torres to Crown, St. Augustine, July 8, 1695, AGI, Santo Domingo, leg. 58–1–26.

50. Crane, *Southern Frontier*, p. 133.

51. Junta de guerra de Indias to Crown, Madrid, Aug. 7, 1693, AGI, Santo Domingo, leg. 58–1–22.

52. Memorial of Thomas Laurence, Whitehall, June 25, 1695, *CSP, Colonial*, XIV, 518; auto, St. Augusine, Oct. 23, 1698, AGI, Mexico, leg. 61–6–22, Stetson Col.

53. Coxe to Board of Trade, Nov. 16, 1699, *CSP, Colonial*, XVII, 522; Crane, *Southern Frontier*, pp. 48–59. It was reported in St. Augustine that England and France had made an agreement providing whichever nation first occupied the Gulf would be allowed to retain it: Lawrence C. Ford, *The Triangular Struggle for Spanish Pensacola, 1689–1739* (Washington, 1939), p. 27.

54. Because of increased foreign interest in the Gulf Coast and because of the threat to New Spain posed by foreign occupation, it had been recommended even in 1689 that St. Augustine be abandoned and that the Gulf Coast be fortified in its place. The Pez Memorial, Mexico City, June 2, 1689, Irving A. Leonard, ed., *Spanish Approach to Pensacola, 1689–1693* (Albuquerque, 1939), pp. 86–90.

Chapter 6

1. Antonio de Ubilla to Marqués del Carpio, Palacio, Jan. 9, 1701, AGI, indiferente general, leg. 147–5–14; mémoire contenant les moyens pour réduire . . . les abitans des Indies à l'obéissance du Roy . . . Charles Troisième, Aug. 24, 1705, Add. MSS, 28056, B. M.

2. Edward Randolph to Board of Trade, Bermuda, May 1, 1699, *CSP, Colonial*, XVII, 184.

3. Charles V to José de Zúñiga y Cerda, Madrid, Jan. 11, 1701, Mark F. Boyd, *et al.*, *Here They Once Stood*, pp. 32–33. Traditionally the Spaniards had been reluctant to furnish firearms to the Indians. Now this policy was starting to break down because the English readily furnished arms to their Indian allies.

4. *Journal of S. C. Commons*, Aug. 28, 1701, p. 32; *ibid.*, Aug. 21, 1702, p. 68.

5. Edward Randolph to Board of Trade, Mar. 5, 1701, *CSP, Colonial*, XIX, 105.

6. *Journal of S. C. Commons*, Aug. 28, 1702, p. 86.

7. Michael Cole to William Blathwayt, Carolina, Dec. 22, 1702, *CSP, Colonial*, XXI, 183; Zúñiga to Charles V, St. Augustine, Jan. 6, 1703, AGI, Santo Domingo, leg. 58–1–27. The best account of the attack on St. Augustine is Charles W. Arnade, *The Siege of St. Augustine in 1702* (Gainesville, 1959).

8. Zúñiga to Charles V, Jan. 6, 1703, St. Augustine, Mark F. Boyd, ed. and trans., "The Siege of Saint Augustine by Governor Moore of South Carolina in 1702 as Reported to the King of Spain by Don Joseph de Zúñiga y Cerda, Governor of Florida," *FHQ*, XXVI (1948), 346–347.

9. Moore and Robert Daniel to Council of Carolina, 1702, *CSP, Colonial*, XX, 746.

10. Zúñiga to Charles V, Jan. 6, 1703, Boyd, "Siege of St. Augustine," p. 349.

11. Moore and Daniel to Council of Carolina, 1702, CSP, *Colonial*, XX, f46; Edward McCrady, *The History of South Carolina under the Proprietary Government, 1670–1719* (New York, 1901), p. 381.

12. Zúñiga to Charles V, Jan. 6, 1703, Boyd, "Siege of St. Augustine," p. 349.

13. *Ibid.*, p. 348; proclamation by the Deputy of Apalachee, San Luis, Dec. 20, 1702, Boyd, *et al.*, *Here They Once Stood*, p. 39.

14. "Present State of Affairs in Carolina, by John Ash, 1706," Salley, *Narratives of Carolina*, p. 272; representation from Carolina to Lords Proprietors of Carolina, June 26, 1705, Saunders, *Colonial Records of N. C.*, II, 904.

15. "Statements Made in the Introduction to the Report on General Oglethorpe's Expedition to St. Augustine," Bartholomew R. Carroll, ed., *Historical Collections of South Carolina: Embracing Many Rare and Valuable Pamphlets, and Other Documents, Relating to the History of That State from Its First Discovery to Its Independence, in the Year 1776* (New York, 1836), II, 351.

16. Moore to Lords Proprietors, Jan. 26, 1703/04, extract, in America, British Colonies, VIII, L. C.; Zúñiga to Charles V, Florida, Mar. 30, 1704, AGI, Santo Domingo, leg. 58–1–27.

17. Moore to Governor of Carolina, 1704, Carroll, *Historical Collections*, II, 574–576. In Moore's letter to the Lords Proprietors of Jan. 26, 1703, he says he returned with only one hundred slaves, while Bienville in Mobile contended that Moore killed and made prisoner six or seven thousand Apalachees: John R. Swanton, *The Indians of the Southeastern United States* (Washington, 1946), p. 90. That Moore returned with four thousand slaves is probably the best estimate.

18. Council of War, St. Augustine, July 13, 1704, Boyd, *et al., Here They Once Stood,* p. 57.

19. Junta de guerra de Indias, Madrid, July 14, 1704, AGI, Santo Domingo, leg. 58–2–2; King to Viceroy of New Spain, Madrid, Feb. 10, 1708, AGN, reales cédulas, originales, tomo 33, expediente 114.

20. Zúñiga to King, St. Augustine, Feb. 3, 1704, Boyd, *et al., Here They Once Stood,* p. 48.

21. Duke of Albuquerque to ?, Mexico, Sept. 20, 1706, AGI, Mexico, leg. 61–1–25, Sp. transcripts, L. C.

22. Declaration of Bartolomé Ruíz de Cuenca before the Governor of New Vera Cruz, Jan. 20, 1705, Boyd, *et al., Here They Once Stood,* pp. 71–72; ? to Viceroy of New Vera Cruz, Feb. 2, 1705, *ibid.,* p. 72.

23. An Impartial Narrative of ye late Invasion of Carolina by ye French and ye Spaniards, Aug. 1706, *CSP, Colonial,* XXIII, 248, 253; Francisco de Córcoles y Martínez to Charles V, St. Augustine, Sept. 30, 1706, AGI, Santo Domingo, leg. 58–1–27.

24. Thomas Nairne to ?, Carolina, July 10, 1708, Salley, *Records Relating to South Carolina,* V, 196.

25. Córcoles to Charles V, St. Augustine, Nov. 12, 1707, AGI, Santo Domingo, leg. 58–1–27.

26. Nairne to Lords Proprietors, May 7, 1707, Salley, *Records Relating to South Carolina,* IV, 196; Ford, *Triangular Struggle for Pensacola,* p. 79.

27. King to Viceroy of New Spain, Madrid, Dec. 4, 1709, AGN, reales cédulas, originales, tomo 34, expediente 88; *ibid.,* June 12, 1713, tomo 36, expediente 18.

28. Nairne to ?, July 10, 1708, Salley, *Records Relating to South Carolina,* V, 196.

29. Max Savelle, *The Origins of American Diplomacy: The International History of Angloamerica, 1492–1763* (New York, 1967), p. 156. There is no comprehensive economic study of the South Sea Company's entire history. Of general value is John G. Sperling, *The South Sea Company: an Historical Essay and Bibliographical Finding List* (Boston, 1962).

30. Anglo-Spanish Treaty, Utrecht, July 13, 1713, Davenport and Paullin, *Treaties,* III, 229, 230.

31. Ibid., p. 230.

32. Secretary Stanhope to Lt. Gov. Moody, Whitehall, May 13, 1715, *CSP, Colonial,* XXVIII, 178.

33. The best account of the Yamasee War is in Crane, *Southern Frontier,* pp. 162–186.

34. Consejo de Indias to crown, Madrid, Jan. 8, 1716, AGI, Santo Domingo, leg. 58–1–20.

35. Córcoles to Spotswood, St. Augustine, May 30, 1716, *CSP, Colonial,* XXIX, 292–293.

36. Andrés de Pez to Charles V, Madrid, Jan. 18, 1716, AGI, Santo Domingo, leg. 58–1–24; consejo pleno de Indias, Feb. 12, 1715, AGI, Santo Domingo, leg. 58–1–20.

37. A good account of the three expeditions is in Mark F. Boyd, ed. and trans., "Diego Peña's Expedition to Apalachee and Apalachicola in 1716,' *FHQ,* XXVIII (1949), 1–27, and in his "Documents Describing the Second and Third Expeditions of Lieutenant Diego Peña to Apalachee and Apalachicola in 1717 and 1718," *FHQ,* XXXI (1952), 109–139.

38. George Bubb to Robert Pringle, Madrid, June 3, 1716, PRO, SP 94/85; Thomas Jefferys, *An Account of the First Discovery and Natural History of Florida with a Particular Detail of the Several Expeditions and Descents Made on that Coast* (London, 1763), p. 90.

39. Notes from the Journal of the House of Burgesses, Dec. 16 and Dec. 20, 1720, *WMQ*, 1st ser., XXI (1913), 254.

40. Governor and Council of S. C. to Board of Trade, Charles Town, Nov. 6, 1719, *CSP, Colonial*, XXXI, 259; answers to queries by the Board of Trade, Jan. 12, 1720, *ibid.*, p. 320.

41. C. Gale to (Gov. Johnson?), 1719, *ibid.*, pp. 260–261; Richard Farrill and Waiger Nicholson to Gov. of Bahama Islands, Havana, Feb. 7, 1720, *ibid.*, p. 352.

42. Ford, *Pensacola*, pp. 109–124.

43. Board of Trade to Secretary Craggs, Whitehall, Dec. 4, 1719, *CSP, Colonial*, XXXI, 274.

44. Jerónimo Becker, *España é Inglaterra, sus relaciones políticas desde las paces de Utrecht* (Madrid, 1906), p. 14.

Chapter 7

1. Robert Montgomery, *A Discourse Concerning the Design'd Establishment of a New Colony to the South of Carolina, in the Most Delightful Country of the Universe* (London, 1717), ed. by J. Max Patrick (Atlanta, 1948).

2. Carolina and Nova Scotia, Defense against the French, Aug. 30, 1720, Grant, *et al., Acts of Privy Council*, VI, 123–125; representation upon the state of his majesties plantations on the continent of America to George I, Sept. 8, 1721, B. M., Add. MSS 35907, Br. transcripts, L. C.

3. Henry Folmer, *Franco-Spanish Rivalry in North America, 1524–1763* (Glendale, 1953), p. 261.

4. Carolina and Nova Scotia, Defense against the French, Aug. 30, 1720, Grant, *et al., Acts of Privy Council*, VI, 123–125.

5. Crane, *Southern Frontier*, pp. 235–237.

6. Board of Trade to George I, 1722, *CSP, Colonial*, XXXIII, 193.

7. Francis Nicholson to Francisco Menéndez Marqués, Mar. 9, 1721/2, *CSP, Colonial*, XXXIII, 211–212.

8. Marqués de Casafuerte to Philip V, Mexico, May 14, 1725, AGI, Santo Domingo, leg. 58-1-29.

9. Arthur Middleton to Col. Chicken, Sept. 18, 1725, Newton D. Mereness, ed., *Travels in the American Colonies* (New York, 1916), p. 159.

10. Capt. Edward Massey to Henry Pelham, South Carolina, Apr. 26, 1727, *CSP, Colonial*, XXXV, 265–266.

11. Massey to Kingsmill Eyre, Charleston, Sept. 2, 1727, *ibid.*, p. 347.

12. William Bull to Board of Trade, May 25, 1738, America, British Colonies, Spanish Papers, II, L. C.

13. Middleton to Newcastle, Charleston, June 13, 1728, *CSP, Colonial*, XXXVI, 132.

14. Ibid., pp. 131–135; Robert Hunter to Charles Townshend, Charleston, Nov. 12, 1726, Vernon-Wager MSS, L. C.

15. Dionisio Suárez de la Vega to Philip v, Havana, Aug. 27, 1728, AGI, Santo Domingo, leg. 58–2–16.

16. Consejo de Indias, Nov. 23, 1724, *ibid.*, leg. 58–1–20; Antonio de Benavides to Crown, St. Augustine, June 16, 1725, *ibid.*, leg. 58–1–29.

17. Instructions for Vice Admiral Francis Hosier, St. James, Mar. 28, 1726, Vernon-Wager MSS; details of impounding and restoring South Sea Company property are in AGI, Contaduría, leg. 2–2–10/23 and leg. 2–2–11/24; Treaty of Seville, Nov. 9, 1729, *A Collection of All the Treaties of Peace, Alliance, and Commerce, between Great-Britain and Other Powers, from the Revolution in 1688, to the Present Time* (London, 1772), I, 5–13.

18. George II's charter to Trustees, June 9, 1732, Allen D. Candler, ed., *The Colonial Records of the State of Georgia* (Atlanta, 1904–1916), I, 11–26.

19. Royal Act, Apr. 3, 1735, *ibid.*, 53–54; Oglethorpe to Andrew Stone, Frederica, Nov. 24, 1742, *Collections of the Georgia Historical Society* (Savannah, 1848), III, 126.

20. Charter to Trustees, Candler, *Ga. Col. Records*, I, 25.

21. E. Merton Coulter, *Georgia, A Short History*, 3rd ed. (Chapel Hill, 1960), p. 34.

22. Journal of Trustees, Palace Court, Nov. 30 and Dec. 7, 1732, Candler, *Ga. Col. Records*, I, 88–89.

23. Moral Sánchez to José Patiño, St. Augustine, Oct. 12, 1735, AGI, Santo Domingo, leg. 87–1–1; William Drake to Charles Pinckney, Santee, July 20, 1736, America, British Colonies, Spanish Papers, II, L. C.

24. The Altamaha River has several mouths and it is debatable whether or not Frederica was within the bounds of the Georgia charter. During this period several Spanish-named islands were renamed: San Pedro to Cumberland, Santa María to Amelia, and Ospo to Jekyll.

25. Account of Dr. Burley, Dec. 8, 1736, James H. Easterby, ed., *The Journal of the Commons House of Assembly* (Columbia, 1951–   ), I, 51; depositions of Messrs. Burleigh and Simpson, *ibid.*, 153; Oglethorpe to Trustees, Frederica, Oct. 7, 1738, Candler, *Ga. Col. Records*, XXII, pt. 1, 278.

26. Newcastle to governors of Jamaica and Virginia, Whitehall, Jan., 1735, *CSP, Colonial*, XLI, 373.

27. Oglethorpe to governor of Havana, Georgia, Aug. 30, 1736, AGI, Santo Domingo, leg. 87–1–1.

28. Perceval diary, Apr. 29, 1737, John Perceval, *Manuscripts of the Earl of Egmont, Diary of the First Earl of Egmont* (London, 1920–1923), II, 395; *ibid.*, May 17, 1740, III, 141.

29. Oglethorpe's treaty with Florida, Oct. 26, 1736, John Pinkerton, *A General Collection of the Best and Most Interesting Voyages and Travels in Various Parts of America; Many of Which Are Now First Translated into English* (Philadelphia, 1810–1812), II, 456.

30. Marqués de Torrenueva to Tomás Geraldino, Madrid, Nov. 28, 1737, AGI, Santo Domingo, leg. 87–1–2. For Sánchez's ultimate fate see John T. Lanning, "The Legend that Governor Moral Sánchez was Hanged," *GHQ*, XXXVIII (1954), 349–355.

31. Felipe de Yturrieta to Governor, Florida, Aug. 28, 1736, AGI, Santo Domingo, leg. 58–2–12.

32. ? to Newcastle, London, Apr. 4, 1737, PRO, SP 94/127.

33. Arredondo to ?, 1738?, AGI, Santo Domingo, leg. 87–1–3.

34. Arredondo to the Governor, Havana, Jan. 22, 1737, AGI, Santo Domingo, leg. 87–1–2.

35. Oglethorpe to Arredondo, Savannah, July 29, 1736, AGI, Santo Domingo, leg. 87–1–3.

36. Arredondo to Governor of Cuba, St. Augustine, Aug. 31, 1736, AGI, Santo Domingo, leg. 58–2–12.

37. Leonard Cocke to Digby Dent, Santiago, Cuba, Nov. 3, 1736, Candler, *Ga. Col. Records*, XXI, 263.

38. Deposition of Capt. Joseph Prew, Apr. 16, 1738, America, British Colonies, Spanish Papers, VI, L. C.

39. Cocke to Dent, Nov. 3, 1736, Candler, *Ga. Col. Records*, XXI, 264.

40. José Patiño to Juan Francisco Güemes y Horcasitas, Jan. 22, 1737, AGI, Santo Domingo, leg. 87–1–3.

41. John Savy to Trustees of Georgia, Cádiz, Oct. 22, 1737, PRO, SP 94/128. Apparently Savy's voluntarily returning to London and disclosing the details of the Spanish attack saved him from serious prosecution. Several years later he was serving in the British army in the West Indies. Here again he tried to betray Britain and enter Spanish employ, but he was imprisoned in Jamaica before he could escape from the island.

42. Easterby, *Commons House Journal*, Feb. 5, 1736/37, I, 209; *ibid.*, Feb. 16, 1736/37, p. 249; *ibid.*, Dec. 14, 1737, p. 367.

43. Crown to Viceroy of Mexico, Madrid, Nov. 28, 1737, AGN, reales cédulas, originales, tomo 57, expediente 99; John Perceval, Earl of Egmont, *The Journal of the Earl of Egmont; Abstract of the Trustees Proceedings for Establishing the Colony of Georgia, 1732–1738,* ed. Robert G. McPherson (Athens, 1962), pp. 249 ff.

44. Perceval, *Diary*, June 29, 1737, II, 417; Newcastle to Benjamin Keene, Whitehall, June 23, 1737, PRO, SP 94/129.

45. Newcastle to Lords of Admiralty, Whitehall, Feb. 10, 1731/2, PRO, SP 94/115; Keene to Sebastián de la Quadra, Mar. 17, 1737/8, *ibid.*, 94/132.

46. Newcastle to William Stanhope, Sept. 27, 1725, *ibid.*, 94/96.

47. Convention of the Pardo, Jan. 14, 1739, *Collection of Treaties between Great-Britain and Other Powers*, I, 38–53.

48. Junta, Madrid, May 13, 1738, AGI, indiferente general, leg. 146–3–7.

49. Perceval, *Diary*, Mar. 10, 1738/9, III, 32; *ibid.*, Mar. 12, p. 33; *A Review of All That Hath Pass'd Between the Courts of Great Britain and Spain, Relating to Our Trade and Navigation from the Year 1721, to the Present Convention; With Some Particular Observations Upon It* (London, 1739), pp. 48–49.

50. Some Observations on the Right of the Crown of Great Britain to the North West Continent of America, by Harman Verelst, Apr. 16, 1739, America, British Colonies, Spanish Papers, VI, L. C.

51. Keene to Marqués de Villadarias, Madrid, May 24, 1739, *ibid.*, v; William Stephens to Verelst, Savannah, Aug. 16, 1738, Candler, *Ga. Col. Records*, XXII, pt. 1, 219; relación que hace el yndio ygnacio de los Reyes, St. Augustine, Aug. 30, 1738, AGI, Santo Domingo, leg. 86–6–5.

52. Geraldino to Newcastle, London, Mar. 13/24, 1738/9, America, British Colonies, Spanish Papers, L. C.

53. The Gentleman's Magazine (London, 1739), IX, 215; Amos A. Ettinger, *James Edward Oglethorpe, Imperial Idealist* (Oxford, 1936), p. 231.

54. Oglethorpe's treaty with Lower Creek Nation, Coweta Town, Aug. 21, 1739, Pinkerton, *Voyages,* II, 463–464.

Chapter 8

1. Much has been written about Jenkins debating if he were a legitimate trader, if the Spaniard who captured him were a duly authorized *guarda costa* commander, if the ear Jenkins displayed to the Commons were not someone else's while his own was still safely tucked away under his wig, or if Jenkins, in fact, ever made a voyage to the West Indies. I am of the opinion that Jenkins was a contrabandist caught by a *guarda costa* crew who more properly should be termed pirates.

2. Deposition of Robert Jenkins, in Newcastle to Greene, June 18, 1731, PRO SP 94/101.

3. Basil Williams, *The Whig Supremacy, 1714–1760* (Oxford, 1939), p. 198.

4. Crown to Edward Vernon, July 16, 1739, Vernon-Wager MSS, L. C.

5. Edward Vernon to Commodore Brown and Captains, *Burford* at Sea, Nov. 7, 1739, B. McL. Ranft, ed., *The Vernon Papers* (London, 1958), pp. 32–34; Vernon's draft reply to Governor's articles of capitulation, Nov. 22, 1739, *ibid.*, pp. 36–37; Dionisio Martínez de la Vega to Crown, Panama, Feb. 12, 1740, Vernon-Wager MSS, L. C.

6. William Stephens' journal, Savannah, Sept. 8, 1739, Candler, *Ga. Col. Records,* IV, 407.

7. Oglethorpe to Trustees, Oct. 5, 1739, *ibid.,* XXII, pt. 2, 217–218.

8. Ibid., Oct. 11, 1739, p. 242.

9. Herbert W. Richmond, *The Navy in the War of 1739–48* (Cambridge, 1920), I, 31, 50.

10. Stephens' journal, Nov. 22, 1739, Candler, *Ga. Col. Records,* IV, 457; *Gentleman's Magazine,* X (1740), 129.

11. Benjamin Martyn, "An Account Showing the Progress of the Colony of Georgia in America from its First Settlement," *Collections of the Georgia Historical Society,* II (1842), 304.

12. Stephens' journal, Jan. 28, 1740, Candler, *Ga. Col. Records,* IV, 500–501.

13. Oglethorpe's estimate of forces, Feb. 4, 1739/40, John T. Lanning, ed., *The St. Augustine Expedition of 1740, a Report to the South Carolina General Assembly, Reprinted from the Colonial Records of South Carolina* (Columbia, 1954), pp. 95–97.

14. Oglethorpe's plan for a sudden attack on St. Augustine, Mar. 29, 1740, *ibid.*, p. 107. Apparently most of the four-hundred-man regiment was raised in North Carolina (Saunders, *Records of North Carolina,* IV, x).

15. Manuel de Montiano to Güemes, Florida, Mar. 25, 1740, in *Letters of Montiano, Siege of St. Augustine,* ed. and trans. C. DeWitt Willcox, *Collections of the Georgia Historical Society,* VII, pt. 1, 48.

16. Ibid.

17. Oglethorpe to Lt. Gov. Bull, Camp in Florida, July 19, 1740, Lanning, *St. Augustine Expedition,* pp. 169–170.

18. Deposition of Capt. William Palmer, South Carolina, Feb. 19, 1740/41, *ibid.*, pp. 122–125.

19. Vincent Pearse to Alexander Vanderdussen, *Flamborough* off the bar of St. Augustine, July 2, 1740, *ibid.*, pp. 55–56.

20. D. Douglass, William Stirling, and Thomas Baillie to Trustees, Savannah, Aug. 10, 1740, *Collections of the Georgia Historical Society*, II (1842), 246–247.

21. William Lea to Wager, London, Mar. 3, 1740, Vernon-Wager MSS, L. C.

22. Consejo de Indias, Madrid, Sept. 1, 1740, AGI, Panama, leg. 107–69–4/38; Wager to Vernon, Admiralty Off., June 10, 1740, Ranft, *Vernon Papers*, p. 109.

23. Vernon to Wager, Portobello Harbor, Apr. 5, 1740, Ranft, *Vernon Papers*, pp. 82–83; articles of capitulation . . . on surrender of Castle St. Lorenzo, Mar. 24, 1740, Vernon-Wager MSS, L. C.

24. Wager to Vernon, Admiralty Off., June 10, 1740, Ranft, *Vernon Papers*, p. 110; *ibid.*, Oct. 11, 1740, p. 137.

25. George Anson, *A Voyage Round the World in the Years MDCCXL, I, II, III, IV . . .* , ed. John Masefield (London, 1911) , pp. 78 ff; S. W. C. Pack, *Admiral Lord Anson; the Story of Anson's Voyage and Naval Events of His Day* (London, 1960).

26. Wager to Vernon, Admiralty Off., Aug. 6, 1740, Ranft, *Vernon Papers*, p. 118.

27. Accounts of the attacks on Cartagena and Santiago with numerous supporting documents are in Ranft's *Vernon Papers*.

28. Wager to Vernon, Parson's Green, Aug. 4, 1742, Ranft, *Vernon Papers*, p. 256.

29. ? to Güemes, Madrid, Oct. 31, 1741, *The Spanish Official Account of the Attack on the Colony of Georgia in America, and of its Defeat on St. Simons Island by General James Oglethorpe*, ed. and trans. C. DeWitt Willcox, *Collections of the Georgia Historical Society*, VII, pt. 3, 21–22.

30. Güemes to Montiano, May 14 and June 2, 1742, *ibid.*, pp. 28–33.

31. *Ibid.*, June 2, 1742, p. 34.

32. Antonio de Arredondo's journal, June 23, 1742, Willcox, *Spanish Official Account*, p. 64.

33. Deposition of Samuel Cloake, Frederica, Aug. 3, 1742, *Gentleman's Magazine*, XII (1742), 661.

34. Oglethorpe to Commander of H. M. Ships at Sea, Frederica, July 14, 1742, *Collections of the Georgia Historical Society*, III (1873), 140. The Spanish naval commanders had a difficult problem. To attack Georgia and Carolina it was necessary to use shallow-draft vessels and minor warships, because most of the coastal harbors would accommodate nothing larger than a twenty-gun vessel. Yet what would happen should the convoy be caught at sea or blockaded in port by larger enemy warships? Charles Wager's observation, Apr. 20, 1737, Vernon-Wager MSS, L. C.

35. Oglethorpe's report after engagement, Frederica?, July 30, 1742, Walter G. Cooper, *The Story of Georgia* (New York, 1938), pp. 243–249.

36. Orders to the commanding officer of the fleet, Willcox, *Spanish Official Account*, p. 46.

37. Oglethorpe's report, Cooper, *Story of Georgia*, pp. 243–249.

38. Oglethorpe to Commander of H. M. Ships, *Collections of the Georgia Historical Society*, III (1873), p. 140; *S. C. Gazette*, July 19, 1742; Montiano to

Fernando Triviño, St. Augustine, Aug. 3, 1742, AGI, Santo Domingo, leg. 87–1–3.

39. Montiano to Philip v, St. Augustine, Aug. 3, 1742, in Willcox, *Spanish Official Account*, p. 96.

40. Extract of a letter from Newport, R. I., Oct. 1, 1742, *Gentleman's Magazine*, XII (1742), 694.

41. Stephens to Verelst, Savannah, Aug. 13, 1742, Candler, *Ga. Col. Records*, XXIII, 284.

42. Thomas Causton to Verelst, Oxted, Ga., Nov. 16, 1742, *ibid.*, p. 428; William Stephens, *The Journal of William Stephens, 1741–1743*, ed. E. Merton Coulter (Athens, 1958–1959), I, 106 ff.

43. S. C. Gazette, Oct. 11, 1742.

44. Montiano to Philip v (?), St. Augustine, Sept. 15, 1742, AGI, Santo Domingo, leg. 87–1–3.

45. Oglethorpe to Lt. Gov. Clarke, Frederica, Apr. 22, 1743, Edmund B. O'Callaghan and Berthold Fernow, eds., *Documents Relative to the Colonial History of the State of New York* (Albany, 1856–1887), VI, 242.

46. Carlos A. Villanueva, *Napoleón y la independencia de América* (Paris, 1912), pp. 19–20.

47. Secret treaty of alliance between France and Spain concluded at Fontainebleau, Oct. 25, 1743, Davenport and Paullin, *Treaties*, IV, 66; Savelle, *Origins of American Diplomacy*, pp. 376–377.

48. Council of War convened by Güemes, Havana, May 10, 1742, AGI, Santo Domingo, leg. 87–1–3.

49. Montiano to Marqués de la Ensenada, St. Augustine, Feb. 8, 1744, AGI, Santo Domingo, leg. 86–6–5.

50. Message from Gov. James Glen to Commons House, June 26, 1744, Easterby, *Commons House Journal*, v, 208.

51. Montiano to crown, St. Augustine, Apr. 15, 1746, AGI, Santo Domingo, leg. 58–1–35, Stetson Col.; Montiano to Triviño, Sept. 25, 1746, *ibid.*, leg. 87–1–1.

52. Martín de Aroztegui to ?, Havana, Aug. 4, 1744, AGI, Santo Domingo, leg. 55–6–35.

53. León to Montiano, Apalachee, May 21, 1745, Lucy L. Wenhold, ed. and trans., "The Trials of Captain Don Isidoro de León," *FHQ*, XXXV (1957), 249 ff; Montiano to Ferdinand VI, St. Augustine, Aug. 3, 1747, AGI, Santo Domingo, leg. 58–1–32.

54. Project for an attempt upon St. Augustine, July 8, 1746, PRO, CO 5, Br. transcripts, L. C.; Montiano to Triviño, Florida, Jan. 19, 1747, AGI, Santo Domingo, leg. 58–1–32.

55. Stephens' journal, Dec. 10, 1739, Candler, *Ga. Col. Records*, IV, 467; Alexander Heron to Verelst, Charles Town, Jan. 2, 1747, *ibid.*, XXV, 251.

56. Oglethorpe to Trustees, Frederica, Mar. 3, 1741/2, *Collections of the Georgia Historical Society*, III, pt. 2 (1873), 119–120.

57. Montiano to Philip v, St. Augustine, June 26, 1745, AGI, Santo Domingo, leg. 58–1–32.

58. Howard M. Chapin, *Rhode Island Privateers in King George's War, 1739–1748* (Providence, 1926), pp. 152–153.

59. John T. Lanning, *The Diplomatic History of Georgia, A Study in the Epoch of Jenkins' Ear* (Chapel Hill, 1936), p. 188; Stephens' journal, Aug. 21, 1741, Candler, *Ga. Col. Records*, IV (supplement), p. 224.

60. Saunders, *Records of North Carolina,* XXII, iii; Gov. Johnston to Board of Trade, Edenton. Apr. 4, 1749, *ibid.,* IV, 922.

61. Treaty of Aix-la-Chapelle, Oct. 18, 1748, *Collection of Treaties between Great Britain and Other Powers,* II, 68–106.

Chapter 9

1. A helpful article in understanding the inter-war period is Jean O. McLachlan, "The Seven Years' Peace, and the West Indian Policy of Carvajal and Wall," *EHR,* LIII (1938), 457–477.

2. J. Potter to Martyn, Whitehall, Feb. 6, 1749, Candler, *Ga. Col. Records,* XXV, 353; Francis Harris and James Habersham to Martyn, Savannah, July 8, 1749, *ibid.,* p. 397.

3. Alexander Heron to Martyn, Savannah, July 7, 1749, *ibid.,* p. 396.

4. Treaty of Madrid, Oct. 5, 1750, *Collection of Treaties between Great-Britain and Other Powers,* II, 107–112.

5. Lucas de Palazio to Gov. and Capt. Gen. of Havana, St. Augustine, Apr. 20, 1753, Brooks Col., L. C.

6. Alonso Fernández de Heredia to Fray Julián de Arriaga, Irene A. Wright, ed. and trans., "Dispatches of Spanish Officials Bearing on the Free Negro Settlement of Gracia Real de Santa Teresa de Mose, Florida," *Journal of Negro History,* IX (1924), 50.

7. William Spencer to Daniel Demetre, Savannah, Nov. 13, 1753, Candler, *Ga. Col. Records,* VI, 417; proceedings of the President and Assistants, Aug. 29, 1754, *ibid.,* p. 451.

8. Palazio to Gov. and Capt. Gen. of Havana, St. Augustine, Apr. 20, 1753, Brooks Col., L. C.

9. Declaration of Jesse Fish, Fla., Apr. 5, 1754, AGN, historia, tomo 436, núm. 754, Mexican transcripts, L. C.

10. Fulgencio García de Solís to Marqués de la Ensenada, St. Augustine, Aug. 25, 1752, AGI, Santo Domingo, leg. 86–5–21; extracto de lo ocurrido . . . , Florida, 1753, AGI, Santo Domingo, leg. 58–1–33.

11. Proceedings of the Council of Maryland, Sept. 13, 1750, William H. Browne, Clayton C. Hall, Bernard C. Steiner, eds., *Archives of Maryland* (Baltimore, 1883–), XXVIII, 481; sheriff of Accomac's account of Spanish wreck, Dec. 27, 1751, William P. Palmer, Sherwin McRae, Raleigh E. Colston, *et al.,* eds., *Calendar of Virginia State Papers and Other Manuscripts* . . . (Richmond, 1875–1893), I, 245.

12. Gilbert Fleming to Board of Trade, St. Christopher Island, Dec. 22, 1750, Great Britain, Board of Trade, *Journal of the Commissioners for Trade and Plantations . . . Preserved in the Public Record Office . . .* (London, 1920–1938), IX, 168.

13. Keene to Holderness, Madrid, Aug. 27, 1755, PRO, SP 94/150.

14. Circular to governors in North America, Whitehall, May 20, 1757, Saunders, *Records of North Carolina,* V, 757.

15. Pitt to William Lyttelton and Henry Ellis, Whitehall, June 10, 1758,

William Pitt, *Correspondence of William Pitt when Secretary of State with Colonial Governors and Military and Naval Commissioners in America,* ed. Gertrude S. Kimball (New York, 1906) , I, 270.

16. Proceeding of the Council of Maryland, Feb. 21, 1757, Browne, *Archives of Md.,* XXXI, 191; Grant, *et al., Acts of Privy Council,* IV, Aug. 9, 1761, p. 357; Joyce E. Harman, *Trade and Privateering in Spanish Florida, 1732–1763* (St. Augustine, 1969), pp. 51–63.

17. Journal of Council, Savannah, July 25, 1760, Candler, *Ga. Col. Records,* VIII, 347.

18. *S. C. Gazette,* Oct. 13, 1757.

19. Pitt to Keene, Aug. 23, 1757, Richard Lodge, "Sir Benjamin Keene, K. B.: a Study in Anglo-Spanish Relations in the Earlier Part of the Eighteenth Century," *Transactions of the Royal Historical Society,* 4th ser., XV (1932), 40; Henry Fox to Keene, Whitehall, Feb. 16, 1756, PRO, SP 94/151.

20. Temple and Pitt to ?, Sept. 18, 1761, B. M., Add. MSS, 35870, f306, Br. transcripts, L. C.; extract of Earl of Bristol's dispatches, Jan. 1759-Apr. 1761, Chatham Papers, XCIII, B. M.

21. Pitt to Earl of Bristol, Whitehall, Sept. 26, 1760, PRO, SP 94/162.

22. Marquis d'Ossun to Duc de Choiseul, Nov. 6, 1759, Allan Christelow, "Economic Background of the Anglo-Spanish War of 1762," *Journal of Modern History,* XVIII (1946), 25.

23. Bristol to Egremont, Escorial, Nov. 2, 1761, PRO, SP 94/164.

24. Jeffery Amherst to James Wright, New York, Apr. 11, 1762, PRO, WO 34/34.

25. Gov. of Nova Scotia to Board of Trade, July 1, 1762, *Jour. of Board of Trade,* XI, 305.

26. *S. C. Gazette,* July 31, 1762.

27. Amherst to Wright, New York, Apr. 9, 1762, PRO, WO 34/34; Journal of Council, Savannah, May 27, 1762, Candler, *Ga. Col. Records,* VIII, 689–690.

28. *Ibid.,* Jan. 12, 1763, IX, 17.

29. *S. C. Gazette,* May 27, 1762.

30. Treaty of Paris, Feb. 10, 1763, *Collections of Treaties between Great-Britain and Other Powers,* II, 272–296; Savelle, *Origins of American Diplomacy,* pp. 497–510.

31. Treaty of Paris, Feb. 10, 1763, *Treaties,* II, 282–283.

32. Instrucción . . . en la evacuación, 1763, AGI, Santo Domingo, leg. 86–7–11.

33. Duvon C. Corbitt, "Spanish Relief Policy and the East Florida Refuges of 1763," *FHQ,* XXVII (1948), 68.

34. Wilbur H. Siebert, "The Departure of the Spaniard and Other Groups from East Florida, 1763–1764," *FHQ,* XIX (1940), 145–149; Robert L. Gold, *Borderland Empires in Transition: The Triple-Nation Transfer of Florida* (Carbondale, 1969), p. 76.

35. William H. Siebert, "How the Spaniards Evacuated Pensacola in 1763," *FHQ,* XI (1932), 54; Robert L. Gold, *Borderland Empires,* pp. 73–101.

36. Journal of Council, Savannah, Sept. 2, 1763, Candler, *Ga. Col. Records,* IX, 86.

37. John Mitchell, *The Present State of Great Britain and North America, with Regard to Agriculture, Population, Trade, and Manufactures, Impartially Considered* (London, 1767), p. 188.

38. During peace negotiations some British statesmen valued the single captured French West Indian sugar island of Guadeloupe more highly than the entire province of Canada.

Chapter 10

1. Vera L. Brown, "The Spanish Court and its Diplomatic Outlook After the Treaty of Paris, 1763," *Smith College Studies in History*, xv, nos. 1–2 (October 1929; January 1930), 1–38.

2. Details of the Spanish occupation of Louisiana are in Charles E. A. Gayarré, *History of Louisiana* (New York, 1854–66), ii and iii, and in Vicente R. Casado, *Primeros años de dominación española en la Luisiana* (Madrid, 1942).

3. Ibid.

4. William Johnson to Cadwallader Colden, Johnson Hall, Jan. 22, 1765, Clarence W. Alvord and Clarence E. Carter, eds., *The Critical Period, 1763–1765* (Springfield, 1915), p. 417.

5. S. C. *Gazette*, Feb. 23, 1769; Príncipe de Masserano to Marqués de Grimaldi, London, Dec. 30, 1766, AGS, estado, leg. 2352. When Britain captured Manila in the past war, the Philippine governor purchased the exemption of private property from plunder by a down payment of two million dollars and the promise of his home government to pay two million more. The authorities at Madrid said this agreement had been extracted by the threat of force and on this or some other pretext refused to pay the additional two million.

6. Treaty of Paris, Feb. 10, 1763, Davenport and Paullin, *Treaties*, iv, 94.

7. John Campbell to Montforte Browne, Pensacola, Oct. 9, 1769, PRO, SP 94/183.

8. Alexandro O'Reilly to Arriaga, New Orleans, Oct. 17, 1769, Lawrence Kinnaird, ed. and trans., *Spain in the Mississippi Valley, 1765–94, Translations of Materials from the Spanish Archives in the Bancroft Library* (Washington, 1945), i, 104–105.

9. John R. Alden, *John Stuart and the Southern Colonial Frontier, A Study of Indian Relations, War, Trade, and Land Problems in the Southern Wilderness, 1754–1775* (Ann Arbor, 1944), pp. 329 ff.

10. Antonio de Ulloa to Grimaldi, New Orleans, Aug. 4, 1768, Kinnaird, *Spain in Miss. Valley*, i, 57–58.

11. Report of the various tribes . . . by Sainte Ange, St. Louis, May 2, 1769, Louis Houck, ed. and trans., *The Spanish Regime in Missouri* (Chicago, 1909), i, 44.

12. Pedro Piernas to Unzaga, St. Louis, Apr. 12, 1773, Kinnaird, *Spain in Miss. Valley*, i, 215–217.

13. John Thomas to George Williamson, Point Iberville, June 16, 1765, Hist. MSS Com., *The Manuscripts of His Grace the Duke of Rutland . . . Preserved at Belvoir Castle* (London, 1888–1905), iv, 233.

14. Juan Joseph Elegio de la Puente to Conde de Ricla, Havana, Sept. 12, 1764, AHN, estado, leg. 3884 bis, expediente 5, núm. 3, Sp. transcripts, L. C.

15. Pierce A. Sinnott to John Stuart, St. Marks, Mar. 2, 1768, *FHQ*, xxi (1942), 137.

16. Thomas Gage to Earl of Hillsborough, New York, July 7, 1770, Clarence E. Carter, ed., *The Correspondence of General Thomas Gage with the Secretaries of State, 1763–1775* (New Haven, 1931), I, 262.

17. Felix de Ferraz, *et al.* to Arriaga, Veracruz, Nov. 26, 1764, AGI, Mexico, leg. 90–2–19, Sp. transcripts, L. C.; Pedro Joseph de Urrutia to Arriaga, Portobello, May 8, 1763, AGI, Panama, leg. 109–2–2; Cecil Johnson, *British West Florida, 1763–1783* (New Haven, 1943), pp. 43, 63–64.

18. Arriaga to Francisco de Croix, San Ildefonso, July 31, 1766, AGN, reales cédulas, originales, tomo 89, expediente 147; Athanase de Mézières to Baron de Ripperda, San Antonio, July 4, 1772, Herbert E. Bolton, ed., *Athanase de Mézières and the Louisiana-Texas Frontier, 1768–1780* (Cleveland, 1914), I, 302–303.

19. Luis de Unzaga y Amezaga to Grimaldi, New Orleans, June 8, 1770, Kinnaird, *Spain in Miss. Valley,* I, 170.

20. Gage to Hillsborough, New York, Apr. 2, 1771, Carter, *Gage Cor.,* I, 294–295.

21. O'Reilly to Grimaldi, Madrid, Sept. 30, 1770, Kinnaird, *Spain in Miss. Valley,* I, 184–185.

22. Arriaga to Unzaga, Aranjuez, June 20, 1771, *ibid.,* pp. 193–194.

23. ? to Grimaldi, Havana, Dec. 10, 1770, AGI, indiferente general, leg. 146–4–2.

24. Arriaga to Unzaga, El Pardo, Mar. 8, 1774, Kinnaird, *Spain in Miss. Valley,* I, 222.

25. For the year 1774 there are many documents relating to the dispute over ownership of Crab Island, PRO, SP 94/195.

26. H. S. Conway to Rochford, St. James, Jan. 3, 1766, *ibid.,* SP 94/173.

Chapter 11

1. An excellent account of the policies of France, Spain, and Britain is in Samuel F. Bemis, *The Diplomacy of the American Revolution,* 4th ed. (Bloomington, 1961); of particular value in regard to Spanish policies is Juan F. Yela Utrilla, *España ante la independencia de los Estados Unidos* (Lérida, 1925).

2. Viscount Weymouth to Baron Grantham, St. James, Nov. 2, 1777, PRO, SP 94/204.

3. Bemis, *Diplomacy of the American Revolution,* p. 93.

4. There are numerous British complaints in 1775, both before and after the outbreak of hostilities, that Spanish ships were trading with the Americans, PRO, SP 94/199.

5. Grantham to Rochford, Madrid, Feb. 20, 1775, PRO, SP 94/197.

6. José de Gálvez to Viceroy of New Spain, San Ildefonso, Sept. 20, 1776, AGN, reales cédulas, originales, tomo 108.

7. Weymouth to Grantham, St. James, Oct. 27, 1778, PRO, SP 94/206; Robert White to George Germain, Pisa Bath, Nov. 15, 1776, Chatham Papers, XCIII.

8. José de Gálvez to Governor of Cuba, Feb. 28, 1776, AGI, Cuba, leg. 1227.

9. Correspondencia con Luciano de Herrera, Oct. 6, 1776, *ibid.;* Katherine

S. Lawson, "Luciano de Herrera, Spanish Spy in British St. Augustine," *FHQ*, XXIII (1945), 170–176.

10. José de Gálvez to Gov. of Havana, San Ildefonso, July 26, 1776, AGI, Cuba, leg. 1227.

11. Bemis, *Diplomacy of American Revolution*, pp. 88–89.

12. Unzaga to José de Gálvez, New Orleans, June 19, 1776, Kinnaird, *Spain in Miss. Valley*, I, 233.

13. Bernardo de Gálvez to Fernando de Leyba, New Orleans, Mar. 9, 1778, *ibid.*, p. 259.

14. Diego José Navarro to José de Gálvez, Havana, Jan. 15, 1778, AHN, estado, leg. 3884, expediente 1/5, Sp. transcripts, L. C.

15. Peter Chester to Germain, Pensacola, June 11, 1777, PRO, SP 94/204.

16. Royal instructions, Dec. 24, 1776, James A. Robertson, ed. and trans., "Spanish Correspondence concerning the American Revolution," *HAHR*, I (1918), 304–305.

17. Masserano to Grimaldi, London, Jan. 12, 1776, AGS, estado, leg. 2362; Francisco Louis Carolinaux to Dalling, Feb. 26, 1780, PRO, CO 137/77.

18. Rafael Altamira y Crevea, *Historia de España y de la civilización española* (Barcelona, 1900–1930), IV, 119.

19. José de Gálvez to Viceroy of New Spain, El Pardo, Mar. 23, 1776, AGN, reales cédulas, originales, tomo 107, expediente 108.

20. Masserano to Grimaldi, London, June 14, 1776, AGS, estado, leg. 2362.

21. José de Gálvez to Viceroy of New Spain, San Lorenzo, Oct. 18, 1776, AGN, reales cédulas, originales, tomo 109, expediente 33.

22. A detailed account of Cook's voyage is in James Cook, *A Voyage to the Pacific Ocean; Undertaken by the Command of His Majesty, for Making Discoveries in the Northern Hemisphere* . . . (Philadelphia, 1818).

23. Real cédula, Madrid, July 8, 1779, AGN, bandos, tomo 11, núm. 19.

24. Franco-Spanish Treaty, Aranjuez, Apr. 12, 1779, Alejandro del Cantillo, ed., *Tratados, convenios, y declaraciones de paz y de comercio que han hecho con las potencias estranjeras los monarcas españoles de la casa de borbon desde el año de 1700 hasta el dia* (Madrid, 1843), pp. 552–554.

25. George Johnstone to Germain, June 19, 1779, Hist. MSS Com., *Report on Manuscripts in Various Collections* (London, 1901–14), VI, 159.

26. Juan Joseph Elegio de la Puente to ?, Havana, May 4, 1778, AHN, estado, leg. 3884 bis, expediente 5/4, Sp. transcripts, L. C.

27. José de Gálvez to Navarro, San Ildefonso, Aug. 29, 1779, Kinnaird, *Spain in Miss. Valley*, I, 355–357.

28. John W. Caughey, *Bernardo de Gálvez in Louisiana, 1776–1783* (Berkeley, 1934), p. 149 ff.; Albert W. Haarmann, "The Spanish Conquest of British West Florida, 1779–1781," *FHQ*, XXXI (1960), 107–114.

29. Caughey, *Gálvez*, 171 ff.; Haarmann, "Spanish Conquest of West Florida," pp. 115–120.

30. Juan de Miralles to Congress, Nov. 24, 1779, Francis Wharton, ed., *The Revolutionary Diplomatic Correspondence of the United States* (Washington, 1889), III, 413; Samuel Huntington to Chevalier de la Luzerne, in Congress, Dec. 16, 1779, *ibid.*, p. 429.

31. Diario de las operaciones de la expedición contra Panzacola, Bernardo de Gálvez, May 12, 1781, AGS, guerra, leg. 6913, expediente 3, Sp. transcripts, L. C.;

see also N. Orwin Rush, *Spain's Final Triumph over Great Britain in the Gulf of Mexico; The Battle of Pensacola, March 9 to May 8, 1781* (Tallahassee, 1966).

32. Leyba to Bernardo de Gálvez, St. Louis, June 8, 1780, Abraham P. Nasatir, "St. Louis during the British Attack of 1780," *New Spain and the Anglo-American West* (Lancaster, 1932), I, 245–247.

33. Ibid., June 20, 1780; Francisco Cruzat to Bernardo de Gálvez, St. Louis, Nov. 12, 1780, Kinnaird, *Spain in Miss. Valley*, I, 395–396.

34. Cruzat to Estevan Miró, Aug. 6, 1781, *ibid.*, 431–434; Spanish act of possession for the valleys of the St. Joseph and Illinois rivers, St. Joseph, Feb. 12, 1781, *ibid.*, p. 418.

35. Bernardo de Gálvez to ?, Guarico, Aug. 5, 1782, Houck, *Spanish Regime in Missouri*, I, 211; Caughey, *Gálvez*, p. 228 ff.

36. Jacobo Debreuil to Miró, May 5, 1783, Fuerte Carlos Tecerco de Arkanzas, in José de Espeleta to Bernardo de Gálvez, Aug. 20, 1783, AGI, Cuba, leg. 2360.

37. Conde de Aranda to Bernardo del Campo, Paris, May 3, 1783, John W. Caughey, ed., *East Florida, 1783–1785, A File of Documents Assembled, and Many of Them Translated by Joseph Byrne Lockey* (Berkeley, 1949), p. 80.

38. Floridablanca to Campo, El Pardo, Mar. 17, 1783, *ibid.*, pp. 65–66.

Chapter 12

1. Valuable for the development of the British empire after 1783 is Vincent T. Harlow, *The Founding of the Second British Empire, 1763–1793* (London, 1952–1964).

2. Extract of a letter from East Florida, Nov. 16, 1783, included in Spanish ambassador? to Floridablanca, London, Mar. 16, 1784, AGS, estado, leg. 2619; the best account of the Florida Loyalists is Wilbur H. Siebert, ed., *Loyalists in East Florida, 1774 to 1785* (De Land, 1929).

3. Thomas Townshend to Richard Oswald, Whitehall, Oct. 26, 1782, Earl of Shelburne Papers, LXX, William L. Clements Library, University of Michigan, Ann Arbor; Patrick Tonyn to Lord Sydney, St. Augustine, June 14, 1784, Caughey, *East Florida Documents*, pp. 289–292; John Cruden to Charles III, St. Mary's, Oct. 28, 1784, *ibid.*, p. 302; Vicente Manuel de Zéspedes to Bernardo de Gálvez, St. Augustine, Feb. 9, 1785, *ibid.*, p. 457.

4. Ibid., July 16, 1784, 224–225. Zéspedes was the governor of only East Florida. The Spaniards after 1783 retained the British division of Florida into two parts, and West Florida already had been conquered during the Revolution.

5. Arthur P. Whitaker, ed. and trans., *Documents Relating to the Commercial Policy of Spain in the Floridas, with Incidental Reference to Louisiana* (De Land, 1931), pp. xxviii–xxix, 225.

6. Zéspedes to José de Gálvez, St. Augustine, Sept. 16, 1785, Caughey, *East Florida Documents*, 725; memorial by Panton, Leslie, and Co. to Spanish Crown, St. Augustine, July 31, 1784, Duvon C. Corbitt, ed., "Papers Relating to the Georgia-Florida Frontier, 1784–1800," *GHQ*, XXI (1937), 80–83.

7. Spanish ambassador? to Floridablanca, London, Aug. 12, 1787, AGS, estado, leg. 2621.

8. Joseph Parker to Arthur St. Clair, New York, Oct. 2, 1787, Clarence W.

Alvord, ed., *Kaskaskia Records, 1778–1790* (Springfield, 1909), p. 411; Capt. Doyle to John Simcoe, July 28, 1793, Ernest A. Cruikshank, ed., *The Correspondence of Lieut. Governor John Graves Simcoe, with Allied Documents relating to His Administration of the Government of Upper Canada* (Toronto, 1923–1931), I, 404.

9. Manuel Perez to Miró, St. Louis, Apr. 5, 1791, Kinnaird, *Spain in Miss. Valley*, II, 411; Zenon Trudeau to Baron de Carondelet, Oct. 20, 1792, *ibid.*, III, 93; Trudeau's report on the English fur trade, May 18, 1793, *ibid.*, pp. 156–160.

10. Lord Dorchester to John Connolly, Quebec, Jan. 15, 1788, PRO, CO 42/60; Dorchester to Lord Sydney, Quebec, June 7, 1789, PRO, CO 42/65; Grenville to Dorchester, Whitehall, Oct. 20, 1789, *ibid.*

11. Phineas Bond to Duke of Leeds, Philadelphia, Nov. 10, 1789, J. Franklin Jameson, ed., "Letters of Phineas Bond, British Consul at Philadelphia, to the Foreign Office of Great Britain, 1790–1794," *Annual Report of the American Historical Association for the Year 1896* (Washington, 1897), I, 649. For further information about British involvement in the Old Southwest after the Revolution see the author's "British Designs on the Old Southwest: Foreign Intrigue on the Florida Frontier, 1783–1803," *FHQ*, XLIV (1966), 265 ff.

12. Observations made by Luis Vidal, London, May 12, 1784, in ? to Floridablanca, San Ildefonso, Aug. 11, 1784, AGS, estado, leg. 2619; proposals made by Don xx and Don xx, London, May 12, 1784, Chatham Papers, CCCLI.

13. Miranda's objectives are ably set forth in William S. Robertson, *Francisco de Miranda and the Revolutionizing of Spanish America, Annual Report of the American Historical Association for the Year 1907* (Washington, 1908), I.

14. Francisco Mendiola made his way from Mexico to New York where he contacted the British consul general who in turn secretly sent him on to London. John Temple to Marquis of Carmarthen, New York, May 7, 1786, PRO, FO 4/4; Torre Lossios, *et al.* to Mendiola, Mexico, Nov. 10, 1785, Chatham Papers, CCCXLV.

15. Representation of William A. Bowles and Creek Indians to George III, London, Jan. 3, 1791, PRO, FO 4/9; Bowles to Miró, frigate *Mississippi*, May 26, 1792, AGS, guerra, leg. 6916, Sp. transcripts, L.C.; William A. Bowles, *Authentic Memoirs of William Augustus Bowles, Esquire, Ambassador from the United Nations of Creeks and Cherokees, to the Court of London* (London, 1791), pp. 109 ff; J. Leitch Wright, Jr., *William Augustus Bowles: Director General of the Creek Nation* (Athens, 1967), pp. 1–35.

16. For an account of McGillivray see John W. Caughey, *McGillivray of the Creeks*, 2nd ed. (Norman, 1959).

17. Zéspedes to Marqués de Sonora, St. Augustine, Mar. 30, 1787, AHN, estado, leg. 3901, apartado 1, núm. 16, Sp. transcripts, L. C.

18. Lord Dunmore to Sir Henry Clinton, Charleston, Feb. 2, 1782, PRO, CO 5/175; Dunmore to Thomas Townshend, London, Aug. 24, 1782, Viscount Sydney Papers, Clements Library; Jack D. L. Holmes, "Robert Ross' Plan for an English Invasion of Louisiana in 1782," *Louisiana History*, v (1964), 161 ff.

19. At the Council Chamber, Whitehall, May 1, 1787, Add. MSS 38390.

20. Declaración de Tomás Miller, Pensacola, Aug. 11, 1788, AGI, Cuba, leg. 1394; Thomas Brown to Zéspedes, 1788?, AHN, estado, leg. 3887, expediente 1, documento 140, Sp. transcripts, L. C.; John Miller to Duke of Portland, May 25, 1801, PRO, CO 23/40.

21. Memorial of William Panton, John Leslie, and Thomas Forbes to William Wyndham Grenville, London, June 19, 1789, PRO, CO 23/29; sobre límites y desavenencias de los indios de las Floridas . . . , AHN, estado, leg. 3887, expediente 1, documento 1, Sp. transcripts, L. C.

22. Bowles to Miró, May 26, 1792, *op. cit.;* Dorchester to Lord Grenville, Quebec, July 26, 1790, PRO, CO 42/68. Dorchester viewed Bowles's project with mixed emotions. Because of a possible war with Spain and the governor's negotiations to win United States's friendship, British support of Bowles's scheme could alienate the United States and disrupt current negotiations. But if there were war with Spain, Bowles could be of value in embarrassing the Spaniards in the Southeast. For the aspirations of Britain and the Six Nations to make the Ohio the boundary see Randolph C. Downes, *Council Fires on the Upper Ohio; A Narrative of Indian Affairs in the Upper Ohio Valley until 1795* (Pittsburgh, 1940), pp. 282–283. Sydney to Dorchester, Whitehall, Apr. 5, 1787, Public Archives of Canada, Governor General Papers, Despatches from Colonial Secretary to Governors, 1, explains Britain's policy at this time toward the Indians in the Old Northwest of the United States.

23. Bowles to Grenville, Adelphi, Jan. 13, 1791, PRO, FO 4/9.

24. Campo to Floridablanca, London, Apr. 15, 1791, AHN, estado, leg. 3889 bis, expediente 10, documento 3, Sp. transcripts, L.C.

25. Robert Leslie to William Panton, Appalachy, Mar. 9, 1792, Corbitt, "Papers Relating to the Georgia-Florida Frontier," *GHQ,* XXII (1938), 184.

26. Campo to Carondelet, Aranjuez, May 29, 1792, AGS, guerra, leg. 6916, Sp. transcripts, L. C.

27. Bowles to Duke of Alcudia, Madrid, July 14, 1793, Add. MSS 37873, B. M.; el consejo de estado, Madrid, Aug. 22, 1793, AHN, estado, leg. 3889 bis, expediente 10, documento 75, Sp. transcripts, L. C.

28. William Wellbank to John Miller, Creek Nation, June 10, 1792, PRO, CO 23/31; John McDonald to Alexander McKee, Lower Cherokees, Dec. 26, 1794, Philip M. Hamer, "The British in Canada and the Southern Indians, 1790–1794," *The East Tennessee Historical Society's Publications,* II (1930), 133–134.

29. Carondelet to Aranda, New Orleans, Aug. 20, 1792, AHN, estado, leg. 3898, apartado 3, carta 11, Sp. transcripts, L. C.

30. Commission granted by Governor Dunmore to Philatoutche Upaiahatche, Bahamas, Feb. 5, 1793, EF, 114J9.

31. Cook, *Voyage to the Pacific Ocean,* I, 353.

32. Cirioco González Carvejal to José de Gálvez, Manila, Feb. 3, 1786, AGI, Guadalajara, leg. 104–5–19, Sp. transcripts, L. C. These ships flew the Portuguese flag either to escape the East India Company's monopoly or to profit from Chinese trading concessions to Portugal. Also of concern to Spain was the possibility that if Britain did not find Botany Bay in Australia a satisfactory region to transport convicts after the loss of the American colonies, then she might try "Nova Albion" on the other side of the Pacific. Diego Gardoqui to Floridablanca, June 25, 1789, Abraham P. Nasatir, ed., *Before Lewis and Clark, Documents Illustrating the History of the Missouri, 1785–1804* (St. Louis, 1952), I, 131.

33. William R. Manning, *The Nootka Sound Controversy. Annual Report of the American Historical Association for the Year 1904* (Washington, 1905), pp. 312 ff.

34. William Eden to Marquis of Carmarthen, Madrid, Feb. 26, 1789, PRO, FO 72/14.

35. Arthur St. Clair to John Jay, Ft. Harmar, Dec. 13, 1788, William H. Smith, ed., *The St. Clair Papers. The Life and Public Services of Arthur St. Clair, Soldier of the Revolutionary War; President of the Continental Congress; and Governor of the North-Western Territory* (Cincinnati, 1882), II, 101–102; observations on the force necessary for the protection of the interior part of Canada

... Nov. 1, 1790, Chatham Papers, CLXXVIII; Dorchester to Connolly, Quebec, Jan. 15, 1788, PRO, CO 42/60.

36. Dorchester to George Beckwith, Quebec, June 27, 1790, PRO, CO 42/68; Thomas Jefferson to James Monroe, New York, July 11, 1790, Thomas Jefferson, *Papers*, ed. Julian P. Boyd (Princeton 1950–   ), XVII, 25.

37. Bond's report of occurrences, Sept. 4–Oct. 7, 1790, PRO, FO 4/8.

38. Francisco de Miranda to Pitt, London, Sept. 8, 1791, Chatham Papers, CCCXLV.

39. Anglo-Spanish Convention, Oct. 28, 1790, Manning, *Nootka Sound Controversy*, pp. 454–456.

40. Floridablanca to Viceroy of Santa Fé and President of Guatemala, Madrid, Dec. 25, 1790, AGN, reales cédulas, originales, tomo 147, expediente 224; Casas to Alcudia, Havana, Feb. 1, 1793, Kinnaird, *Spain in Miss. Valley*, III, 136.

41. Anglo-Spanish Convention, Jan. 11, 1794, Manning, *Nootka Sound Controversy*, p. 470.

42. Conde de Revilla Gigedo to Marqués de Brancifort, June 30, 1794, *Instrucciones de los virreyes*, II, 269; Revilla Gigedo to Alcudia, Feb. 18, 1793, AGN, correspondencia de los virreyes, primera serie, tomo 173, núm. 54.

43. George Vancouver, *A Voyage of Discovery to the North Pacific Ocean and Round the World* ... (London, 1798), III, 326–338.

44. Campo to Viceroy of New Spain, Aranjuez, Mar. 25, 1793, AGN, reales cédulas, originales, tomo 154, expediente 259.

45. ? to Baron St. Helens, Whitehall, Nov. 30, 1793, PRO, FO 72/28.

46. Carondelet to Simcoe, New Orleans, July 22, 1794, Cruikshank, *Simcoe Cor.*, II, 335.

47. Simcoe to Carondelet, Rapids of Miamis, Apr. 11, 1794, PRO, CO 42/100.

48. Charles Stevenson to Simcoe, Orchard St., Aug. 1, 1793, Cruikshank, *Simcoe Cor.*, I, 413.

49. George Washington to Thomas Jefferson, Mount Vernon, Aug. 23, 1792, John C. Fitzpatrick, ed., *The Writings of George Washington from the Original Manuscript Sources, 1745–1799* (Washington, 1931–1944), XXXII, 130.

50. Dorchester to Carondelet, Montreal, Aug. 24, 1794, PRO, CO 42/104; details of the organization of the Missouri Company before Todd stepped in are in Abraham P. Nasatir, "The Formation of the Missouri Company," *Missouri Historical Review*, XXV (1930), pp. 10 ff.

51. Alcudia to Campo, San Ildefonso, Aug. 6, 1794, AGS, estado, leg. 2624; Stevenson to Henry Dundas, July 31, 1793, Cruikshank, *Simcoe Cor.*, I, 413.

52. Grenville to Hammond, Whitehall, Apr. 25, 1792, PRO, FO 115/1.

53. Carondelet to Carlos Howard, New Orleans, Nov. 26, 1795, Houck, *Spanish Regime in Missouri*, II, 128–129; Robert Liston to Robert Prescott, Philadelphia, Nov. 28, 1796, PRO, CO 42/108.

54. Duke of Portland to Simcoe, Whitehall, Oct. 24, 1795, Cruikshank, *Simcoe Cor.*, IV, iii; Hawkesbury's comment on Grenville project, 1794, Bradford Perkins, ed., "Lord Hawkesbury and the Jay-Grenville Negotiations," *MVHR*, XL (1953), 295.

Chapter 13

1. Crown to Miguel Joseph de Azanza, San Lorenzo, Oct. 7, 1796, AGN, reales cédulas, originales, tomo 165, expediente 78.

2. Carondelet to Howard, New Orleans, Nov. 26, 1796, *Collections of the State Historical Society of Wisconsin* (Madison, 1908), XVIII, 449–452.

3. Liston to Prescott, Philadelphia, Nov. 28, 1796, PRO, CO 42/108; Prescott to Portland, Quebec, Oct. 1, 1798, PRO, CO 42/111.

4. Carondelet to Prince of Peace, New Orleans, Jan. 8, 1796, AHN, estado, leg. 3900, apartado 1/65, Sp. transcripts, L. C.

5. Juan Ventura Morales to Gardoqui, Dec. 10, 1796, *ibid.*, leg. 3902, apartado 2/63.

6. Carondelet to Prince of Peace, New Orleans, June 3, 1796, Nasatir, *Before Lewis and Clark*, I, 355; extracts of John Evans' Journal, *ibid.*, II, 496.

7. ? to Earl of Bute, Downing St., June 3, 1796, PRO, FO 72/41. In the 1783 treaty with the United States, an article guaranteed Britain free navigation of the Mississippi River, and this provision was reaffirmed in the Jay Treaty. The United States, also anxious to win free navigation of the Mississippi River, in the past, as in the Jay Treaty, generally supported Britain's demand. Hammond to Grenville, Philadelphia, July 3, 1792, PRO, FO 115/1.

8. Nicholas Romayne to William Pulteney, New York, June 12, 1798, Viscount Melville Papers, Clements Library; William H. Masterson, *William Blount* (Baton Rouge, 1954), pp. 303–307; Thomas P. Abernethy, *The South in the New Nation, 1789–1819* (Baton Rouge, 1961), pp. 169 ff.

9. Ebenezer Jacob to Dundas, Dec. 28, 1797, Melville Papers.

10. Liston to Grenville, Philadelphia, Feb. 15, 1797, PRO, FO 115/5; *ibid.*, Mar. 16, 1797; Prescott to Portland, Feb. 18, 1797, PRO, CO 42/108.

11. Statement of John Chisholm to Rufus King, London, Nov. 29, 1797, Frederick J. Turner, ed., "Documents on the Blount Conspiracy, 1795–1797," *AHR*, X (1905), 596–597.

12. Liston to Grenville, Philadelphia, May 10, 1797, PRO, FO 115/5; Consul-General Létombe to Charles Delacroix, Philadelphia, June 18, 1797, Frederick J. Turner, ed., *Correspondence of the French Ministers to the United States, 1791–1797* (Washington, 1904), p. 1039.

13. Alexander Hamilton to King, New York, Aug. 22, 1798, Charles R. King, ed., *The Life and Correspondence of Rufus King; Comprising His Letters Private and Official, His Public Documents, and His Speeches* (New York, 1894–1900), II, 659; Grenville to Liston, Downing St., June 8, 1798, PRO, FO 115/6; John C. Miller, *Alexander Hamilton, Portrait in Paradox* (New York, 1959), pp. 466 ff.

14. Andrés Álvarez to Viceroy of New Spain, Aranjuez, June 26, 1798, AGN, reales cédulas, originales, tomo 170, expediente 67; Miranda to Castlereagh, London, Jan. 10, 1808, Charles Vane, Marquess of Londonderry, ed., *Memoirs and Correspondence of Viscount Castlereagh* (London, 1848–1853), VII, 406.

15. William Windham to ?, Oct. 5, 1799, Add. MSS 37878, B. M.

16. Malmesbury's notes on conference with French, July 8, 1797, James Harris, 1st Earl of Malmesbury, *Diaries and Correspondence of James Harris, First Earl of Malmesbury . . .* , ed. 3d Earl of Malmesbury (London, 1844), III, 370.

17. Carlos Martínez de Irujo to Carondelet, Philadelphia, Mar. 13, 1797, Houck, *Spanish Regime in Missouri,* II, 125–129.

18. Létombe to Delacroix, Philadelphia, June 10, 1797, Turner, *Correspondence of French Ministers,* p. 1032.

19. Richard K. Murdoch, "Elijah Clarke and Anglo-American Designs on East Florida, 1797–1798," *GHQ,* XXXV (1951), 173 ff.

20. Bowles to Grenville, June 5, 1798, AGI, Cuba, leg. 2371; "General Bowles," *Public Characters of 1801–1802* (London, 1804), pp. 147–148.

21. Irujo to Someruelos, Philadelphia, May 3, 1799, AHN, estado, leg. 3889 bis, expediente 10, documento 119, Sp. transcripts, L. C.

22. Bowles to John Reeves, Portsmouth, Mar. 1, 1799, Add. MSS 37878, B. M.; Windham to ?, Pall Mall, Nov. 3, 1802, Earl of Rosebury, ed., *The Windham Papers; the Life and Correspondence of the Rt. Hon. William Windham, 1750–1810, a Member of Pitt's First Cabinet and the Ministry of "All the Talents," Including Hitherto Unpublished Letters . . .* (London, 1913), II, 201–202; Bowles to ?, Kingston, July 14, 1799, AGI, Cuba, leg. 212B; Elisha P. Douglass, "The Adventurer Bowles," *WMQ,* VI, 3rd ser. (1949), 18–20.

23. Félix Berenguer de Marquina to Junto Superior, Mexico, Sept. 6, 1800, AGN, marina, tomo 143; Marqués de Casa Calvo to Antonio Cornel, New Orleans, Oct. 19, 1800, AGS, guerra, leg. 6929, núm. 6; Pedro Cevallos to ?, London, May 24, 1803, AGS, estado, leg. 2631. Apparently these troops would have been sent to Florida had they not been diverted to Egypt.

24. Irujo to Mariano Luis de Urquijo, Philadelphia, May 19, 1800, AHN, estado, leg. 3897, apartado 3/161, Sp. transcripts, L. C.

25. John Leslie to George Chalmers, Winchester St., May 21, 1800, Add. MSS 22901, B. M.

26. Many of the details are in AGI, Cuba, leg. 183A and leg. 2355. The best published account is in Arthur P. Whitaker, *The Mississippi Question, 1795–1803, A Study in Trade, Politics, and Diplomacy* (New York, 1934), p. 169.

27. Henry Dundas, memorandum for consideration of His Majesties Ministers, Wimbledon, Mar. 31, 1800, Chatham Papers, CCXLIII; Ford S. Stuart to Dundas, Walworth, Feb. 13, 1800, Melville Papers.

28. AGI, Cuba, leg. 183A and leg. 2355; Whitaker, *Mississippi Question,* p. 171.

29. Decree of Vice Admiralty Court of Nassau, Sept. 14, 1802, AGI, Cuba, leg. 2372; T. Halkett to John Sullivan, Government House, Oct. 13, 1802, PRO, CO 23/42.

30. Halkett to Someruelos, New Providence, Sept. 26, 1802, AGI, Cuba, leg. 2355. Since the American Revolution there had been a bitter dispute between the original "Old Settlers" of the Bahamas and the Loyalists or "New Settlers" who came there in large numbers after the war. That Dunmore and Bowles, even though Loyalists, were associated with the "Old Settler" faction and that the new governor was supported by the "New Settlers" was in part responsible for the harsh treatment meted out to Bowles's adherents.

31. Journal of a voyage to the Creek Nation from Pensacola, 1803, AGI, Cuba, leg. 2372; Whitaker, *Mississippi Question,* pp. 173–175.

32. Marquina to Crown, Nov. 26, 1800, AGN, correspondencia de los virreyes, primera serie, tomo 204, expediente 50.

33. Carondelet to Jacques Clamorgan, New Orleans, July 9, 1796, Nasatir, *Before Lewis and Clark,* II, 442–443.

34. Crown to Viceroy of New Spain, San Lorenzo, Dec. 11, 1799, AGN, reales cédulas, originales, tomo 174.

35. Peace treaty between Spain, France, Batavia, and Britain, Amiens, Mar. 27, 1802, Cantillo, *Tratados*, pp. 702–706.

36. Irujo to Cevallos, Philadelphia, Dec. 5, 1805, AHN, estado, leg. 5546, apartado 1, Sp. transcripts, L. C.

37. Ibid., Jan. 28, 1807, leg. 5633, apartado 1/803.

38. The best account of all aspects of this conspiracy is Thomas P. Abernethy, *The Burr Conspiracy* (New York, 1954).

39. Antonio Ballesteros y Beretta, *Historia de España y su influencia en la historia universal* (Barcelona, 1918–1941), VI, 166–175.

40. There was disagreement in British councils as to how an expeditionary force should be employed against Spanish America. Miranda's idea, with which some cabinet members agreed, was that British troops could not forcibly make themselves masters of Spanish America even if they wanted to, and that these troops should be employed merely to aid the Spanish Americans in winning independence. Wellington and other Tories had a genuine dread of Jacobinism, democracy, and everything else associated with the French Revolution and were reluctant to promote revolution anywhere. Wellington recommended that British troops take Veracruz, march to Mexico City, and substitute British for Spanish authority. Arthur Wellesley, Memorandum, Nov. 18, 1806. Arthur Wellesley, First Duke of Wellington, *Supplementary Despatches and Memoranda of Field Marshal Arthur, Duke of Wellington*, ed. Arthur R. Wellington (London, 1858–72), VI, 35–38; *ibid.*, Nov. 20, 1806, 42; *ibid.*, Nov. 20, 45–47; William Walton to William Grenville, Apr. 26, 1806, Hist. MSS Com., *The Manuscripts of J. B. Fortescue, Esq., Preserved at Dropmore* (London, 1892–1927), X, 458–459.

41. Lord Melville to Castlereagh, Dunira, June 8, 1808, Londonderry, *Correspondence of Castlereagh*, VII, 445; on the establishment of naval stations, and survey of the states of America, by General Dumouriez, 1807, *ibid.*, pp. 367–370.

42. Prince of Peace to Viceroy of New Spain, Madrid, Dec. 4, 1806, AGN, historia, tomo 49, núm. 36.

43. William W. Kaufmann, *British Policy and the Independence of Latin America, 1804–1828* (New Haven, 1951), p. 41.

Chapter 14

1. Arthur Wellesley, Memorandum, 1808, Wellington, *Supplementary Despatches*, VI, 80–81.

2. ? to Henry Wellesley, Foreign Office, Mar. 13, 1810, PRO, FO 72/93.

3. Representaciones del consulado . . . , Cádiz, 1810, AGI, indiferente general, leg. 151–6–12; Saavedra to Viceroy of New Spain, Seville, July 10, 1809, AGN, reales cédulas, originales, tomo 201, expediente 149; ? to Governor of Carmen, Mexico, Mar. 25, 1809, AGN, historia, tomo 537.

4. William S. Robertson, *The Life of Miranda* (Chapel Hill, 1929), II, 23.

5. George Prevost to Castlereagh, Halifax, June 17, 1808, PRO, CO 217/83; Isaac J. Cox, "Hispanic-American Phases of the Burr Conspiracy," *HAHR*, XII (1932), 171–172.

6. Rogue Abarca to Lizana, Guadalajara, Apr. 10, 1810, AGN, reales cédulas, duplicadas, tomo 7, expediente 87; Robertson, *Miranda*, II, 18; on the establishment of naval stations, and survey of the states of America by General Dumouriez, 1807, Londonderry, *Correspondence of Castlereagh*, VII, 367 ff.; John Morier to crown, Washington, Dec. 3, 1810, PRO, FO 115/21.

7. Isaac J. Cox, *The West Florida Controversy, 1798–1813; A Study in American Diplomacy* (Baltimore, 1918), pp. 312 ff.

8. Onís to Eusebio Bardaxi y Azara, Philadelphia, Jan. 12, 1811, AHN, estado, leg. 5637/5, Sp. transcripts, L. C.

9. George Canning to Richard Wellesley, Foreign Office, Aug. 12, 1809, PRO, FO 72/75; Richard Wellesley to Augustus Foster, Apr. 10, 1811, Bernard J. Mayo, ed., *Instructions to the British Ministers to the United States, 1791–1812* (Washington, 1941), p. 320.

10. Jos. Hibberson to Richard Wellesley, Liverpool, Jan. 5, 1811, PRO, FO 72/125; Foster to Richard Wellesley, Washington, July 5, 1811, PRO, FO 115/22.

11. Onís to Bardaxi, Philadelphia, Jan. 31, 1811, AHN, estado, leg. 5637, Sp. transcripts, L. C.

12. Special meeting of Council of State, Cádiz, Aug. 6, 1812, *ibid.*, leg. 5556, expediente 1.

13. ? to British ambassador, Cádiz, Aug. 10, 1812, *ibid.*

14. Castlereagh to Henry Wellesley, Foreign Office, Sept. 9, 1812, PRO, FO 72/128.

15. Admiral Cochrane to Earl Bathurst, July 14, 1814, PRO, WO 1/141; Ferdinand S. Stuart to Bathurst, Bloomsbury Sq., Aug. 3, 1814, PRO, CO 42/159.

16. The most recent account of Tecumseh is Glenn Tucker, *Tecumseh, Vision of Glory* (New York, 1956).

17. John S. Bassett, *The Life of Andrew Jackson* (New York, 1916), I, 109 ff.

18. Edward Nicholls to Morier, Durham Lodge, Eltham, Sept. 25, 1815, PRO, WO 1/143.

19. Cochrane to Indian Chiefs, Bermuda, July 1, 1814, PRO, FO 5/139.

20. Nicholls to Bathurst, Durham Lodge, Eltham, Aug. 24, 1814, PRO, FO 5/140; A. Gordon and Nicholls to Governor of Pensacola, Oct. 2, 1814, PRO, FO 72/219.

21. Nicholls to Juan Ruiz de Apodaca, *Seahorse* off Barrancas, Nov. 9, 1814, PRO, FO 72/219.

22. Mark F. Boyd, ed., "Events at Prospect Bluff on the Apalachicola River, 1808–1818, An Introduction to Twelve Letters of Edmund Doyle, Trader," *FHQ*, XVI (1937), 70; Stuart to Bathurst, Aug. 3, 1814, PRO, CO 42/159.

23. Abernethy, *South in the New Nation*, 373 ff.; John K. Mahon, "British Strategy and Southern Indians: War of 1812," *FHQ*, XLIV (1966), 285 ff.

24. Bassett, *Jackson*, I, 135–141.

25. George Salkeld to John Wilson Croker, Liverpool, Jan. 3, 1815, PRO, WO 1/143. After Jackson's capture of Pensacola the Spaniards became more diligent in enforcing Florida's neutrality. At first they justified Nicholls' and Woodbine's intrigues because of Britain's "ancient alliance" with the Creeks. After Pensacola's fall, however, Spain took positive measures to cut off communication between the British and the Indians. Sebastian Kindelan to George Woodbine, St. Augustine, Dec. 30, 1814, Lockey Col., University of Florida Library, Gainesville.

26. The most recent account of the battle of New Orleans is Charles B. Brooks, *The Siege of New Orleans* (Seattle, 1961).

27. E. Cooke to Castlereagh, Foreign Office, Apr. 29, 1814, Londonderry, *Correspondence of Castlereagh*, IX, 528.

28. Pedro Cevallos to Fernan-Nuñez, Madrid, Apr. 21, 1815, AGS, estado, leg. 2675, expediente 692; Abernethy in his *South in the New Nation* supports this position.

29. Stuart to Bathurst, Aug. 3, 1814, PRO, CO 42/159; Wellington to Liverpool, Paris, Nov. 9, 1814, Wellington, *Supplementary Despatches*, IX, 426; Edward Kendall to Duke of York, Beddington, Dec. 1, 1814, PRO, CO 42/159.

30. Wenceslao R. de Villa-Urrutia, *Relaciones entre España é Inglaterra durante la guerra de la independencia, apuntes para la historia diplomática de España de 1808 á 1814* (Madrid, 1911–1914), III, 413.

31. Cevallos to Fernan-Nuñez, Madrid, Dec. 23, 1814, AGS, estado, leg. 8289; Charles Vaughan to Castlereagh, Madrid, Nov. 16, 1815, Charles K. Webster, ed., *Britain and the Independence of Latin America, 1812–1830, Select Documents from the Foreign Office Archives* (London, 1938), II, 344.

Chapter 15

1. Cochrane to Indian Chiefs, Bermuda, July 1, 1814, PRO, FO 5/139.

2. Edward Cooke to Henry Goulburn, Foreign Office, May 20, 1816, PRO, FO 5/118.

3. Acceptance of 9th Article by Creeks, British Fort on Apalachicola River, Apr. 2, 1815, PRO, FO 5/139; J. Leitch Wright, Jr., "A Note on the First Seminole War as Seen by the Indians, Negroes, and Their British Advisers," *Journal of Southern History* (1968), pp. 567–568.

4. Bassett, *Jackson*, I, 233–234.

5. Cochrane to Bathurst, 19 Upper Harley St., Mar. 12, 1816, PRO, WO 1/144; Bathurst to Governor Cameron, June 8, 1816, statement of correspondence which took place in 1816 and 1817 . . . , Lockey Col.

6. Cochrane to Pulteney Malcolm, off Mobile Bay, Feb. 17, 1815, PRO, WO 1/143.

7. Nicholls to Anthony Baker, Amelia Island, June 12, 1815, PRO, FO 5/139.

8. Proposal of the Muscogee Nation for an alliance with Britain, Mar. 10, 1815, *ibid.*; Nicholls to Morier, Durham Lodge, Eltham, Sept. 25, 1815, PRO, WO 1/143.

9. Bathurst to Hillis Hadjo, London, Sept. 21, 1815, PRO, FO 5/140. Hillis Hadjo was better known to the American frontiersman as the Prophet Francis.

10. Bathurst to Cameron, Downing St., Jan. 11, 1817, *ibid.*; William Hamilton to John Croker, Foreign Office, Sept. 14, 1818, *ibid.*

11. In time, however, Hambly became convinced that the Americans were going to acquire Florida. He began courting their friendship and abandoned pretensions that he was a British agent.

12. Boyd, "Events at Prospect Bluff," pp. 74–81.

13. Onís to Cevallos, Washington, Jan. 1, 1816, AHN, estado, leg. 5641/1, Sp. transcripts, L. C.

14. Bassett, *Jackson*, I, 233 ff.

15. Andrew Jackson to Rachel Jackson, St. Marks, Apr. 8, 1818, John S. Bassett, ed., *Correspondence of Andrew Jackson*, (Washington, 1926–1935), II, 357–358; Jackson to William Davenport, Ft. Gadsden, May 4, 1818, *ibid.*, p. 364.

16. Chargé d'affaires to Crown, London, July 15, 1817, AGS, estado, leg. 2675; Joaquín Francisco Campuzano to Castlereagh, Portland Place, Aug. 13, 1817, *ibid.*

17. Castlereagh to Henry Wellesley, Foreign Office, Mar. 27, 1818, PRO, FO 72/209.

18. An account of the United States's policy in relation to Florida is in Samuel F. Bemis, *John Quincy Adams and the Foundations of American Foreign Policy* (New York, 1949), I, 300 ff.

19. Ibid., pp. 327–328.

20. Bassett, *Jackson*, I, 234.

21. Salvador de Madariaga, *Bolivar* (New York, 1952), p. 317; Bathurst to Duke of Manchester, Downing St., Feb. 5, 1818, PRO, Adm. 1/269. Richard G. Lowe, "American Seizure of Amelia Island," *FHQ*, XLV (1966), 18 ff. McGregor was primarily interested in East Florida and temporarily occupied Amelia Island in 1817. However, there was a small piece of West Florida not taken over by the United States between the Perdido and Suwannee rivers, including Pensacola, which McGregor would have liked to have had under his control.

22. Adams-Onís Treaty, Feb. 22, 1819, David Hunter Miller, ed., *Treaties and Other International Acts of the United States of America* (Washington, 1931–   ), III, 3 ff.

23. Apéndice formado . . . a las instrucciones extendidas por . . . Manuel González Salmon, London, July 18, 1820, AGS, estado, leg. 8288.

24. Joseph B. Lockey, "The Florida Intrigues of José Alvarez de Toledo," *FHQ*, XII, (1934), 178.

25. Conferences between Gen. Vives and Castlereagh, London, Feb. 24, 1820, AHN, estado, leg. 5646, Sp. transcripts, L. C.

Bibliography

I. Manuscripts

Archivo General de Indias, Seville
    Audiencia de Guatemala, 1570–1820
    Audiencia de Mexico, 1528–1820
    Audiencia de Panama, 1570–1751
    Audiencia de Santo Domingo, 1539–1820
    Contaduría, 1510–1600
    Contratación, 1507–1779
    Cuba, 1580–1820
    Estado, 1700–1820
    Indiferente general, 1492–1820
    Justicia, 1515–1600
    Patronato, 1523–1620

Archivo General de la Nación, Mexico
    Bandos, vols. 1–32
    Correspondencia de los virreyes, primera serie, vols. 1–275
    Correspondencia de los virreyes, segunda serie, vols. 1–58
    Historia, vols. 1–572
    Marina, vols. 1–162
    Reales cédulas, duplicadas, vols. 1–39
    Reales cédulas, originales, vols. 1–238

Archivo General de Simancas, Simancas
    Estado (England), legs. 806–8325
    Guerra, legs. 2035–2040; 6912–6932

British Museum, London
  Cotton Galba
  Cotton Vespasian
  Harleian Manuscripts
  Stowe Manuscripts
  Additional Manuscripts: 22900–901, 27859, 28056, 32093, 37873–890,
    38235, 38310, 38390

Library of Congress, Washington
  John Archdale Papers
  British transcripts:
    America, British Colonies
    America, British Colonies, Spanish Papers
    Marquis of Bath's Library, Longleat, Coventry Papers
    British Museum, Additional Manuscripts: 35870, 35907
    Public Record Office, Colonial 5 (America and West Indies)
    Public Record Office, War Office 34 (Amherst Papers)
    The Royal Society, Classified Papers
  A. M. Brooks Collection
  Jeannette T. Connor Collection
  G. R. G. Conway Collection
  East Florida Papers
  Woodbury Lowery Collection
  Spanish Transcripts:
    Archivo General de Indias
      Audiencia de Guadalajara
      Audiencia de Mexico
      Audiencia de Santa Fé
      Audiencia de Santo Domingo
      Cuba
      Indiferente general
    Archivo General de Simancas: Estado and Guerra
    Archivo Histórico Nacional: Estado
  Vernon-Wager Manuscripts

Public Archives of Canada, Ottawa
  Governor General Papers: Despatches from the Colonial
    Secretary to Governor, vols. 52–58

Public Record Office, London
  Admiralty 1 (In-letters), vols. 505–511
  Colonial 5 (America and West Indies), vol. 175
  Colonial 23 (Bahamas), vols. 10–46
  Colonial 42 (Canada), vols. 1–166
  Colonial 137 (Jamaica), vols. 1–160
  Colonial 217 (Nova Scotia and Cape Breton), vol. 83
  Chatham Papers, vols. 1–373
  Foreign Office 4 (United States), vols. 1–16

Foreign Office 5 (United States), vols. 1–150
Foreign Office 72 (Spain), vols. 1–220
Foreign Office 115 (United States), vols. 1–27
State Paper Office, Foreign 94 (Spain), vols. 1–255
War Office 1 (In-letters), vols. 141–144
War Office 34 (Amherst Papers), vols. 1–250

State Department of Archives and History, Raleigh
Spanish Records of the North Carolina Historical Commission,
vols. 1–24

P. K. Yonge Library of Florida History, University of Florida, Gainesville
Joseph B. Lockey Collection
John B. Stetson Collection

William L. Clements Library, University of Michigan, Ann Arbor
Viscount Melville Papers
Earl of Shelburne Papers
Viscount Sydney Papers

II. *Newspapers and Contemporary Periodicals*

The Gentleman's Magazine (London, 1731–1820)
South-Carolina Gazette (1732–1775)

III. *Published Records, Correspondence, Diaries, and Contemporary Works*

Alvord, Clarence W., ed. *Kaskaskia Records, 1778–1790*. Springfield, 1909.
Alvord, Clarence W. and Carter, Clarence E. eds. *The Critical Period, 1763–1765*. Springfield, 1915.
Anson, George. *A Voyage Round the World in the Years MDCCXL, I, II, III, IV, Compiled from Papers and Other Materials of the Right Honorable George Lord Anson, and Published under His Direction by Richard Walter, M. A.* Ed. John Masefield. London, 1911.
Arber, Edward and Bradley, Arthur G., eds. *Travels and Works of Captain John Smith, President of Virginia, and Admiral of New England, 1580–1631*. 2 vols. Edinburgh, 1910.
Arredondo, Antonio de. *Arredondo's Historical Proof of Spain's Title to Georgia*. Ed. Herbert E. Bolton. Berkeley, 1925.

Barcia Carballido y Zúñiga, Andrés G. de. *Ensayo cronológico para la historia general de la Florida.* Trans. Anthony Kerrigan. Gainesville, 1951.

Barlow, Roger. *A Brief Summe of Geographie.* Ed. Eva G. R. Taylor. London, 1923.

Bassett, John S., ed. *Correspondence of Andrew Jackson.* 7 vols. Washington, 1926–1935.

Biggar, Henry P., ed. *The Precursors of Jacques Cartier, 1497–1534, A Collection of Documents Relating to the Early History of the Dominion of Canada.* Ottawa, 1911.

Bland, Edward. *The Discovery of New Brittaine. Began August 27, Anno Dom. 1650.* London, 1651.

Bolton, Herbert E., ed. *Athanase de Mézières and the Louisiana-Texas Frontier, 1768–1780.* 2 vols. Cleveland, 1914.

Bowles, William A. *Authentic Memoirs of William Augustus Bowles, Esquire, Ambassador from the United Nations of Creeks and Cherokees, to the Court of London.* London, 1791. Reprinted in *The Magazine of History with Notes and Queries,* extra number 46 (1916), 103–127.

Boyd, Mark F., ed. and trans. "Diego Peña's Expedition to Apalachee and Apalachicola in 1716," *Florida Historical Quarterly,* XXVIII (1949), 1–27.

————. "Documents Describing the Second and Third Expeditions of Lieutenant Diego Peña to Apalachee and Apalachicola in 1717 and 1718," *Florida Historical Quarterly,* XXXI (1952), 109–139.

————. "Events at Prospect Bluff on the Apalachicola River, 1808–1818, an Introduction to Twelve Letters of Edmund Doyle, Trader," *Florida Historical Quarterly,* XVI (1937), 55–96.

————. "The Siege of St. Augustine by Governor Moore of South Carolina in 1702 as Reported to the King of Spain by Don Joseph de Zúñiga y Cerda, Governor of Florida," *Florida Historical Quarterly,* XXVI (1948), 345–352.

Browne, William H.; Hall, Clayton C.; and Steiner, Bernard C., eds. *Archives of Maryland.* Baltimore, 1883–.

Calendar of Letters and State Papers Relating to English Affairs Preserved Principally in the Archives of Simancas, ed. M. A. S. Hume. 4 vols. London, 1892–1899.

Calendar of Letters, Despatches, and State Papers relating to the Negotiations between England and Spain, Preserved in the Archives at Vienna, Brussels, Simancas and Elsewhere, ed. G. A. Bergenroth, Pascual de Gayangos, M.A.S. Hume, *et al.* London, 1862–.

Calendar of State Papers, Colonial, ed. W. N. Sainsbury, J. W. Fortescue, C. Headlam, and A. P. Newton. London, 1860–.

Calendar of State Papers, Domestic, Anne, ed. R. P. Mahaffy. London, 1916–.

Calendar of State Papers, Domestic, Charles I, ed. John Bruce, W. D. Hamilton, and S. C. Lomas. 23 vols. London, 1858–1897.

Calendar of State Papers, Domestic, Charles II, ed. Everett Green, F. H. B. Daniell, and F. Bickley. 28 vols. London, 1860–1947.

Calendar of State Papers, Domestic, the Commonwealth, ed. Everett Green. 13 vols. London, 1875–1886.

Calendar of State Papers, Domestic, Edward VI, Mary, Elizabeth and James I, ed. R. Lemon and Everett Green. 12 vols. London, 1856–1872.

Calendar of State Papers, Domestic, Home Office Papers, George III, ed. J. Redington and R. A. Roberts. London, 1878–.

Calendar of State Papers, Domestic, William III, ed. W. J. Hardy and E. Bateson. 11 vols. London, 1896–1937.

Calendar of State Papers, Foreign, Edward VI, ed. W. B. Turnbull. London, 1861.

Calendar of State Papers, Foreign, Elizabeth, ed. J. Stevenson, A. J. Crosby, A. J. Butler, *et al.* London, 1863–.

Calendar of State Papers, Foreign, Mary, ed. W. B. Turnbull. London, 1861.

Candler, Allen D., ed. *The Colonial Records of the State of Georgia.* 26 vols. Atlanta, 1904–1916.

Cantillo, Alejandro del, ed. *Tratados, convenios, y declaraciones de paz y de comercio que han hecho con las potencias estranjeras los monarcas españoles de la casa de borbon desde el año de 1700 hasta el dia.* Madrid, 1843.

Carroll, Bartholomew R., ed. *Historical Collections of South Carolina; Embracing Many Rare and Valuable Pamphlets, and Other Documents, Relating to the History of That State from Its First Discovery to Its Independence, in the Year 1776.* 2 vols. New York, 1836.

Carter, Clarence E., ed. *The Correspondence of General Thomas Gage with the Secretaries of State, 1763–1775.* 2 vols. New Haven, 1931.

Caughey, John W., ed. *East Florida, 1783–1785. A File of Documents Assembled and Many of Them Translated by Joseph Byrne Lockey.* Berkeley, 1949.

A Collection of All the Treaties of Peace, Alliance, and Commerce, between Great-Britain and Other Powers, from the Revolution in 1688, to the Present Time. 2 vols. London, 1772.

Collinson, Richard, ed. *The Three Voyages of Martin Frobisher, in Search of a Passage to Cathaia and India by the North-West, A. D. 1576–8, Reprinted from the First Edition of Hakluyt's Voyages, with Selections from Manuscript Documents in the British Museum and State Paper Office.* London, 1867.

Connor, Jeannette T., ed. and trans. *Colonial Records of Spanish Florida.* 2 vols. De Land, 1925.

————. *Pedro Menéndez de Avilés; Memorial by Gonzalo Solís de Merás.* Gainesville, 1964.

Cook, James. *A Voyage to the Pacific Ocean; Undertaken by the Command of His Majesty, for Making Discoveries in the Northern Hemisphere; Performed under the Direction of Captains Cook, Clerke, and Gore in the Years 1776, 1777, 1778, 1779, 1780, Compiled from the Various Accounts of That Voyage Hitherto Published*. 2 vols. Philadelphia, 1818.

Corbett, Julian S., ed. *Papers Relating to the Navy During the Spanish War, 1585–1587*. London, 1898.

Corbitt, Duvon C., ed. "Papers Relating to the Georgia-Florida Frontier, 1784–1800," *Georgia Historical Quarterly*, xxi (1937)–xxv (1941).

Cruikshank, Ernest A., ed. *The Correspondence of Lieut. Governor John Graves Simcoe, with Allied Documents relating to His Administration of the Government of Upper Canada*. 5 vols. Toronto, 1923–1931.

Dalrymple, John. *Memoirs of Great Britain and Ireland from the Dissolution of the Last Parliament of Charles II, until the Sea-Battle off La Hogue*. 2 vols. Edinburgh, 1771–1778.

Davenport, Frances G. and Paullin, Charles O., eds. *European Treaties Bearing on the History of the United States and Its Dependencies*. 4 vols. Washington, 1917–1937.

Davis, T. Frederick, ed. "History of Juan Ponce de Leon's Voyages to Florida, Source Records," *Florida Historical Quarterly*, xiv (1935), 5–66.

Dickinson, Jonathan. *God's Protecting Providence, Man's Surest Help and Defense, in Times of Greatest Difficulty, and Most Eminent Danger, Evidenced in the Remarkable Deliverence of Robert Barrow, with Divers Other Persons, from the Devouring Waves of the Sea, Amongst Which They Suffered Shipwreck, and Also from the Cruel Devouring Jaws of the Inhuman Cannibals of Florida*. Philadelphia, 1699.

Easterby, James H., ed. *The Journal of the Commons House of Assembly 1736–*. Columbia, 1951–.

Fitzpatrick, John C., ed. *The Writings of George Washington from the Original Manuscript Sources, 1745–1799*. 39 vols. Washington, 1931–1944.

Grant, William L.; Munro, James; and Fitzroy, Almeric W., eds. *Acts of the Privy Council of England, Colonial Series*. London, 1908– .

Great Britain, Board of Trade. *Journal of the Commissioners for Trade and Plantations . . . Preserved in the Public Record Office*. . . . 14 vols. London, 1920–1938.

Great Britain, Historical Manuscripts Commission. *The Manuscripts of His Grace the Duke of Rutland . . . Preserved at Belvoir Castle*. 4 vols. London, 1888–1905.

———. *The Manuscripts of J. B. Fortescue, Esq., Preserved at Dropmore*. 10 vols. London, 1892–1927.

———. *Report on Manuscripts in Various Collections*. 8 vols. London, 1901–1914.

————. *Report on the Pepys Manuscripts, Preserved at Magdalene College, Cambridge.* London, 1911.

————. *Third Report.* London, 1872.

Hakluyt, Richard. *The Principal Navigations, Voyages, Traffiques, and Discoveries of the English Nation.* 12 vols. New York, 1903.

Hening, William W., ed. *The Statutes at Large, Being a Collection of All the Laws of Virginia from the First Session of the Legislature in the Year 1619.* 13 vols. Richmond, 1809–1823.

Hilton, William; Goldsmith, Samuel; Greenlese, Lucas; *et al.* "William Hilton's Voyage to Carolina in 1662," ed. J. Leitch Wright, Jr. *Essex Institute Historical Collections,* cv (1969), 96–102.

Hilton, William; Long, Anthony; and Fabian, Peter. *A True Relation of a Voyage upon Discovery of Part of the Coast of Florida from the Latitude of 31° to 33°45′ North Latitude. . . .* In *Collections of the South Carolina Historical Society,* v (1857–1897), 18–25.

Houck, Louis, ed. and trans. *The Spanish Regime in Missouri.* 2 vols. Chicago, 1909.

Ingram, David. *The Land Travels of Davyd Ingram and Others in the Years 1568–9. From the Rio de Minas in the Gulph of Mexico to Cape Breton in Acadia.* In P. C. J. Weston, ed. *Documents Connected with the History of South Carolina.* London, 1856.

Instrucciones que los vireyes de Nueva España dejaron a sus sucesores. 2 vols. Mexico, 1873.

Jameson, J. Franklin, ed. "Letters of Phineas Bond, British Consul at Philadelphia, to the Foreign Office of Great Britain, 1790–1794," *Annual Report of the American Historical Association for the Year 1896,* I (Washington, 1897), 513–659.

Jefferson, Thomas. *Papers,* ed. Julian P. Boyd. Princeton, 1950–.

Jefferys, Thomas. *An Account of the First Discovery and Natural History of Florida with a Particular Detail of the Several Expeditions and Descents Made on That Coast.* London, 1763.

"A Journal of John Forbes, May, 1803," *Florida Historical Quarterly,* ix (1931), 279–289.

King, Charles R., ed. *The Life and Correspondence of Rufus King; Comprising His Letters Private and Official, His Public Documents, and His Speeches.* 6 vols. New York, 1894–1900.

Kingsbury, Susan M., ed. *The Records of the Virginia Company of London.* 4 vols. Washington, 1906–1935.

Kinnaird, Lawrence, ed. and trans. *Spain in the Mississippi Valley, 1765–94, Translations of Materials from the Spanish Archives in the Bancroft Library.* 3 vols. Washington, 1945.

Lanning, John T., ed. *The St. Augustine Expedition of 1740, A Report to* the South Carolina General Assembly, Reprinted from the Colonial Records of South Carolina. Columbia, 1954.

Londonderry, Charles Vane, Marquess of, ed. *Memoirs and Correspondence of Viscount Castlereagh.* 12 vols. London, 1848–1853.

Malmesbury, James Harris, 1st Earl of. *Diaries and Correspondence of James Harris, First Earl of Malmesbury. . . ,* ed. 3d Earl of Malmesbury. 4 vols. London, 1844.

Markham, Clements R., ed. *The Hawkins' Voyages during the Reigns of Henry VIII, Queen Elizabeth, and James I.* London, 1878.

Martyr, Peter. *The Decades of the Newe Worlde or West India. . . ,* trans. Richard Eden. London, 1555.

Mayo, Bernard J., ed. *Instructions to the British Ministers to the United States, 1791–1812.* Washington, 1941.

Mereness, Newton D., ed. *Travels in the American Colonies.* New York, 1916.

Miller, David Hunter, ed. *Treaties and Other International Acts of the United States of America.* Washington, 1931–.

Mitchell, John. *The Present State of Great Britain and North America, with Regard to Agriculture, Population, Trade, and Manufactures, Impartially Considered.* London, 1767.

Montgomery, Robert. *A Discourse Concerning the Design'd Establishment of a New Colony to the South of Carolina, in the Most Delightful Country of the Universe,* ed. J. Max Patrick. Atlanta, 1948.

Montiano, Manuel de. *Letters of Montiano, Siege of St. Augustine,* ed. and trans. C. DeWitt Willcox. Vol. VII, part 1 of *Collections of the Georgia Historical Society.* Savannah, 1909.

Nasatir, Abraham P., ed. *Before Lewis and Clark, Documents Illustrating the History of the Missouri, 1785–1804.* 2 vols. St. Louis, 1952.

Navarrete, Martín Fernández de, ed. *Collección de los viages y descubrimientos que hicieron por mar los españoles desde fines del siglo XV, con varios documentos inéditos concernientes á la historia de la marina castellana y de los establecimientos españoles en Indias.* 5 vols. Madrid, 1825–1837.

Navarrete, Martín Fernández de; Salvá, Miguel; Sainz de Baranda, Pedro; et al., eds. *Colección de documentos inéditos para la historia de España.* 113 vols. Madrid, 1845–1895.

Nichols, Philip. *Sir Francis Drake Revived: Calling Upon This Dull or Effeminate Age, to Folowe His Noble Steps for Golde & Silver, by This Memorable Relation, of the Rare Occurances (Never Yet Declared to the World) in a Third Voyage, Made by Him Into the West-Indies, in the Years 72. & 73. . . .* London, 1628.

Nuttall, Zelia M. M., ed. and trans. *New Light on Drake, A Collection of Documents Relating to His Voyage of Circumnavigation, 1577–1580.* London, 1914.

Oré, Luís Jerónimo de. *The Martyrs of Florida (1513–1616)*, trans. Maynard Geiger. New York, 1936.

Oviedo y Valdés, Gonzalo Fernández de. *Historia general y natural de las Indias, islas y tierra-firme del mar océano*. 4 vols. Madrid, 1851–1855.

Pacheco, Joaquín; Cárdenas, Francisco de; Mendoza, Luis Torres de; *et al.*, eds. *Colección de documentos inéditos relativos al descubrimiento, conquista, y colonización de las posesiones españolas en América y Oceania, sacados en su mayor parte, del real Archivo de Indias*. 42 vols. Madrid, 1864–1884.

Palmer, William P.; McRae, Sherwin; Colston, Raleigh E.; *et al.*, eds. *Calendar of Virginia State Papers and Other Manuscripts . . . Preserved in the Capitol at Richmond*. 11 vols. Richmond, 1875–1893.

Parker, Mattie E. E., ed. *North Carolina Charters and Constitutions, 1578–1698*. Raleigh, 1963.

Penzer, Norman M., ed. *The World Encompassed and Analogous Contemporary Documents Concerning Sir Francis Drake's Circumnavigation of the World*. London, 1926.

Perceval, John, Earl of Egmont. *The Journal of the Earl of Egmont; Abstract of the Trustees Proceedings for Establishing the Colony of Georgia, 1732–1738*, ed. Robert G. McPherson. Athens, 1962.

————. *Manuscripts of the Earl of Egmont, Diary of the First Earl of Egmont*. 3 vols. London, 1920–1923.

Perkins, Bradford, ed. "Lord Hawkesbury and the Jay-Grenville Negotiations," *Mississippi Valley Historical Review*, XL (1953), 291–304.

Pinkerton, John. *A General Collection of the Best and Most Interesting Voyages and Travels in Various Parts of America; Many of Which Are Now First Translated into English*. 6 vols. Philadelphia, 1810–1812.

Pitt, William. *Correspondence of William Pitt when Secretary of State with Colonial Governors and Military and Naval Commissioners in America*, ed. Gertrude S. Kimball. 2 vols. New York, 1906.

Purchas, Samuel. *Hakluytus Posthumus or Purchas His Pilgrimes, Contayning a History of the World in Sea Voyages and Lande Travells by Englishmen and Others*. 20 vols. Glasgow, 1905–1907.

Quinn, David B., ed. *The Roanoke Voyages, 1584–1590, Documents to Illustrate the English Voyages to North America Under the Patent Granted to Walter Raleigh in 1584*. 2 vols. London, 1955.

————. *The Voyages and Colonizing Enterprises of Sir Humphrey Gilbert*. 2 vols. London, 1940.

Ranft, B. McL., ed. *The Vernon Papers*. London, 1958.

A Review of All That Hath Pass'd between the Courts of Great Britain and Spain, Relating to Our Trade and Navigation from the Year 1721, to the Present Convention; With Some Particular Observations Upon It. London, 1739.

Robertson, James A., ed. and trans. "Spanish Correspondence Concerning the American Revolution," *Hispanic American Historical Review*, I (1918), 299–316.

Rosebury, Earl of, ed. *The Windham Papers; the Life and Correspondence of the Rt. Hon. William Windham, 1750–1810, a member of Pitt's First Cabinet and the Ministry of "All the Talents," including hitherto Unpublished Letters.* . . . 2 vols. London, 1913.

Rymer, Thomas, ed. *Foedera, Conventiones, Literae, et Cujuscunque Generis Acta Publica, Inter Reges Angliae et Alios Quosvis Imperatores, Reges, Pontifices, Principes.* . . . 2d ed. 20 vols. London, 1726–1735.

Salley, Alexander S., Jr., ed. *Journals of the Commons House of Assembly of South Carolina for the Two Sessions of 1697.* Columbia, 1913.

————. *Narratives of Early Carolina, 1650–1708.* New York, 1911.

————. *Records in the British Public Record Office Relating to South Carolina, 1663–1710.* 5 vols. Atlanta, 1928.

Saunders, William L., ed. *The Colonial Records of North Carolina.* 10 vols. Goldsboro, 1886–1890.

Siebert, Wilbur H., ed. *Loyalists in East Florida, 1774–1785.* 2 vols. De Land, 1929.

Smith, William H., ed. *The St. Clair Papers. The Life and Public Services of Arthur St. Clair, Soldier of the Revolutionary War; President of the Continental Congress; and Governor of the North-Western Territory.* 2 vols. Cincinnati, 1882.

Stephens, William. *The Journal of William Stephens,* ed. E. Merton Coulter. 2 vols. Athens, 1958–1959.

Stock, Leo F., ed. *Proceedings and Debates of the British Parliaments Respecting North America.* 5 vols. Washington, 1924–1941.

Taylor, Eva G. R., ed. *The Original Writings and Correspondence of the Two Richard Hakluyts.* 2 vols. London, 1935.

Turner, Frederick J., ed. *Correspondence of the French Ministers to the United States, 1791–1797.* Washington, 1904.

————. "Documents on the Blount Conspiracy, 1795–1797," *American Historical Review*, x (1905), 574–606.

————. "English Policy Toward America in 1790–1791," *American Historical Review*, VII (1902), 706–735 and VIII (1902), 78–86.

Vancouver, George. *A Voyage of Discovery to the North Pacific Ocean and Round the World; in Which the Coast of North-West America Has Been Carefully Examined and Accurately Surveyed . . . in the Years 1790, 1791, 1792, 1793, 1794, and 1795.* . . . 3 vols. London, 1798.

Velasco, Juan López de. *Geografía y descripción universal de las Indias, recopilada por el cosmógrafo-cronista Juan López de Velasco, desde el año de 1571 al de 1574.* Madrid, 1894.

Ware, Horace E., ed. and trans. "Letters of Pedro Menéndez de Avilés," *Proceedings of the Massachusetts Historical Society*, VIII (1892–1894), 2d series, 416–468.

Webster, Charles K., ed. *Britain and the Independence of Latin America, 1812–1830, Select Documents from the Foreign Office Archives.* 2 vols. London, 1938.

Wellington, Arthur Wellesley, First Duke of. *Supplementary Despatches and Memoranda of Field Marshal Arthur, Duke of Wellington,* ed. Arthur R. Wellington. 15 vols. London, 1858–1872.

Wenhold, Lucy L., ed. and trans. "The Trials of Captain Don Isidoro de León," *Florida Historical Quarterly,* xxxv (1957), 246–265.

Wharton, Francis, ed. *The Revolutionary Diplomatic Correspondence of the United States.* 6 vols. Washington, 1889.

Whitaker, Arthur P., ed. and trans. *Documents Relating to the Commercial Policy of Spain in the Floridas, with Incidental Reference to Louisiana.* De Land, 1931.

Willcox, C. DeWitt, ed. and trans. *The Spanish Official Account of the Attack on the Colony of Georgia in America, and of Its Defeat on St. Simons Island by General James Oglethorpe.* Vol. vii, part 3, *Collections of the Georgia Historical Society.* Savannah, 1913.

Williams, Edward. *Virginia: More Especially the South Part Thereof, Richly and Truly Valued: Viz. the Fertile Carolana, and No Lesse Excellent Isle of Roanoak, of Latitude from 31. to 37. Degr. relating the Means of Raysing Infinite Profits to the Adventurers and Planters....* London, 1650.

Winthrop, John. *Winthrop's Journal, "History of New England,"* 1630–1649, ed. James K. Hosmer. 2 vols. New York, 1908.

Winwood, Ralph. *Memorials of Affairs of State in the Reigns of Q. Elizabeth and K. James I. Collected (Chiefly) From the Original Papers of the Right Honourable Sir Ralph Winwood, Kt. Sometime One of the Principal Secretaries of State....* 3 vols. London, 1727.

Wright, Irene A., ed. "Dispatches of Spanish Officials Bearing on the Free Negro Settlement of Gracia Real de Santa Teresa de Mose, Florida," *Journal of Negro History,* ix (1924), 144–195.

————. *Documents Concerning English Voyages to the Spanish Main, 1569–1580.* London, 1932.

————. *Further English Voyages to Spanish America, 1583–1594, Documents from the Archives of the Indies at Seville Illustrating English Voyages to the Caribbean, the Spanish Main, Florida, and Virginia.* London, 1951.

————. *Historia documentada de San Cristóbal de la Habana en el siglo XVI, basada en los documentos originales existentes en el Archivo General de Indias en Sevilla.* 2 vols. Havana, 1927.

————. *Spanish Documents Concurning English Voyages to the Caribbean, 1527–1568.* London, 1929.

IV. Secondary Works

Abernethy, Thomas P. *The Burr Conspiracy*. New York, 1954.

————. *The South in the New Nation, 1789–1819*. Baton Rouge, 1961.

Alden, John R. *John Stuart and the Southern Colonial Frontier, A Study of Indian Relations, War, Trade, and Land Problems in the Southern Wilderness, 1754–1775*. Ann Arbor, 1944.

Altamira y Crevea, Rafael. *Historia de España y de la civilización española*. 5 vols. Barcelona, 1900–1930.

Andrews, Charles M. *The Colonial Period of American History*. 4 vols. New Haven, 1934–1938.

Andrews, Kenneth R. *Drake's Voyages; A Re-assessment of Their Place in Elizabethan Maritime Expansion*. New York, 1967.

Andrews, Matthew P. *Virginia, The Old Dominion*. New York, 1937.

Arnade, Charles W. *Florida on Trial, 1593–1602*. Coral Gables, 1959.

————. *The Siege of St. Augustine in 1702*. Gainesville, 1959.

Ballesteros y Beretta, Antonio. *Historia de España y su influencia en la historia universal*. 11 vols. Barcelona, 1918–1941.

Bancroft, Hubert H. *History of the Pacific States of North America*. 34 vols. San Francisco, 1882–1890.

Barbour, Philip L. "Captain George Kendall, Mutineer or Intelligencer?," *Virginia Magazine of History and Biography*, LXX (1962), 297–313.

Bassett, John S. *The Life of Andrew Jackson*. 2 vols. New York, 1916.

Baxter, James P., ed. *Sir Ferdinando Gorges and His Province of Maine. Including the Brief Relation, the Brief Narration, His Defence, the Charter Granted to Him, His Will, and His Letters*. 3 vols. Boston, 1890.

Becker, Jerónimo. *España é Inglaterra, sus relaciones políticas desde las paces de Utrecht*. Madrid, 1906.

Bemis, Samuel F. *The Diplomacy of the American Revolution*. 4th ed. Bloomington, 1961.

————. *John Quincy Adams and the Foundations of American Foreign Policy*. New York, 1949.

Biggar, Henry P. "An English Expedition to America in 1527," *Mélanges d'histoire offerts à M. Charles Bémont par ses amis et ses élèves à l'occasion de la vingt-cinquième année de son enseignement à l'École pratique des hautes études* (1913), pp. 459–472.

Bolton, Herbert E. "Spanish Resistance to the Carolina Traders in Western Georgia (1680–1704)," *Georgia Historical Quarterly*, IX (1925), 115–130.

Boyd, Mark F. "The Fortifications at San Marcos de Apalache," *Florida Historical Quarterly*, XV (1936), 3–34.

Boyd, Mark F.; Smith, Hale G.; and Griffin, John W. *Here They Once Stood, the Tragic End of the Apalachee Missions*. Gainesville, 1951.

Brooks, Charles B. *The Siege of New Orleans*. Seattle, 1961.

Brown, Alexander, *The Genesis of the United States*. 2 vols. Boston, 1890.

Brown, Vera Lee. *Anglo-Spanish Relations in America in the Closing Years of the Colonial Era, 1763–1774*. Baltimore, 1923.

———. "Spanish Claims to a Share in the Newfoundland Fisheries in the Eighteenth Century," *Canadian Historical Association Report* (1925), pp. 64–82.

———. "The Spanish Court and Its Diplomatic Outlook After the Treaty of Paris, 1763," *Smith College Studies in History*, xv (October, 1929; January, 1930), nos. 1–2.

Carande Thobar, Ramón. *Carlos V y sus banqueros, la vida económica de España en una fase de su hegemonía, 1516–1556*. Madrid, 1943.

Casado, Vicente R. *Primeros años de dominación española en la Luisiana*. Madrid, 1942.

Caughey, John W. *Bernardo de Gálvez in Louisiana, 1776–1783*. Berkeley, 1934.

———. *McGillivray of the Creeks*, 2d ed. Norman, 1959.

Chapin, Howard M. *Rhode Island Privateers in King George's War, 1739–1748*. Providence, 1926.

Chatelain, Verne E. *The Defenses of Spanish Florida, 1565–1763*. Washington, 1941.

Chaunu, Hugette et Pierre. *Seville et l'Atlantique, 1504–1650*. 8 vols. Paris, 1955–1959.

Christelow, Allan. "Economic Background of the Anglo-Spanish War of 1762," *Journal of Modern History*, xviii (1946), 22–36.

Connell-Smith, Gordon. *Forerunners of Drake, A Study of English Trade with Spain in the Early Tudor Period*. London, 1954.

Cooper, Walter G. *The Story of Georgia*. 4 vols. New York, 1938.

Corbitt, Duvon C. "Spanish Relief Policy and the East Florida Refugees of 1763," *Florida Historical Quarterly*, xxvii (1948), 67–82.

Coulter, E. Merton. *Georgia, A Short History*. 3d ed. Chapel Hill, 1960.

Covington, James. "Drake Destroys St. Augustine: 1586," *Florida Historical Quarterly*, xliv (1965), 81–93.

Cox, Isaac J. "Hispanic-American Phases of the Burr Conspiracy," *Hispanic American Historical Review*, xii (1932), 145–175.

———. *The West Florida Controversy, 1798–1813; A Study in American Diplomacy*. Baltimore, 1918.

Crane, Verner W. *The Southern Frontier, 1670–1732*. Durham, 1928.

———. "The Southern Frontier in Queen Anne's War," *American Historical Review*, xiv (1919), 379–395.

Craven, Wesley F. "The Earl of Warwick, a Speculator in Piracy," *Hispanic American Historical Review*, x (1930), 457–479.

———. *The Southern Colonies in the Seventeenth Century, 1607–1689*. Baton Rouge, 1949.

Davies, David W. *Elizabethans Errant; The Strange Fortunes of Sir Thomas Sherley and His Three Sons as well in the Dutch Wars as in Muscovy, Morocco, Persia, Spain and the Indies.* Ithaca, 1967.

Davies, Godfrey. *The Early Stuarts, 1603–1660.* 4th ed. Oxford, 1949.

Douglass, Elisha P. "The Adventurer Bowles," *William and Mary Quarterly,* VI (1949), 3d series, 3–23.

Downes, Randolph C. *Council Fires on the Upper Ohio; a Narrative of Indian Affairs in the Upper Ohio Valley until 1795.* Pittsburgh, 1940.

Dunn, William E. *Spanish and French Rivalry in the Gulf Region of the United States, 1678–1702; the Beginnings of Texas and Pensacola.* University of Texas Bulletin, No. 1705. Austin, 1917.

Ettinger, Amos A. *James Edward Oglethorpe, Imperial Idealist.* Oxford, 1936.

Fisher, Lillian E. *Viceregal Administration in the Spanish-American Colonies.* Berkeley, 1926.

Folmer, Henry. *Franco-Spanish Rivalry in North America, 1524–1763.* Glendale, 1953.

Ford, Lawrence C. *The Triangular Struggle for Spanish Pensacola, 1689–1739.* Washington, 1939.

Gámez, José D. *Historia de la costa de Mosquitos, hasta 1894.* Managua, 1938.

Gayarré, Charles E. A. *History of Louisiana.* 4 vols. New York, 1854–1866.

"General Bowles," *Public Characters of 1801–1802* (1804), 118–154.

Giménez Fernández, Manuel. *Nuevas consideraciones sobre la historia, sentido y valor de las bulas alejandrinas de 1493 referentes a las Indias.* Seville, 1944.

Gipson, Lawrence H. "British Diplomacy in the Light of Anglo-Spanish New World Issues, 1750–1757," *American Historical Review,* LI (1946), 627–648.

Girard, Albert. *Le commerce français à Séville et Cadix au temps des Habsbourg contribution à l'étude du commerce étranger en Espagne aux XVIᵉ et XVIIIᵉ siècles.* Paris, 1932.

Gold, Robert L. *Borderland Empires in Transition: The Triple-Nation Transfer of Florida.* Carbondale, 1969.

————. "The Settlement of the Pensacola Indians in New Spain, 1763–1770," *Hispanic American Historical Review,* XLV (1965), 567–576.

Haarmann, Albert W. "The Spanish Conquest of British West Florida, 1779–1781," *Florida Historical Quarterly,* XXXIX (1960), 107–134.

Hamer, Philip M. "The British in Canada and the Southern Indians, 1790–1794," *The East Tennessee Historical Society's Publications,* II (1930), 107–134.

Hanke, Lewis U. *The Spanish Struggle for Justice in the Conquest of America.* 2d ed. Philadelphia, 1959.

Haring, Clarence H. *The Spanish Empire in America.* New York, 1947.

————. *Trade and Navigation between Spain and the Indies in the Time of the Hapsburgs.* Cambridge, 1918.

Harlow, Vincent T. *The Founding of the Second British Empire, 1763–1793.* 2 vols. London, 1952–1964.

Harman, Joyce E. *Trade and Privateering in Spanish Florida, 1732–1763.* St. Augustine, 1969.

Harrisse, Henry, *John Cabot, the Discoverer of North-America and Sebastian His Son, a Chapter of the Maritime History of England Under the Tudors, 1496–1557.* London, 1896.

Hart, Francis R. *The Disaster of Darien; the Story of the Scots Settlement and the Causes of Its Failure, 1699–1701.* Boston, 1929.

Holmes, Jack D. L. "Robert Ross' Plan for an English Invasion of Louisiana in 1782," *Louisiana History,* v (1964), 161–177.

Humphreys, Robert A. "Richard Oswald's Plan for an English and Russian Attack on Spanish America, 1781–1782," *Hispanic American Historical Review,* xviii (1938), 95–101.

Innis, Harold A. *The Cod Fisheries; the History of an International Economy.* New Haven, 1940.

————. "The Rise and Fall of the Spanish Fishery in Newfoundland," *Transactions of the Royal Society of Canada,* xxv (1931), 3d series, 51–70.

Insh, George P. *The Company of Scotland Trading to Africa and the Indies.* London, 1932.

————. *Scottish Colonial Schemes, 1620–1686.* Glasgow, 1922.

Izon, John. *Sir Thomas Stucley, c. 1525–1578, Traitor Extraordinary.* London, 1956.

Jacquemin, Jeanine, "La colonisation protestante en Floride et la politique européenne au XVIe siècle," *Bulletin de la Société de l'Histoire du Protestantisme Français,* ci (1955), 181–208.

Johnson, Cecil. *British West Florida, 1763–1783.* New Haven, 1943.

Julien, Charles A. *Les voyages de découverte et les premiers établissements (XVe–XVIe siècles).* Paris, 1948.

Kaufmann, Wiliam W. *British Policy and the Independence of Latin America, 1804–1828.* New Haven, 1951.

Kinnaird, Lawrence. "The Significance of William Augustus Bowles' Seizure of Panton's Apalachee Store in 1792," *Florida Historical Quarterly,* ix (1931), 156–192.

————. "The Spanish Expedition against Ft. St. Joseph in 1781, a New Interpretation," *Mississippi Valley Historical Review,* xix (1932), 173–191.

Lanning, John T. "The American Colonies in the Preliminaries to the War of Jenkins' Ear," *Georgia Historical Quarterly,* xi (1927), 129–155; 191–215.

————. *The Diplomatic History of Georgia, A Study of the Epoch of Jenkins' Ear.* Chapel Hill, 1936.

————. "Don Miguel Wall and the Spanish Attempt Against the Existence of Carolina and Georgia," *North Carolina Historical Review,* x (1933), 186–213.

————. "The Legend that Governor Moral Sánchez was Hanged," *Georgia Historical Quarterly,* xxxviii (1954), 349–355.

————. *The Spanish Missions of Georgia.* Chapel Hill, 1935.

La Roncière, Charles G. M. B. de. *La Floride française, scène de la vie indienne, peintes en 1564 par Jacques LeMoyne de Morgues.* Paris, 1928.

————. *Histoire de la marine française.* 6 vols. Paris, 1899–1932.

Lawson, Katherine S. "Luciano de Herrera, Spanish Spy in British St. Augustine," *Florida Historical Quarterly,* xxiii (1945), 170–176.

Leonard, Irving A., ed. *Spanish Approach to Pensacola, 1689–1693.* Albuquerque, 1939.

Lewis, Clifford M. and Loomie, Albert J. *The Spanish Jesuit Mission in Virginia, 1570–1572.* Chapel Hill, 1953.

Linden, Herman vander. "Alexander vi and the Demarkation of the Maritime and Colonial Domains of Spain and Portugal, 1493–1494," *American Historical Review,* xxii (1916), 1–20.

Lockey, Joseph B. "The Florida Intrigues of José Álvarez de Toledo," *Florida Historical Quarterly,* xii (1934), 145–178.

Lodge, Richard. "Sir Benjamin Keene, K. B.: a Study in Anglo-Spanish Relations in the Earlier Part of the Eighteenth Century," *Transactions of the Royal Historical Society,* xv (1932), 4th series, 1–44.

Lounsbury, Ralph G. *The British Fishery at Newfoundland, 1634–1763.* New Haven, 1934.

Lowe, Richard G. "American Seizure of Amelia Island," *Florida Historical Quarterly,* xlv (1966), 18–30.

Lowery, Woodbury. *The Spanish Settlements within the Present Limits of the United States, 1513–1561.* 2d ed. New York, 1959.

————. *The Spanish Settlements within the Present Limits of the United States, Florida, 1562–1574.* 2d ed. New York, 1959.

Mackie, John D. *The Earlier Tudors, 1485–1558.* Oxford, 1952.

Madariaga, Salvador de. *Bolívar.* New York, 1952.

Mahan, Alfred T. *The Influence of Sea Power Upon History, 1660–1783.* Boston, 1890.

————. *The Influence of Sea Power Upon the French Revolution and Empire, 1793–1812.* 2 vols. Boston, 1892.

Mahon, John K. "British Strategy and Southern Indians: War of 1812," *Florida Historical Quarterly,* xliv (1966), 285–302.

Manning, William R. *The Nootka Sound Controversy. Annual Report of the American Historical Association for the Year 1904.* Washington, 1905.

Masterson, William H. *William Blount.* Baton Rouge, 1954.

McCrady, Edward. *The History of South Carolina Under the Proprietary Government, 1670–1719.* New York, 1901.

McLachlan, Jean O. "The Seven Years' Peace, and the West Indian Policy of Carvajal and Wall," *English Historical Review,* LIII (1938), 457–477.

————. *Trade and Peace with Old Spain, 1667–1750; a Study of the Influence of Commerce on Anglo-Spanish Diplomacy in the First Half of the Eighteenth Century.* Cambridge, 1940.

Means, Philip A. *The Spanish Main, Focus of Envy, 1492–1700.* London, 1935.

Miller, John C. *Alexander Hamilton, Portrait in Paradox.* New York, 1959.

Morison, Samuel E. *Admiral of the Ocean Sea, A Life of Christopher Columbus.* Boston, 1942.

Mowat, Charles L. *East Florida as a British Province, 1763–1784.* Berkeley, 1943.

Murdoch, Richard K. "Elijah Clarke and Anglo-American Designs on East Florida, 1797–1798," *Georgia Historical Quarterly,* XXXV (1951), 173–190.

Murga Sanz, Vicente. *Juan Ponce de León: fundador y primer gobernador del pueblo puertorriqueño, descubridor de la Florida y del Estrecho de las Bahamas.* San Juan, 1959.

Nasatir, Abraham P. "Anglo-Spanish Frontier in the Illinois Country during the American Revolution, 1779–1783," *Journal of the Illinois State Historical Society,* XXI (1928), 29–358.

————. "The Anglo-Spanish Frontier on the Upper Mississippi, 1786–1796," *Iowa Journal of History and Politics,* XXIX (1932), 155–232.

————. "Anglo-Spanish Rivalry on the Upper Missouri," *Mississippi Valley Historical Review,* XVI (1929), 359–382 and (1930), 507–528.

————. "The Formation of the Missouri Company," *Missouri Historical Review,* XXV (1930), 10–22.

————. "St. Louis during the British Attack of 1780," *New Spain and the Anglo-American West,* I (1932), 239–261.

Norris, John M. "The Policy of the British Cabinet in the Nootka Crisis," *English Historical Review,* LXX (1955), 562–580.

Pack, S. W. C. *Admiral Lord Anson; the Story of Anson's Voyage and Naval Events of His Day.* London, 1960.

Pares, Richard. *War and Trade in the West Indies, 1739–1763.* Oxford, 1936.

Parkman, Francis. *France and England in North America, Pioneers of France in the New World.* Boston, 1865.

Pike, Ruth. "Seville in the Sixteenth Century," *Hispanic American Historical Review,* XLI (1961), 1–30.

Preston, Richard A. *Gorges of Plymouth Fort; a Life of Sir Ferdinando Gorges, Captain of Plymouth Fort, Governor of New England, and Lord of the Province of Maine.* Toronto, 1953.

Priestley, Herbert I. *The Mexican Nation, A History.* New York, 1923.

Prowse, Daniel W. *A History of Newfoundland from the English, Colonial, and Foreign Records.* London, 1895.

Quinn, David B. "The Argument for the English Discovery of America between 1480 and 1494," *The Geographical Journal,* CXXVII (1961), 277–285.

——. *Raleigh and the British Empire.* New York, 1949.

——. "Some Spanish Reactions to Elizabethan Enterprises," *Transactions of the Royal Historical Society,* I (1951), 5th series, 1–23.

Richmond, Herbert W. *The Navy in the War of 1739–48.* 3 vols. Cambridge, 1920.

Robertson, William S. *Francisco de Miranda and the Revolutionizing of Spanish America. Annual Report of the American Historical Association for the Year 1907.* Vol. 1, Washington, 1908.

——. *The Life of Miranda.* 2 vols. Chapel Hill, 1929.

Ross, Mary. "The French on the Savannah, 1605," *Georgia Historical Quarterly,* VIII (1924), 167–194.

——. "The Restoration of the Spanish Missions in Georgia, 1598–1606," *Georgia Historical Quarterly,* X (1926), 171–199.

Ruidíaz y Caravia, Eugenio. *La Florida, su conquista y colonización por Pedro Menéndez de Avilés.* 2 vols. Madrid, 1893.

Rush, N. Orwin. *Spain's Final Triumph over Great Britain in the Gulf of Mexico; The Battle of Pensacola, March 9 to May 8, 1781.* Tallahassee, 1966.

Savelle, Max. *The Origins of American Diplomacy: The International History of Angloamerica, 1492–1763.* New York, 1967.

Scott, James B. *The Spanish Origins of International Law, Francisco de Vitoria and His Law of Nations.* London, 1934.

Siebert, Wilbur H. "The Departure of the Spaniard and Other Groups from East Florida, 1763–1764," *Florida Historical Quarterly,* XIX (1940), 145–154.

——. "How the Spaniards Evacuated Pensacola in 1763," *Florida Historical Quarterly,* XI (1932), 48–57.

Simpson, Richard, ed. *The School of Shakespere.* 2 vols. London, 1878.

Sirmans, M. Eugene. *Colonial South Carolina; A Political History, 1663–1763.* Chapel Hill, 1966.

Southall, James P. C. "Captain John Martin of Brandon on the James," *Virginia Magazine of History and Biography,* LIV (1946), 21–67.

Sperling, John G. *The South Sea Company: An Historical Essay and Bibliographical Finding List.* Boston, 1962.

Swanton, John R. *Early History of the Creek Indians and Their Neighbors.* Washington, 1922.

——. *The Indians of the Southeastern United States.* Washington, 1946.

Taylor, Eva G. R. "Early Empire Building Projects in the Pacific Ocean," *Hispanic American Historical Review,* XIV (1934), 296–306.

TePaske, John J. *The Governorship of Spanish Florida, 1700–1763.* Durham, 1964.

Tucker, Glenn. *Tecumseh, Vision of Glory.* New York, 1956.

Turner, Frederick J. "The Diplomatic Contest for the Mississippi Valley," *Atlantic Monthly,* xciii (1904), 676–691; 807–817.

Unwin, Rayner. *The Defeat of John Hawkins; A Biography of His Third Slaving Voyage.* New York, 1960.

Villanueva, Carlos A. *Napoleón y la independencia de América.* Paris, 1912.

Villa-Urrutia, Wenceslao R. de. *Relaciones entre España é Inglaterra durante la guerra de la independencia, apuntes para la historia diplomatica de España de 1808 á 1814.* 3 vols. Madrid, 1911–1914.

Whitaker, Arthur P. *The Mississippi Question, 1795–1803, A Study in Trade, Politics, and Diplomacy.* New York, 1934.

————. *The Spanish-American Frontier: 1783–1795, the Westward Movement and the Spanish Retreat in the Mississippi Valley.* Boston, 1927.

Williams, Basil. *The Whig Supremacy, 1714–1760.* Oxford, 1939.

Williamson, James A. *The Age of Drake.* 4th ed. London, 1960.

————. *The Cabot Voyages and Bristol Discovery Under Henry VII; with the Cartography of the Voyages by R. A. Skelton.* Cambridge, 1962.

————. *Sir John Hawkins, the Time and the Man.* Oxford, 1927.

————. *The Voyages of the Cabots and the English Discovery of North America under Henry VII and Henry VIII.* London, 1929.

Wright, Irene A. "Spanish Policy Toward Virginia," *American Historical Review,* xxv (1920), 448–479.

Wright, J. Leitch, Jr. "Andrew Ranson: Seventeenth Century Pirate?" *Florida Historical Quarterly,* xxxix (1960), 135–144.

————. "British Designs on the Old Southwest: Foreign Intrigue on the Florida Frontier, 1783–1803," *Florida Historical Quarterly,* xliv (1966), 265–284.

————. "A Note on the First Seminole War as Seen by the Indians, Negroes, and Their British Advisors," *Journal of Southern History,* xxxiv (1968), 565–575.

————. Sixteenth Century English-Spanish Rivalry in la Florida," *Florida Historical Quarterly,* xxxviii (1960), 265–279.

————. "Spanish Reaction to Carolina," *North Carolina Historical Review,* xli (1964), 464–476.

————. *William Augustus Bowles: Director General of the Creek Nation.* Athens, 1967.

Yela Utrilla, Juan F. *España ante la independencia de los Estados Unidos.* 2 vols. Lérida, 1925.

Zavala, Silvio A. *Hispanoamérica septentrional y media; período colonial.* Mexico, 1953.

Index